*Reclaiming African
Religions in Trinidad*

Reclaiming African Religions in Trinidad

The Socio-Political Legitimation of the Orisha and Spiritual Baptist Faiths

Frances Henry

THE UNIVERSITY OF THE WEST INDIES PRESS
Barbados • Jamaica • Trinidad and Tobago

University of the West Indies Press
1A Aqueduct Flats   Mona
Kingston 7   Jamaica

© 2003 by The University of the West Indies Press
All rights reserved. Published 2003

07 06 05 04 03   5 4 3 2 1

CATALOGUING IN PUBLICATION DATA

Henry, Frances, 1931–
Reclaiming African religions in Trinidad: the socio-political
legitimation of the Orisha and Spiritual Baptist faiths / Frances Henry
p. cm.
Includes bibliographical references.

ISBN: 976-640-129-2

1. Orishas – Trinidad and Tobago. 2. Spiritual Baptists –
Trinidad and Tobago. 3. Trinidad and Tobago – Religion –
African influences. 4. Trinidad and Tobago –
Religious life and customs. I. Title.

BL2566.T7H47 2003   299'6.07298321

Set in Adobe Garamond 11/14.5 x 24
Cover photo: Babalorisha Sam Phills at Orisha Family Day celebration, 2000.
Courtesy of Vincent Goldberg.

Book and cover design by Robert Harris.
E-mail: roberth@cwjamaica.com

Printed on acid-free paper.
Printed in Canada

*To my "spiritual father", the late
Ebenezer "Pa Neezer" Elliott,
whose influence on my life I'm just
beginning to understand.*

Contents

List of Illustrations / *viii*
Preface / *ix*
Acknowledgements / *xi*
Introduction / *xiii*
Note on Terms and Spellings / *xxx*

1. The Orisha Religion in Trinidad Today / *1*
2. Spiritual/Shouter Baptism in Trinidad Today / *30*
3. The Formal Processes of Political Legitimation / *49*
4. The Orisha Religion from Sacred to Secular: The Evolution of the Shango Cult into the Orisha Movement / *78*
5. Contested Theologies in the Orisha Religion: Discourses of Authenticity and Inauthenticity / *108*
6. The Role of Syncretism in the Orisha Religion Today / *137*
7. African Religions and Popular Culture: Calypsos, Steelband and Carnival / *157*
8. Conclusion / *193*

Appendix: My Life with Ebenezer Elliott (Pa Neezer) / *202*

Notes / *211*

Glossary / *224*

Illustrations

1. Prime Minister Panday participating in a candle ceremony at the Spiritual Baptist national holiday celebration, 1996 / *52*
2. President A.N.R. Robinson with Archbishop Randoo, Archbishop Clarence Baisden and Senator Barbara Burke at the Spiritual Baptist national holiday celebration, 1997 / *54*
3. Leader of the opposition Patrick Manning with Baptist dignitaries at the Spiritual Baptist national holiday celebration, 1998 / *56*
4. Senator Barbara Burke, Prime Minister Panday and Minister of Culture Daphne Phillips at the Spiritual Baptist national holiday celebration, 1999 / *59*
5. "Spirit lash" cartoon, *Trinidad Guardian* / *64*
6. "Honorary pupil" cartoon, *Trinidad Express* / *64*
7. Broadside protesting PNM policy / *70*
8. Water festival to Oshun, August 2000 / *120*
9. Prime Minister Panday with Orisha elders blessing the ancestral memorial at the Orisha Family Day, 1999 / *122*
10. President Robinson hosting a dinner for delegates to the Sixth World Orisha Congress, 1999 / *128*
11. Babalorisha Sam Phills at Orisha Family Day celebration, 2000 / *31*

Preface

I STARTED THIS PROJECT as a fairly traditional ethnography that focused on the research questions that informed the project – the increasing socio-political legitimation of African religions in Trinidad and the attempt to explain why these changes are taking place. From the outset I felt that it would probably reach several audiences in the academic world and people interested in the development of African religions, especially in the Caribbean.

As the work progressed, the question of audience as well as my own perspective began to change. I realized that the changes in the Orisha faith were of the moment – happening in front of my eyes, so to speak – and that the whole movement was very much in the public discourse. Writing this book therefore began to take on a slightly different perspective.

There is dialogue and debate within the Orisha and, to a lesser extent, the Spiritual Baptist communities and I hope that this book will assist as that dialogue continues. My wish is that this book will further the debate and that my work can be used by devotees as a means of informing and continuing the process. I also wanted to present the community with an objective analysis of how their religion is changing. That might seem presumptuous on my part, but I have tried wherever possible to have people speak in their own voices so that it is their voices that inform and articulate the debate. Thus, the audience for this book became directed more and more towards the community itself and less towards the scholarly community. Naturally, I also hope that the book will be of value to social scientists, Caribbeanists and scholars of comparative religion.

During the course of the fieldwork, it also became apparent to me that the Orisha religion is already over-researched. Two or three students and researchers from abroad, as well as many undergraduate and graduate students from the University of the West Indies who also are now interested in researching the Orisha and Spiritual Baptists, are busy studying aspects of the faith. The problem with much of this kind of work, however, is that it is rarely published; it remains buried in academic files. Some of the students are working on undergraduate and Master's theses that rarely if ever see the light of day. Aside from my earlier work, that of George Simpson and more recent books by James Houk and Kenneth Lum, very little has been published on Orisha, yet so much research is being undertaken.[1] The actual communities, many of whose members are so generous with their time, rarely receive anything in return from many of these researchers. In view of this situation, I wanted to make sure that my findings would come out fairly. By publishing it with a Caribbean publisher, I hope also to ensure that the book will be more readily accessible in the region.

Finally, I made an attempt to write the book in a manner that is accessible to many levels of readership, and have therefore attempted to avoid not only excessive jargon but also too much of the theorizing that is comprehensible only to academic specialists. I hope that members of the Orisha and Spiritual Baptist religions around the world will read this book because their issues of changing ritual, practice and behaviour are more than local – they are universal and speak to the human condition.

Acknowledgements

I AM DEEPLY GRATEFUL to the many members of both the Orisha and Spiritual/Shouter Baptist faiths who took the time and trouble to talk to me and answer my many questions. This book would not have been possible without their cooperation.

I need to express my special thanks to Eintou Pearl Springer, who not only was giving of her time throughout the course of this project but who read the manuscript in draft. Her many helpful suggestions and additional information made this a better book. Her assistant Merlyn Atwell-Dick provided help throughout the course of this project. Michael Cyrus also read several sections and corrected some mistakes. Bishop Carlotta John read and reviewed the chapter on the Spiritual Baptist religion.

Iyalorisha Melvina Rodney was warmly welcoming and helpful. Babalorisha Sam Phills was always ready with support and encouragement. Mrs Patricia McCleod, Ella Andall and Brother Oludari were exceptionally generous with their time.

Drs Ken and Sheri Deaver, long-time calypso fans and collectors, sent me some important calypsos that I used in chapter 7. I am happy to acknowledge the help of Dr Ann Lee in the research and writing of the chapter on calypsos and popular culture.

Two graduate students – Keith McNeal and Vincent Goldberg – were doing research in Trinidad during the course of my own fieldwork. I am grateful to them for help, shared materials and particularly some of the photographs used in this book. I wish to also give special credit to Mr Lennox Grant, the then editor of the *Trinidad Guardian,* who made some photos available to me, and to the *Trinidad Express,* which also supplied some photos. Mr Chapman of the photography unit of the government information ministry was very helpful in finding more photos.

Professor John Stewart read the manuscript in draft, and I am hugely indebted to him for the many excellent revisions he suggested. His profound insights helped inform my thinking on many of the issues addressed in this book. My long-time associate in Toronto, Carol Tator, also read the manuscript and made excellent suggestions.

The Social Science Humanities and Research Council of Canada provided support for this project.

Finally, I always need to acknowledge with heartfelt thanks the contributions of my husband, Jeff Henry. Not only did he frequently come with me to some of these events but he also read every draft of this book. This book could not have been written without his constant encouragement.

Introduction

I FIRST TRAVELLED TO TRINIDAD in 1956 as a young doctoral student, hoping to do a study of what was then known as the "Shango Cult". I was living in the United States at that time and studying at an American university. I had already completed a Master's thesis on the forms of worship in a fundamentalist black church in Ohio and had developed a keen interest in the subject of New World African religious forms. One of my professors had studied the Vodou religion in Haiti, and suggested to me that I work on this as well. Since I had very little language facility in French, I looked for an English-speaking area in order to pursue my interest in African-derived religion. Reading Herskovits's *Trinidad Village,* with its brief mentions of the "Shango Cult" in Trinidad, convinced me that I should go to Trinidad.

Accordingly, I arrived in Port of Spain in June of 1956 knowing no one, and certainly not any member of this religious group. I began to ask Trinidadians whom I met about Shango and was surprised to be greeted with horrific stares and exclamations. Most middle-class people I encountered and questioned said they knew nothing about it, but their shocked faces had already given them away. Working-class people I managed to meet said it existed but they were certainly not part of it because "they did the work of the devil". No one would admit to any knowledge or experience of the group, least of all to knowing where their worshippers might be found. I interviewed a few religious leaders who told me that they had vaguely heard that some misguided and ignorant people did still believe in "that sort of African belief" but, of course, no one of any respectability. I was also told, and later confirmed, that the Roman Catholic Church in some areas of the country at that time denied communion to any known practitioner of the "Shango Cult". Members of the academic establishment were no help either, since no one had really looked into this form of religion. The friends I began to make viewed the subject of my inquiry with horror, saying that not only was this not a religion but it was shameful African barbarism. Moreover, it would be dangerous for a foreign white woman like me to even go to the areas where it was practised, much less participate in its rituals. But they could not, or would not, tell where these "areas" were. Gradually I began to get the idea that there was something very wrong in the way this "cult" was perceived by the majority of the population. People were so afraid of it that they would not admit to any knowledge or experience of it.

In those days I travelled in taxis and would always engage the driver and other passengers in conversation, and gradually would raise the subject of Shango. "No, no, madam, you don't want to get involved in that" was the usual reply, until one day I ran into a bit of luck. I was in a private taxi and asked my usual question. The driver looked at me – I could see his surprised eyes in his rear mirror – and asked why I wanted to know. As I told him the reason for my inquiry, he admitted that he did know of a place and would take me there whenever I wanted to go. I said, how about now, and off we went. The rest, as they say, is history.

The driver took me to Tanti Silla's *palais* on St François Valley Road in Belmont, and I immediately saw significance in the name of the road being the same as my own first name. I boldly walked into her yard, where I met Tanti's husband who greeted me cordially and said that she was busy at the moment but would be out soon. She came out of the house a bit later and was somewhat suspicious of me at first. I pressed upon her the reasons for my interest, and she warmed up and invited me to attend her feast that, again luckily for me, was only two weeks away. In the meantime, I was free to speak with her and her associates at any time.

Thus began one of the most exciting, rewarding and beneficial periods of my life. In addition to Tanti Silla and the many other Orisha practitioners whom I met through her, the most important introduction was to Ebenezer

Elliott, "Pa Neezer", the undisputed leader of this religion in all of Trinidad. He came to officiate at Tanti's feast, and when I began talking to him, he was a bit suspicious at first. Later that evening we talked again and he asked me why I wanted to know about the religion. I said that it was unknown outside of Trinidad and I wanted to share the knowledge with my students and others in North America. I also mentioned that I already knew his knowledge was extensive; I told him that he knew more about Shango than anyone else. "It's not Shango, it's the African work, the Orisha work", he said. I knew then that he had accepted me and shortly before he left, he invited me to come down and stay with him at Lengua.

I lived in his house on the Moruga Road for many months, and was able to observe at first hand his spiritual and medical "healing practice", as he was a renowned bush doctor. He also invited me to accompany him when he went to the numerous feasts given by his many spiritual children. We became quite a familiar sight, as a taxi driven by one of Pa's associates containing him, one or two of his special drummers and me would pull up at the home of some Orisha leader. Although occasionally a few eyebrows would be raised, being in Pa's presence meant that I had been given the stamp of approval. Through him I met other leaders and attended many ceremonies, and my ethnographic research went very smoothly for the remainder of my time in Trinidad.

Background to the Present Study

I returned to Trinidad in 1958 for some follow-up research and also spent time in Grenada studying the Orisha religion there. On my many subsequent trips to Trinidad I spent time with Orisha people, and completed a re-study of changes in ritual, practice and observances in 1984. In the early 1990s it became increasingly clear that the Orisha religion, as it was now officially called, was again evolving. The major change was that people were beginning to take notice of it, were less suspicious and were more accepting. Moreover, the government was beginning to take the group seriously and was discussing some policy decisions regarding its status as a religion.

Accordingly my interest was sparked by this new and growing relationship between not only Orisha and the government but also the other major African-derived religion practised in Trinidad: Spiritual and Shouter

Baptism. The relationship between politics and African-derived religions became increasingly interesting, especially when the government allotted a day of official holiday to celebrate the Spiritual and Shouter Baptist religions while declaring a day of celebration for Orisha. I began seriously thinking of undertaking research on this dynamic relationship, developed a research proposal and began fieldwork in 1997 that carried through to 2000.[1]

As so often happens during the course of anthropological fieldwork, as I began my inquiries into the political legitimation of African religions, another dimension of interest began to emerge. As I visited and spoke with Orisha leaders and members it soon became apparent that a major dynamic of change was also taking place particularly *within* the Orisha religion. This was the move towards Africanization or Yorubaization of the ritual, and the elimination of its syncretic Christian elements. What these changes in ritual and doctrine involve is the issue of authenticity – a topic of great importance in the anthropological literature, particularly in the anthropology of religion. It is a major point of contestation within all religions that have had to change as a result of colonization, foreign influences, diffusion, differing interpretations of their own dogma by different leaders and the like. The authenticity or inauthenticity of beliefs, practices and rituals is especially contested in modern and postmodern societies experiencing massive social change, globalization and transnationalism. Although in earlier times Orisha worshippers were not especially concerned with issues of authenticity, that topic has surfaced recently because a group of "innovators" are attempting to develop an infrastructure for this formally decentralized and atomistic religion. Today is a period of transition between the traditional syncretic and the more "modern" African approach to the religion. Both the increasing public or *external* legitimation of African religions by the government and their growing presence on the public agenda, as well as the *internal* processes and dynamics of authentication are influenced by the larger societal changes taking place in the country as it modernizes.

This book therefore presents two levels of analysis. On the one hand there is the macroscopic societal level, in which the development of the sociopolitical changes with respect to marginalized African religions takes place. It provides the overarching framework within which the African religions, especially the Orisha movement, are also changing in structure and ideology. At a more microscopic level, the changes within the religion, especially

with respect to administrative structures and theological and ideological understanding of the ritual, will be examined.

The focus of this book is therefore twofold:

- The growing political and social legitimation of African-derived religions, primarily the Orisha movement, as they move from oppression and marginalization to occupying a more accepted role in mainstream Trinidad society;
- The dynamics of change with respect to the challenge of authenticity within the Orisha religion.

A number of research questions inform this book. These are:

- Why have these formerly despised religions become almost mainstream?
- Why are they increasing their membership and their activities, both ceremonial and secular?
- Why has the government, in terms of both benefits and legislation, increasingly recognized them?
- How has public legitimation affected the internal dynamics of the religions, especially the Orisha movement?
- What motivates the need to Africanize or Yorubanize the Orisha religion?

Legitimation Processes

Political Legitimation

The political legitimation of the African religions can be studied from several perspectives. In the first instance, official or legislative actions are a good indicator of how change is effected. In recent times there has been some significant legislation with respect to the religions; one of the most important is the granting of a public holiday to the Spiritual Baptists that involved changing the legislation regulating public holidays in the country. Most recently, the government legislated a marriage act for the Orisha faith. Other official benefits have been granted to both religions.

Public Ceremonies

These are events that are developed by the religions but that include the full participation of government and officialdom. The Orisha religion now celebrates a public Family Day to which members of government and officials, the public at large, and notable people are invited, and many attend. The public celebration of the Spiritual Baptist holiday, in which large numbers of political and other notables participate, is another example.

Media Coverage

The extensive coverage by the media of all Orisha and Spiritual Baptist events is a relatively new phenomenon and reflects the growing legitimation of these groups. The media coverage can be used as both an indicator of legitimation and a creator of it, in the sense that the more the media participates in these events, the more attention and legitimation the groups receive.

Popular Culture

Contributing to the growing acceptance of these groups is the way in which their portrayal in the popular culture, especially in calypso music, has changed. In early calypsos the religions were mocked and reviled, but in more recent times their image has changed in positive directions. Also, several outstanding exponents of this popular art form are themselves members or supporters of the religions. The importance of the African religions to the development of the steelband and their relationship to Carnival are only now beginning to be explored.

Internal Changes

Identity

As public or official changes are taking place the religions, and especially the Orisha, are undergoing significant internal changes. At the level of organization, a group of younger innovators are attempting to develop a centralized infrastructure for the management of the religions. With respect to social organization, the religion is continuing to attract younger members who are concerned with their personal and cultural identities and are trying to establish a connection to the African origin of their ancestors.

These more private or internal aspects of the process appear to relate to the need, in postmodern societies, to re-establish personal and national identities. At the personal level, particularly among younger people, the need to establish an identity apart from that which was imposed during the colonial era becomes an important part of the socialization process. Black nationalism and the Black Power movement brought this into sharp relief. It is not surprising therefore that African-derived people look back to their historical origins and the culture from which they were taken to reshape their identities. In Trinidad the most dominant African cultural form has been the Orisha religion, which has survived, albeit with changes, over the many years of its suppression. Thus, it is through the belief in African religion as it is practised here that a growing number of younger people are attracted to it. The need to reaffirm African identity is made all the more urgent in recent times, since an "Indian" government has come to power and there is a resurgence of Indianness in Trinidad society. Afro-Trinidadians have become quite apprehensive about what they perceive to be Indian favouritism and a loss of power within their own group. Reaffirming African identity, through commitment to an African religion, has become even more crucial today.

Authenticity and Syncretism

As newer members are reclaiming their African identity through involvement with Orisha, they are also attempting to transform some ritual and ceremonial practices to conform more closely to the religion's African origins. One of the most important of these is the desire to eliminate or reduce the Christian syncretism that affected the religion from its beginnings in the Caribbean. The need to become more African and "authentic" has become a sharply contested discourse within the largely amorphous group. It pits the younger innovators against the older and more traditional members of the faith, many of whom cling to their learned ways and continue Christian practices. This new movement within the Trinidadian group has, however, also resulted in the addition of ritualistic and ceremonial practices derived from its African Yoruba source. It also raises the question of how "authentic" the Orisha religion is as practised in a changing Nigeria where its source, the Yoruba, were exposed to missionaries under colonial rule.

The components of legitimation and the internal dynamics of change will be discussed in subsequent chapters. Both dynamics must be understood within the context of the general and more overarching impact of globalization on Trinidadian society and its political and socio-economic infrastructures. In addition to being influenced by the economic and political dynamics of globalization, the society of Trinidad and Tobago is characterized by some particular and even unique elements that play a role in motivating some of the external and internal changes taking place in the Orisha and Spiritual Baptist faiths. The fact that Trinidad is a plural society in which two ethnic groups, virtually equal in numbers, compete for place, power and resources must also be considered in understanding the strong position taken by the government in granting benefits and guaranteeing rights to these religious groups.

The oil boom of the late 1980s had a great impact on Trinidad. It has become a modern, even a postmodern society, characterized by the challenging of tradition, rapid rates of change and the importance of materialism and consumerism. Modernism also brings with it an increased focus on issues relating to national and personal identity. At the national level, this plays out in the often tense relationship between the two main ethnic groups, and the role that politics plays in trying to maintain a stable and accommodating society. This brings into play the need for any government to win the support of members of both ethnic groups. The present government of the United National Congress (UNC), headed by Prime Minister Basdeo Panday, is widely perceived to be an "Indian" government largely favouring its own ethnic group at the expense of the Afro-Trinidadian community.[2]

The government is therefore eager to demonstrate that it also grants benefits to the Afro-Trinidadians, who make up the majority of worshippers in African-derived religions. Certainly one way of demonstrating support, as well as, in all likelihood, trying to gain electoral support from this community is by appealing to the deeply felt religious fervour so characteristic of Trinidadian people and by providing them with assistance.

Theoretical Orientation

In attempting to present some systematic analysis of the research questions that frame this book, several theoretical perspectives have been drawn upon. In general terms, religion is viewed as part of a *cultural system* constantly constructed and reconstructed in response to human experience and the changing socio-political realities of society.[3] Religion as such cannot be understood as a static institutional category because religious practices are in a state of constant change and are influenced by the social and historical contexts in which they are found. Like any institution in society, religion is a constructed and interpretative category.[4] As such, studies of religion must take into account the power relations and ideological structure of a society. As John Nelson notes, "anthropological studies of religion can not be separated from the study of power, ideology, or semiotics any more than heart surgery can proceed without a knowledge of the interrelation of the body's circulatory, nervous, and muscular structures".[5]

While it has been assumed that modernism and its reliance on science and technology would reduce the need for religion,[6] in fact, social scientists who study religion and modern social movements have found that there has been an increase in socio-religious movements even in technologically advanced countries. It has been suggested that such movements fill a need because of the fragmentation and alienation produced in modern and postmodern societies. People feel insecure and in need of ideological assurance. As well, they feel increasingly marginalized from the centres of power. Many of the new religions therefore are committed to finding new ways and a new ideology in order to "empower the individual" and to seek "a direct correspondence between human action and a meaningful context for its expression (often in the embrace of a sanctioned institution), and at providing a sense of community, support, and guidance".[7]

While Orisha and Spiritual Baptism cannot be considered new religious movements, their new status of legal, political and social acceptance almost puts them into that category. These religions are, moreover, empowering individuals in new ways. What the innovators in Orisha are attempting in bringing back Africanisms is not only to reaffirm African identity and ideologies but also to empower the group and its members. These formerly despised religions, whose members were mocked and powerless, are now positioning themselves in new spaces within their society.

Earlier it was mentioned that globalization plays a role in the transformation of African religions in Trinidad. Globalization theory therefore also informs this project. How is this international dynamic relevant to the present study of religious change? The term "globalization" is used loosely in public discourse, but a more concise definition is required here. Scholte defines the dynamics of globalization as "the emergence and spread of a supraterritorial dimension of social relations. It impacts all the institutions of society through the growth of transnational corporations and regulatory agencies, round the world financial markets' production lines and consumption patterns."[8] As Lorne Dawson (quoting Jan Aart Scholte) explains, it also influences the values of society by establishing common scales of measurement and universal human rights, as well as

> "non-territorial networks of collective solidarity (e.g., among women, the disabled or indigenous peoples.)" . . . A comprehensive shift in the basic conditions of social relations is being effected, whereby the world is becoming a "single place" . . . growing cognizance that our identities, both as individuals and as societies, are now being shaped to an ever greater extent by a larger interactive order of societies stretching around the globe.

Globalization has also affected the relationship of individuals to society, and it has therefore

> produced a heightened cultural and individual comprehension of the socially constructed character of particular identities . . . [and] heightens the need felt by individuals and their governments to self-consciously fashion strong collective identities. Fostering such group identities is, of course, another of the conventional functions served by traditional religious belief systems and more recently by systems of civil religion.

Thus, the changes taking place within and to African and especially the Orisha religions in Trinidad and Tobago today can be seen as part of a larger dynamic of international globalization and its impact on both societal institutional restructuring and the often stressful relationships between individuals and society.

Another useful approach is provided by the literature on "popular" religion, defined as a religion of the people that "flourishes on the margins . . . and is always peripheral to institutions", as opposed to an official state religion.[9] "Popular" religion is one that is continually being redefined and reinterpreted, appeals primarily to the masses as opposed to the elite in society, and emphasizes problem solving and survival strategy for its largely disadvantaged followers. Popular religion has many uses, one of which is to minimize the distinction between it and the official religions. In so doing, the popular religion loses some of its marginal appeal and becomes more official in perspective. Some of the changes in the societal positioning of both

Spiritual Baptism and Orisha worship in Trinidad can be understood from this perspective.

Another useful orientation is that provided by the literature on cultural and national identity. Stuart Hall's distinction, between cultural identity understood as shared culture and history and cultural identity viewed as always in flux and in a state of becoming rather than being, is extremely useful.[10] Cultural identities have histories but are also constantly undergoing transformations as they are subjected to the continuous play of history, culture and power. Cultural identities are not always integrated into a national cultural identity. Membership and participation in Spiritual Baptism and Orisha are important to the way in which people define themselves. However, it is clear from the marginalized histories of both religious groups that they have never been defined as part of the national culture that "imagines" itself as constructed solely from denominational Christian origins and South Asian–derived religious traditions, including Hinduism and Islam. There was no identified role in the national culture for African-based religions until recently. Africanization, which started with the Black Power movement in the 1970s and 1980s, is today being given impetus by the politics of identity as a counterforce to the resurgence of Indian ethnicity, culture and political power. This leads to greater involvement of young people who need to reaffirm their black African identity and Orisha, as an African-based religion, provides one such vehicle. Thus, the increasing political legitimation of both groups can also be understood in terms of the recognition of the vitality of these religions in defining individual cultural identity and as part of the emerging reconstruction of Trinidadian national cultural identity.

Of particular interest in this project is the role of younger innovators who are at the forefront of attempting to change and Africanize the Orisha religion. Basic to their motivation is the need to reaffirm black African identity, in addition to their national identity as Trinidadians. The notion of identity is also related to the notion of representation. New, younger members of Orisha want to represent themselves as "Africans" rather than, or in addition to, Afro-Trinidadians, and Orisha presents one mechanism for such representation. Rahier stresses the changing nature of black identity when he notes that

> Black identities cannot be defined once and for all by pointing to – more or less vaguely – "their origin", as some sort of immutable entities. . . . Black identities

are defined and redefined, imagined and re-imagined, performed and performed again within the flux of history and within specific, changing, spatially determined societal structures.[11]

Black identity formation and its changes relate strongly to black cultural forms as being the site of resistance. Throughout history, black resistance has taken many forms and cannot be essentialized. The notion of resistance, therefore, is also important to the analysis of legitimation. Keeping Orisha traditions alive during the periods of slavery and colonialism was an important form of black resistance in the Caribbean. The current attempt to eliminate the Christian elements brought into it because of slavery and colonialism can also be considered a form of resistance through insisting that Orisha should only be practised according to its original Yoruba source.

Another important dimension of the theoretical analysis is how the various ideological, doctrinal and ritual changes that have occurred in these religions, and especially within the Orisha movement, can be analysed from the perspective of the notions of *authenticity* and *inauthenticity* as contested sites within the study of African-derived religions.

The topic of authenticity can be fraught with difficulty. Authenticity is self-evident to believers in a tradition who know that their form of religious expression is not only authentic and true but also hegemonic because it is the right and only path to follow. Thus, authenticity also means that "divergences from the tradition are *inauthentic*" (italics mine). (Some religions are, however, "henotheistic" in that they accept the interpretation of not only other religions but also members of their own faiths whose interpretations of an event, text or statement may differ from that of others. Hinduism and Tibetan Buddhism are examples of such faiths.)[12] Many scholars in this field state that they do not study the metaphysical claims to authenticity but rather the "authentication process".[13] This is defined as "the processes through which orthodoxy or legitimacy is determined and this can be studied independently of theological claims and theological categories". These processes constitute the legitimate inquiry of sociological analysis and include "the status of religious views, institutions, personnel, texts, behavior patterns, sacred sites . . . when understood and practised as authoritative by individuals and/or groups".[14] This book stays within this sociological perspective. It does not challenge the supernatural or metaphysical bases of the claims to authenticity made by members of these African-derived religions.

Rather, its focus is on "authentication processes" that involve the work of living human beings today.

The issue of authenticity is not new to Caribbean studies. As Glazier notes, early controversies between Herskovits and Frazier revolved around the issue of whether African survivals could be found in the New World. Herskovits spent his scholarly life searching for them and was the first to recognize that in the area of religions Orisha (Shango, Candomblé and so on) was among the purest of these survivals. Today the participants themselves conduct the battles over authenticity.[15]

The need for African authenticity on the part of the innovators in the Orisha movement is powerful but so is the resistance of average worshippers, especially older members, who wish to worship the way they initially learned to. Arguments take place between members and even between elders over this issue, and it is clearly a major site of contestation. (Chapter 6 explores the case study of a congress held in 1999 in which this issue surfaced as a major dynamic.) And, as Glazier also notes, African religions have changed, and therefore the question must be raised as to what is authentic. In view of the work of missionaries in African societies, it is highly doubtful that the Yoruba Orisha religion as practised in Nigeria today is what it used to be.[16] Africans travel to the New World because they believe that some of the Caribbean versions of their religion, which date back in time, are more authentic than what is practised in Nigeria today. The president of the World Orisha Steering Committee stated publicly at a conference held in Trinidad that he travels to Brazil every year and has been doing so for twenty years in order to learn and relearn his religion. Moreover, the African delegates to the congres, including the chair and leading executive committee members, are themselves Christians. The Ooni of Ife, titular and symbolic head of the Orisha religion worldwide, is a Methodist. This raises questions about the meaning of "authenticity" and, if that construct is contested, how "inauthenticity" can be defined (see chapter 5).

A Note on Methodology

The main data-gathering instruments during the course of this fieldwork consisted of approximately one hundred hours of participant observation at Orisha and Spiritual Baptist events and intensive interviewing of leaders, members, politicians, notables and others associated with either religion. Formal interviews were conducted with forty-five persons but many more were informally questioned or interviewed at the many events that I attended. I tried to talk to every major figure in the Orisha movement as well as a sampling of Baptist leaders and practitioners. I would estimate that I talked to hundreds of members over the course of the fieldwork period of nine months (spread out over a three-year period).

Another very important source was archival records. These included transcriptions of Hansard covering the various parliamentary debates over the Orisha and Spiritual Baptist holidays and celebrations. In addition, back issues of the main newspapers, the *Trinidad Guardian* and the *Trinidad Express* going back to the early 1980s, were searched for their coverage of events that took place prior to the fieldwork. I collected a newspaper file of nearly seventy articles.

For the analysis of African religious representation in calypsos, several collectors were contacted who searched through their collections of materials and supplied lyrics. Musicians such as Andre Tanker, David Rudder and Ella Andall were interviewed and they also supplied some lyrics. Their views and perceptions were especially useful in framing the analysis of the role of popular culture in legitimating African religions.

Finally, a very important aspect of the methodology involves my own historical involvement with Orisha and Spiritual Baptism, which spans over forty-six years – half a lifetime! This gives me a sense of the development of the religions and a time perspective rare in anthropological fieldwork. Some of my early respondents were the very "ancestors" virtually worshipped today by the modern generations of believers. I met Bishop Griffith, the force behind the abolition of the Shouters Prohibition Act (see chapter 2), personally while he was on a crusade mobilizing support for these political objectives. He discussed with me the need for the repeal of this repressive legislation and he also allowed me to take photos of him and some of his colleagues. Today, Bishop Griffith is only a historical icon to this generation of Baptists.

This early involvement has stood me in good stead in conducting this study. I was remembered by Mother Rodney, the current spiritual head of the movement, from my time with Pa Neezer. She reminded me that she used to work in his kitchen during feasts and at that time she kept shyly in the background. She knew well the "white, foreign lady who Pa uses to talk to – she lived in his very house", she explained to one of her associates when I first came to visit her. Some of the younger members were amazed that I knew their mothers or grandmothers.

In writing this book, I have attempted wherever possible to cite the actual words of respondents as they talked to me or were quoted in the press. The danger of appropriating the culture of others and attaching meanings to their behaviour not necessarily applied by them presents a constant threat to social anthropologists. I have consciously tried to steer away from interpretations and explanations that would not be consistent with the beliefs of the people I have studied. I have also tried not to be offensive to any members of the religious groups that are the object of this book and hope that, for the most part, I have been successful. If my words are taken wrongly, however, I apologize and state unequivocally that no offence was meant. I have included a substantial number of case studies taken directly from interviews and many actual quotes, so that the voice of the people can be heard clearly throughout the work.

Finally, I need to state my own subjective biases with respect to these religions and especially Orisha. Because of my lifetime experience with it, I feel very close to the religion and its adherents. Although I have never been initiated because I cannot in honesty profess faith, I strongly believe in the Orisha as part of the supernatural forces that dwell in the universe. Although I was born Jewish I have never practised this religion with any fervour. I do define myself and part of my identity as Jewish, and am committed to its culture though not necessarily to its religious practices. I do not believe in a God as such, but do believe in supernatural forces of which the Orisha, in my personal cosmology, are included.

I also identify myself as an advocate for African religions in Trinidad and elsewhere because their adherents and practitioners were, and to some extent still are, oppressed, marginalized and excluded from the religious structure of this society. I firmly believe in their right to worship as they choose, and welcome the changes brought about by legislative and social action to bring them into the mainstream of society.

Outline of the Book

Chapters 1 and 2 provide the reader with the ethnographic background to both religions, describing their ritual practices then and now. History, ritual, ceremonials and doctrines of Spiritual Baptism and Orisha worship in Trinidad are described.

Chapter 3, "The Formal Processes of Political Legitimation", begins the analysis by examining, in detail, the societal or external level within Trinidad society in which the growing legitimation of African religions has taken place. It describes the various governmental and legislative changes that are helping to bring them from the margins towards the mainstream of religious life in the country.

Chapter 4, "The Orisha Religion from Sacred to Secular: The Evolution of the Shango Cult into the Orisha Movement", continues this theme by describing how the religions are reorganizing and restructuring themselves by moving towards more centralized and standardized forms of decision making. It focuses on the need to develop the secular aspects of these organizations.

This chapter discusses the structure and organization of the two religions as they are practised today. It contains an analysis of the attempt to create a national infrastructure in both groups, and the difficulties faced by them as they attempt to modernize and move away from the traditionally individualistic form of organization. The establishment of the Council of Elders and nominating official public relations officers and other administrative personnel are part of this process.

Chapter 5, "Contested Theologies in the Orisha Movement: Discourses of Authenticity and Inauthenticity", provides a detailed discussion of contested areas within the Orisha movement, beginning with the notions of Africanization centring around the ideas of authenticity and inauthenticity.

This chapter describes in detail the Yorubanization of what used to be called "the Shango Cult" into its present form of the Orisha movement. Using my earlier ethnographic study of Shango, the changes that have taken place in the intervening years will be described. Most of these involve the increasing Africanization of the religion and the attempt, by some groups, to decrease the number and extent of Christian elements.

Chapter 6, "The Role of Syncretism in the Orisha Religion Today", continues this analysis by examining in more detail the nature of syncretism – how syncretic the religion still is, as well as the need on the part of the innovators who want only African ritual to remove its syncretisms. The move towards Yorubaization has inspired the contested issues of authenticity and syncretism, discussions that occupied most of the proceedings of a world congress of Orisha worship held in Trinidad in 1999. These proceedings will be presented in this chapter as a case study.

Chapter 7, "African Religions and Popular Culture: Calypsos, Steelband and Carnival", returns to the more overarching societal level by showing how African religions are featured in popular culture, especially calypso. The roles of Orisha and Spiritual Baptism in the popular art form of calypso are explored, showing that, while most references to these African religions in earlier times were extremely negative, increasingly they are being praised by calypsonians as true and authentic. Calypsos dating back to the 1930s and up to the present day, in particular some of the Orisha-framed songs of David Rudder, are analysed in this chapter. As well, the important role of Orisha in the development of *ole mas* characters in Carnival and the influence of these religions in the development of the steelband are discussed.

The concluding chapter addresses the issue of whether these African traditions as they exist in Trinidad today can properly be classified as "religions".

Note on Terms and Spelling

IT IS ALWAYS DIFFICULT to find terms that accurately represent people and groups without offending them. I have used the term "innovators" to describe the group that is in the forefront of bringing about changes in the internal rituals and practices of the Orisha movement. The term "traditionalists", however, is fraught with ideological connotations that are not consistent with the aims of this group, and has therefore not been used. Descriptors such as "Africanizers" or "Yorubanizers" also did not appear to be appropriate.

In the popular discourse, especially as reflected in the press, the members of the religion are increasingly referred to as "Orishas". I do not think that this identifier is in keeping with the meaning of this Yoruba term (spirit or deity), nor does it reflect the practice of the people. I have rarely heard a worshipper refer to him- or herself as an "Orisha". I therefore use the more awkward phraseology "members of the Orisha religion", or something close to that.

In keeping with the trend towards Africanization, some Yoruba spellings are now used by practitioners and journalists. For example, "Orisha" is now often spelled without the "h". Similarly, there is some confusion around the spelling of the Yoruba *ase* (power), which is sometimes spelled *ashe*. Much of the written literature, however, still retains the older usages, and I have also decided to retain them. Wherever possible I have used the spellings that appeared to be used most often.

> When Nezer of Moruga walked this earth
> Mighty Babalorisha,
> Papa Nezer
> Father to them all,
> And still remembered . . .
> – *Eintou Pearl Springer, "The Yard"*

CHAPTER ONE

The Orisha Religion in Trinidad Today

THE ORISHA RELIGION IN Trinidad is historically derived from the complex of religious beliefs found among the Yoruba people of Nigeria.[1] Its religious system is syncretic; that is, elements of Catholicism have become fused with native African beliefs. This is most striking in the identification of African gods with Catholic saints; for example, Shango, the Yoruba god of thunder, has become identified with John the Baptist. In more recent times, elements of Hinduism have also found their way into the religion, and some scholars suggest that Kabbalistic elements can also be found in the practices of a few leaders.[2] Orisha worship is found throughout the Caribbean but only in those countries that were colonized by the Spanish or the French, who brought Roman Catholicism with them. The syncretism between Orisha and Catholicism developed in part because of the multiplicity of saints who could be identified with Orisha deities.[3] Similar syncretic belief systems have been described in Haiti,[4] Brazil[5] and Cuba.[6] It is thought that the Orisha religion began in the middle of the nineteenth century in Trinidad, as slaves from Yoruba lands were sent there in significant numbers.[7] More recently, Orisha worship derived from the Caribbean or from Africa directly is a rapidly growing religion among African Americans and migrants from the Caribbean.[8] Recent studies of these religions in the United States include works by George Brandon, Kamari Clarke and Marta Vega.[9]

The annual ceremony performed by active leaders was formerly called a "feast" or "sacrifice" but today the Yoruba term *Ebo*, meaning "sacrifice", is in common usage. This takes place in the courtyard of the leader's home. In earlier times, leaders were sometimes called priests or more often just addressed as "leader". Today the terms *baba* and *iya* are often used. The courtyard is now called a "shrine" and, in the more progressive groups, the Yoruba *Ile* is used. It is composed of the leader's house, a separate kitchen, the *palais, chapelle* and the "tombs". The *palais*, where the major part of the ceremony takes place, is an area of approximately thirty by thirty feet that used to be covered by a palm thatched or "carrat" roof, supported by four or more upright log beams planted in the ground. Today, it is more usual to find corrugated tin or galvanized roofing. The beams are interconnected by rough boards reaching about one-third of the distance from the ground to the thatched roof. The boards, serving as partial walls about five feet in height, have extensions built into the *palais* area. These board extensions serve as benches for the spectators. In two corners of the structure there is an opening that serves as a door. The floor is made of packed earth in order to ensure greater contact with the spirit world. In more modern *palais* the structure tends to be more elaborate, with whitewashed walls and real benches. In one well-known shrine, there is a separate seating gallery for visitors and the entire compound is considerably larger than most others.

The *chapelle* is a small (approximately ten by ten feet) one- or two-room "church" with wattle and daub or wooden walls; the ground consists of packed or flattened earth. The *chapelle* is generally located near the *palais* and contains altars, lithographs of the saints and the implements used by the gods. There are usually three to five altars dedicated to various important gods that hold both Catholic and African symbols. Crosses, rosaries, colourful holy statues and thunderstones (Carib or Arawak celts), obi seeds and axes are mingled in profusion. Chromolithographs of the saints hang on the walls, while various implements of the gods lay scattered in corners on the earthen floor. On feast days large coloured flags are hung in the *chapelle*.

Despite the attempts at Africanization and the removal of syncretic Christian elements, most *chapelles* still contain pictures of Catholic saints.

Near the gate or entrance to the courtyard (or, in some cases, scattered about the *chapelle*) is a small secluded area. Here the "tombs" (also called "stools" or "pere-oguns" or "memorial stones") to the Orisha are placed. There are five to seven such "tombs" dedicated to the major gods. These are generally flat, raised, cement platforms (but sometimes merely mounds of earth) on which are placed candles, flowers, pottery jugs, bottles of olive oil and other sacred items. Protruding from the centre of each "tomb" is an implement that is associated with the particular god. When these are metal they are charred or burned. Two of the gods (Ogun-St Michael and Shakpana-St Jerome), as well as others, have flags of their sacred colour set on long bamboo poles waving over their "tombs". Shakpana-St Jerome has a forked branch with a burned pottery jug resting in the fork implanted in his "tomb". Leaders, who are more often today designated by the title *Baba* or the feminine *Iya* or the honorific title of "elder", hold a major feast once a year, usually beginning after Easter or around Christmas time. *Ebo*s are sometimes scheduled on a particular saint's day venerated by the leader. The feast begins on a Tuesday evening and continues uninterrupted until the final animal sacrifice on Saturday morning. Following an interval of one week, and if the leader can afford the expense, another feast is held from Wednesday evening until Saturday morning. This is known as "the return" and is explained thus: "when you give somebody something, it's nice to get a return". The "return" does not appear to be practised much today; a one-week ceremony usually suffices. Sometimes a leader will depart from the Tuesday schedule and begin a feast on a Sunday evening if divining or a dream has said to begin on that day. Occasionally some leaders give one- or two-day feasts to commemorate special events at odd times during the year, for example, on New Year's Day.

A typical feast begins anywhere between nine and eleven in the evening. In earlier times, approximately twenty-five to fifty people were seated in the *palais* on rough wooden benches and a comparable number circulated about the courtyard. Today the numbers attending a feast have dropped markedly; there can be as few as ten. At this time the atmosphere is rather casual: people joke with each other, renew friendships, eat dinner, play with children and the like. Despite the mood of jocularity, the air is filled with tension and suspense. Occasionally a few people in the *palais* begin singing, with or without the accompaniment of the drums. As soon as the leader and the *mongba* (teacher) who leads the singing enter, the latter frequently holding a rosary and a candle, and kneel in the centre of the *palais*, people come to attention. The *mongba* begins chanting the Lord's Prayer, Hail Marys, sometimes the Catholic Litany of the Saints and other Catholic prayers. He recites line by line as the audience responds with antiphonal chants. At times he interrupts the prayers to sprinkle water from a pottery jug into the four corners of the *palais*. The same prayers are constantly repeated and the entire prayer period can last as long as two hours. (In some *Ebos* today there is an attempt to eliminate, or at least reduce, the number of Christian prayers chanted. In one *Ebo* given by a well-known elder, however, the prayers lasted for well over an hour with worshippers kneeling throughout this lengthy period.) At some of the progressive *iles*, the evening begins with Yoruba song followed by Yoruba prayers to each of the major deities being honoured at the feast. If a member can pronounce the Yoruba, the prayers are read in that language and an English translation is then provided.

During this time more and more people enter the *palais*. As the prayer period comes to an end a hymn may or may not be sung, depending in large part upon the whim of the leader. After this, one or more members, "servants to the powers", place a candle flanked by two calabashes containing water and ashes, respectively, at the centre of the *palais*. A circle of olive oil is drawn around it by slowly pouring the oil from a bottle. The three drummers and the *chac-chac* players enter and sit at one end of the *palais*; the leader is in front of them, often resting on a chair. He begins the first song to Eshu, the trickster deity, who in earlier times was also identified as the devil. The drums pick up the beat and the audience begins singing. At the same time a circle of approximately twenty people, mostly women, forms. The women begin to dance in a slow shuffle around the candle and calabash. This dance is said to ensnare or encircle Eshu to keep him from coming to the *Ebo* and disrupting the procedures. One leader recently referred to this practice as "Eshuing". Seven songs are sung to Eshu and each new song is marked by a reversal of the dancing circle. At the conclusion of the sixth song the candle and calabashes are thrown out by the same "servant to the powers". The circle procedure is known as "getting rid of the devil" or "giving him his due". However, few people today refer to Eshu as the devil.

The Orisha Religion in Trinidad Today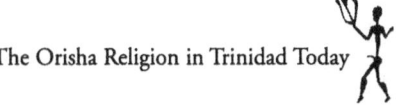

Immediately following the last song to Eshu singing begins to Ogun, who is identified as St Michael, the leading deity in the Orisha pantheon. At least seven songs must be sung to Ogun to equal the number sung to the devil, because "the saints are higher than the devil".

Usually, after three or four songs to Ogun, the first possession manifesting the characteristics ascribed to Ogun begins. (Possessions today are generally known as "manifestations". In earlier times, "getting the power" was the more usual description.) Generally a woman dancing in the circle begins violently swaying back and forth. Her eyes become glazed and dilated and her face undergoes a radical transformation, becoming quite masculine, with lips and chin protruding. She falls back and is supported by several bystanders, thereby breaking the circle of dancers. Singing and drumming cease temporarily. One bystander ties a red (Ogun's colour) headband about the possessed woman's head, another ties a sash underneath her stomach, and her jewellery and shoes are removed. During this dressing period the possessed woman is held by others so that the god or "power" may be dressed properly and given a chance to "settle". This "power" then breaks away and begins dancing in the *palais*. Meanwhile the drumming and singing have resumed. At times the "power" may run into the *chapelle* and kneel on the floor or run to the "tomb" area or anywhere about the courtyard. The "power" calls for his implements, a sword or cutlass in Ogun's case, and dances with them. Ogun greets the audience, generally in a mixture of English and patois, for example, "Bon Soir, tout monde, good night all." He may bless all present by distributing olive oil either to drink or to be rubbed onto the head and face. The singing to Ogun continues either until Ogun decides that he has had enough songs or until the leader sings to another power.[10] After the arrival of Ogun-St Michael, different powers "manifest" upon other individuals.[11]

Most active Orisha participants have one or more special patrons who "manifest" upon them regularly. Such individuals are often, even today, termed "horses" or "saint horses" and identified as "she Ogun [St Michael] horse", or "she take Ogun [Michael]", "Ogun [Michael] manifest on her". Among modern worshippers, the Yoruba Orisha name is more likely to be used, but older members still tend to refer to the saints' names. The more patrons one has, the greater the prestige, so that the leaders can and do "take any power" or "have many manifestations".

Singing, drumming and spirit possessions continue until three to five o'clock in the morning. The duration depends to some degree upon general fatigue. People then go to sleep for a few hours, finding themselves berths anywhere in the courtyard. Many leave to go home to rest briefly and then go to work. When dawn comes, activities begin again. At sunrise, selected animals are washed and sacrificed to the powers, with the accompaniment of drums. The killing, preceded by the casting of obi seeds to determine if the powers will accept the sacrifice, takes place in the *chapelle*, and the blood of the animals is splashed over the "tombs". More drum beating and manifestations may take place following the sacrifice until about ten in the morning. People who have regular jobs leave sometime in the morning and return again the following evening. Today, more people tend to leave for their workplaces during the day. One or two of the women remain and spend the day cooking the sacrificed animals. Some food is cooked without salt and this is offered to the powers on large leaves, in front of their particular "tombs". The rest, cooked with salt, is eaten by the participants. At approximately the same time on the next evening the entire ceremony begins again until its conclusion on Saturday morning.

Occasionally, during the late afternoon, one of the water powers may "manifest" upon his or her "horse" and call for a special river ceremony. Then a procession, sometimes dressed in white, marches to the river. Food is placed on the banks of the river and singing and drumming to the particular water power takes place. This only occurs when the leader's courtyard is situated near a river. However, several leaders now routinely hold ceremonies dedicated to the water goddess Oshun. At one such ceremony, as many as 250 people attended the beach ceremony during which flags were placed on the beach and the congregants sang as they formed concentric circles. There were also several short manifestations of Oshun. A high point of the water ceremony was the placing of food sacrifices in the water as offerings to Oshun. The tide is supposed to carry them out but it did not appear strong enough, so several participants waded out into the water and pushed the offerings out.

With the increasing Africanization of this religion, more Yoruba festivals are being recreated. Recently, a ceremony honouring the rain was started by one prominent leader and another held a special festival honouring the Orisha Olukun.

Orisha Cosmology

The Orisha, gods or "powers" inhabit the heaven and are called "heavenly powers". Other powers exist, but these are the powers of darkness and evil that inhabit the "nether" regions. In my first Orisha study, a well-known leader talked about evil powers: "It have plenty. Not here, you know. It have its place – circle work Joe Steele, Skull and Crossbones, Prince of Darkness. It have plenty who say they giving Shango dance, but call evil. They do all kinds of wrong, say they do Orisha work, but use the black hand."

The reference here is clearly to Kabbalistic practices, which then, as today, are widely performed. Occasionally during an *Ebo* such an evil spirit can appear despite the fact that he has not been summoned. These evil spirits are then exorcized by the major heavenly powers, usually Ogun-St Michael. Groups working with these supposed evil powers are greatly feared. There appears to be a relationship between the familiarity of the "horse" to the group and this interpretation. Thus, unfamiliar "horses" were frequently accused of manifesting evil spirits or non-recognized powers.

The deities or powers are believed to lead ordinary lives in heaven. Indeed, it seems that the powers are looked upon as if they lived on earth, "always around working". The chief deity is Oludumare, the supreme being, who is thought of as "everything", while the rest of the Orisha are deities who control and protect aspects of the environment and, at the same time, are able to influence the lives of people. While, theoretically, the Orisha live in heaven, the concept of heaven as home for the powers is vague and nebulous. The Orisha may arrive with or without being summoned, especially in the latter case, when they have "work to do". The nature of this work, aside from dancing at feasts, appears to be diagnosing and suggesting cures for ills and delivering messages to "warn of something going wrong or something going happen". The specific behaviour of an Orisha is said to be a function of what activity he or she was engaged in at the time of being summoned. For example, if Ebejee-St Peter calls for a dagger when he arrives, this means that he has been fishing. If, however, he calls for a key, he has just been opening or closing the heavenly gate. Similarly, Ogun-St Michael will call for a cutlass if he has merely been protecting heaven and his dancing and activity will be relatively subdued. If he has been fighting he will call for a sword and dance violently and behave aggressively.

The Orisha can "manifest" on any person. Generally a "horse" will have one or two special patrons who regularly manifest upon him or her. Indeed, an Orisha is recognized after his arrival not so much by his behaviour, but by the regularity of the manifestation on the same person or "horse". The deities are free to choose their "horses", and very frequently individuals become "overshadowed" with a power. They do not fall into the deep trancelike state of active spirit possession but may become dizzy, fall down or shake violently for a few moments and then return to normal. When this occurs it is said to be a power trying to find a "horse" to settle upon.

This may happen, for example, to two or three individuals at the same time, and then a fourth individual may suddenly become completely possessed. In order to receive a power the "horse" must be "living clean" or abstaining from sexual activities and from consuming alcohol two to three days prior to and during the feast. Rejected individuals, that is, those who do not "manifest or catch power", are assumed to have lived "unclean" and are considered "not proper horses". In at least one orthodox Orisha shrine or yard, women who are menstruating are not allowed into the ceremonial area because they are said to be unclean. It is feared that this condition will prevent the Orisha from attending and blessing the *Ebo*.

At the time of first possession, or when a person first "falls under a power or manifests an Orisha", the leader at whose shrine this event takes place interprets to the new person the name of the god who possesses him. The behaviour of a newly possessed person is erratic. For example, he may call for several conflicting implements or use different dance steps. When this occurs it is said that several powers are competing for the new "horse"; that is, one power says to the other, "See what a nice new horse I have." The other powers become jealous and attempt to compete for possession of the new "horse". Newer and younger Orisha members recognize that this signifies the beginning or learning of a manifestation.

The powers of Orisha are said to come in threes. Thus, for example, three individuals may simultaneously be possessed by Shango–St John. However, each is possessed by a different form of St John, for example, the Baptist, the Evangelist and of the Cross. While, in theory, this is supposed to occur with all powers, it was noted in the earlier study that only Saints John and Francis have multiple manifestations, as might be expected in view of the fact that the several saints bearing these names respectively are particularly well known. No multiple manifestations were observed at more recent *Ebos*.

In earlier times most Orisha worshippers had little knowledge concerning the African origins of the deities. The major leaders and a handful of active participants (those who became possessed frequently) were able to cite African names; the rest seemed more comfortable referring to and following the Catholic saints. Respondents spontaneously talked about the saints rather than the African gods. To illustrate this point, one major leader was asked if Shango and Oya were married. His reply was, "St John the Baptist never married." On the whole, most of the participants were primarily concerned with the feasting, singing, drumming and possession aspects of the ceremonies and indicate little knowledge of, or concern with, the theology underlying the practices that they accepted and shared unquestioningly.

Today the African origins of the Orisha are understood by many more worshippers. The supreme deity, Olodumare, is mentioned often and more of the original Yoruba Orisha are now recognized. The role of the ancestors and ancestor worship is also being brought into the religion by innovating individuals.[12] Many more worshippers have been taught Yoruba words and phrases, and a great deal is now known about the Orisha in their original Nigerian home. Some elders have travelled to Africa and have been ordained there, bringing a considerable degree of knowledge back with them.

The Social Organization of Orisha

The Orisha religion was and remains very individualistic. There was no centralized administration or authority structure. In earlier times there was no official head of the religion, although Pa Neezer (Ebenezer Elliott, a great leader and healer who lived in the Fifth Company Village in southern Trinidad) held that position unofficially because of the respect members had for him. During the 1970s and 1980s Isaac "Sheppy" Lindsay was also acknowledged by many as an unofficial head because of the extent of his knowledge of the faith. Today Iyalorisha Melvina Rodney and Baba Clarence Forde are recognized as the heads of the religion because their organizations were officially registered with the government and the Council of Elders was incorporated. The two are therefore automatically central leaders. This is a recent development.

Despite these developments, the religion can still be characterized as individualistic rather than formally organized. Any person can become a leader by opening a shrine, furnishing it with the proper implements and convincing a group of followers that he or she has been called by the Orisha to a position of leadership. This rather fluid method of leadership means that shrines rise and fall depending upon the health, wealth and general position of the leader. Shrines often close upon the death of the leader. At present, it is estimated that there are about sixty shrines with about five thousand active members; twenty of the shrines have registered with the newly formed National Council of Orisha Elders.

There is no real attempt at the centralization of ritual and activity. Although younger modern members are calling for some sort of standard, ritual, beliefs and behaviour may vary from shrine to shrine. This is especially apparent today as some innovators are attempting to eliminate Christian elements. Similarly, some leaders incorporate a few elements of Hinduism while others maintain Christianity. Some leaders practise both Orisha and Spiritual Baptism, and sometimes elements of both religions are found in the same ceremonial. A number of Orisha shrines include a Christian church or sanctum on the compound. Today, on some compounds, there is a concerted attempt to Yorubanize the lyrics of the songs whereas in more traditional compounds, the songs still contain English, French, patois and sometimes merely vocal sounds. While these differences are particularly evident today, some differences were evident previously.[13]

If one examines the structure of the Orisha religion in the country it becomes apparent that there has been some significant change. In earlier times there were distinct networks of Orisha leaders, joined together primarily because they were all the spiritual children of one particular leader or they lived in close proximity. The network that Pa Neezer worked in, for example, included about one dozen or so leaders whose compounds or shrines he would visit and at whose feasts he would officiate. The spiritual kinship that bound a "child" to his or her spiritual father or mother created bonds of ritual kinship between members. They would regularly attend each other's feasts, travelling together in a kind of circuit, and an informal attempt would be made to schedule feasts so that they would not overlap.

Today Orisha leaders and their shrines seem to operate quite independently of each other. There are still a few networks but little attempt is made to avoid conflicting schedules. There is also a much greater tendency towards the independent operation of each shrine, nor do members of one shrine travel to the feasts of other leaders. A few people still attend more than one, especially if the feasts are taking place in close geographical proximity. However, the attachment to one's own shrine and leader seems far more intense today than it was in former times. The newly formed Council of Elders is attempting to standardize the calendar of *Ebos* or feasts. In 2000 Baba Forde complained that there were several feasts taking place at the same time as his, although his feast day of Osain is well known and should, he thought, be respected by others.

There was always a rather strong division between the city of Port of Spain and the countryside, especially the south. This division was also found in Orisha observance and it is still quite evident. There are shrines operating in the south – Siparia, Fyzabad and Gasparillo – that are relatively out of touch with the modernizing dynamic affecting the religion today. Their ritual practices are relatively unchanged and they have not been influenced by the movement away from Christianity. There is also little movement or contact between groups operating in various parts of the country.

One result of this atomized social organization is that there is much competition among leaders for members and other resources. There is also a considerable amount of "bad talking" of leaders by each other. A leader will always mention one or two others who "don't do it right" and whose members are not being taught correctly. The behaviour of people at feasts is also strongly criticized. Leaders exert their influence to keep their members faithful to them. They discourage their attendance at other feasts, telling the members they will learn negative things from them. Another important reason for the increased individualism of the religion is that some shrines that have introduced more Yoruba ritual have suffered a drop in membership. Iyalorisha Rodney, the co-leader of the religion, used to have substantial attendance at her feast, but this has dropped off considerably because of the absence of Christian prayers. (The day of the feast honouring cattle was very well attended, however) This competition and ill-will among leaders brings about "disunity". The plea is often made publicly that "we need to stop our differences, we need to pull together, we need to respect the ancestors". The cry for unity is the single most important discourse in the religion today. What is meant is not so much the unity between the two

Orisha groups (now only one) as between individual leaders, their shrines and their membership.

During the late 1950s and 1960s the social stratification of each shrine or compound was quite evident. Observations about the stratification patterns in 1965 are still relevant today:

> The relatively small group, or more accurately, clique of high status people form a non-permeable, tightly-knit group and are virtually cut off socially from other members. Most people fall into the intermediate class, those who have some measure of status but are constantly striving to increase it. The third group of people, those with extremely low status, is small and often quite transitory. Finding little reinforcement or little need satisfaction, these people either leave or attend feasts sporadically. Members of this latter group have minimal communication with other members and their often, somewhat pathetic, efforts at possession are generally ignored and sometimes ridiculed. The people constituting this group are in the unfortunate position of being relatively unknown in the group and thus do not have the prior knowledge of cult proceedings needed to become a known participating member. They may come from villages quite distant, or from other cities or their familial background may be unknown. Occasionally, such an individual receives a "lucky break" in some way thereby giving him higher status in the group. For the most part, the vicious circle of status leading to more status is in operation and these people have no foundation upon which to build.
>
> One sees status operating most significantly in the intermediate group in which there are the most active status strivers; the individuals who actually count the number of possessions and patrons that a particular person may have, and who often imitate the behavior of high status people even in the non-possessed state. The high status group consists predominantly of leaders and very active followers, those persons who become possessed frequently. Respect, admiration, and complete obedience, both in the possessed and non-possessed state are commanded by this group. The behaviour of the high status people in possession is extremely self-confident, authoritarian and often quite aggressive. They control and take command of the situation so thoroughly that other gods of lesser status yield to them. Power, which may be considered a major behavioral referent of status, is the outstanding characteristic of this small clique; there are little or no restrictions upon their behavior and they are free to structure any situation according to their own wishes....
>
> This division of members into several different groups seems related to other important patterns which have significant influences upon the way in which

interpersonal relations are structured. One such pattern is a type of ritual kinship whereby a spiritual family is formed among the high status leaders and their followers. One of the functions of the leader is to interpret to a person possessed for the first time or to an already established follower who manifests a new god, the name of the god who is possessing him and also the behaviors which are appropriate to that god. The new person then considers the leader to be his spiritual mother or father and the two often will call each other by the appropriate terms. "Children" of the same leader consider themselves to be spiritual siblings and the spiritual family may take on major numerical proportions. Often this family is socially and psychologically more significant to the individual than his actual biological family. Leaders attempt to compete with each other for new followers since this too enhances their own positions. Similarly, a new person may approach a wellknown and high status leader to serve as his mentor, thereby attaining membership in a more important spiritual family. Friendship patterns to a great extent follow the lines of the spiritual family and friendship across status lines was never observed.[14]

It has been observed today that fewer persons seem to "manifest" power or become possessed than in earlier times. One reason for this might be the increase in middle-class members wearing well-made and -designed African style clothing. Perhaps such persons feel that being in the state of possession might soil their clothing. Another possible reason might be the apparent decrease in the number of high-status persons who surround the leader. Today this high-status group, while always relatively small in the past, appears to have decreased even further. This means fewer people manifest the high-status deities and more of the middle and observer group tend to participate in the ceremonial only to demonstrate their belief and support, but without "manifesting" Orisha power. What has also been observed today is that, as each evening's Orisha is sung to and invoked, that Orisha may appear in the head of the leader or a close follower but no other Orisha grace the evening by their presence. Several evenings were observed in which the evening's Orisha was diligently sung to but the leader, perhaps for reasons of fatigue or ill-health, did not become possessed and neither did any other member present. This appears to add some validity to the notion that it is really only the small number of high-status persons who do manifest power.

Of greater significance, however, in limiting manifestations is that as the religion attracts more members from the middle class, time and the demands of occupation cut into Orisha attendance, as well as the draining and tiring experience of possession. As more members, including women, are employed, they no longer have the time or energy to manifest the vigorous possessions of the deities. There is also more interest among new and younger members in the cosmology of this African religion, and less emphasis on old rituals such as possession.

Case Study

Iyalorisha Melvina Rodney

The highlights of an interview conducted with Iyalorisha Melvina Rodney, the spiritual leader of the religion today, is relevant to this chapter. She talks of how she came to be an Orisha worshipper at a young age, the influence of Pa Neezer on her religious life and especially his method of teaching by interpreting her dreams and visions. She concludes with her observations and feelings about the visit of the Ooni of Ife in 1989. Iyalorisha Rodney therefore spans a long period of Orisha history, and her words make a fitting end to this ethnographic description of the Orisha religion.

At eighty-six, Iya Rodney is still a sprightly woman who takes her role as a religious very seriously. Although she says little about her personal life, one is given to understand that it has been a hard one. Her husband did not, apparently, provide much material support to her and her children, as he seemed to be a heavy drinker. After some years and a few children, she left him and the marriage.

She still lives in her own home and maintains an active Orisha shrine, giving her major *Ebo* in September every year. She has hundreds of spiritual children and most of the "notable" members in the Orisha movement today, described in chapter 4, are her spiritual children. She is happy with her large extended family of spiritual kin. Iyalorisha Rodney was anointed by Pa Neezer just before he died in 1969, and her position as spiritual head of the religion was again confirmed by being anointed by the Ooni of Ife during his visit in 1989. Iyalorisha Rodney is the last living link to the great Orisha tradition as practised by Ebenezer Elliott from the 1940s to the 1960s. As such she encompasses the heritage that came from Africa and was maintained in Trinidad throughout the long periods of slavery and colonialism by what are today called "the elders" but then were generally known as "old heads". Iyalorisha Rodney's life in Orisha also brings a totality to the practice, since as a young child she was anointed, blessed and confirmed by Pa Neezer and towards the end of her life she was again confirmed by the Ooni of Ife as not only an Orisha elder but as the leader of the faith. Today, she is generally recognized by most members of the faith as the spiritual head of the religion, but one or two persons do dispute her authority and position.

In the following interview Iyalorisha Rodney speaks broadly about a number of issues. In order to capture the flavour of her memories, I have recorded her words as she spoke them in dialect but as an aid to the non-Trinidadian reader, I have included something of a "translation". At this point, she is not quite four years old:

MR: It start to come on an come on, an ah day ah could remember feeling dat ah reach to a certain age it going on an going on an going on ah was done have three years ah stop in in meh fourth, ah was going into meh four years and ah morning ah get a spin an ah catch mehself and was wet an ah change meh cloths an meh grandmother say like dis ting . . . an she went back to him an she leave meh home with meh cousin an when she start preparing tings she say well ah will give yuh, yuh want dis ting to leave yuh ah say yes, she say ah will carry yuh somewhere, ah will get de ting, de ting will stop taking yuh an she will stay with meh yuh say no, ah say well ma I wouldn't stay cause I is de capt. But ah was two months to make four years 'cause ah remember dat good, cause yuh know is always is be July is feast, an it happen ah think . . . September month, because October to November is meh birthday, September perspiring an hot an den I wouldn't know much animal is dat, an well I tell yuh I doh think it have anybody like Pa again when de night I hearing de birds bawling an yuh know how, an I start to bawl I say I want to go home, well I bawling because dey say she gorn, dey say she gorn to come back, ah say ah want to go home dey say she come back an she coming back just now, an I cry until because ah ent seeing nothing ah only hearing de birds an dem bawling because yuh know how there was an eventually dey ask for him an dey gorn in de back an start to cry an when ah catch mehself power mus' be take meh an had meh head well tie up everything an lady who does make dey business good a lady was from Caratal dey used to call she "Safa" she was with meh in de chapel an when I start to bawl dey had to call Pa an I doh know what he did again I call out but first night I cyar remember ah start to cry out part of de night but all ah hearing now like is "chack chack" . . . dey wake meh up to like drums although is night, de following day a lady had to bathe meh and first I tell her I say I doesn't bathe myself yuh know, well she start to bathe meh she say is alright I'll bathe yuh, when she bathe meh dey put orn a piece a business an ah want to know what dat for, I had was to sleep with dat de night in de chapel, say em yuh might want to pee pee any time you want to pee pee an yuh in ting an ah could remember date ah say where Ma, dey say Ma coming later, dey hadn't a big crowd dem call a big crowd because like he didn't want somebody to look like he didn't want to spread an ah could remember he told me "yuh could keep a secret" an some lady tell meh doh say Pa but I remembering now as a malicious little child dat I leave Pa home an how I call yuh call yuh sister Pa an say well everybody calling him Pa, but calling Pa an dat was dat, well I know is power now, I could say is power, ting start an ah come an ah hear an I well everytime dat ah come out every morning when ah change meh cloths an ah start getting meh visions an dem an I uses to tell dem, an ah could remember as a young child if I dream you going out de road and yuh stump yuh foot and yuh buss yuh toe in yuh shoes believe it an when I was five-and-a-half years when he start, ah tink is five it came, ah cyar remain de feast Bastor Hall an Mother B . . .

FH: Mother B, I remember her well.

MR: . . . an he was in de em chapel head first dey say he with em Shango an Munja an long after I get to know ah long, long long after is when Pa done gorn den dey tell meh about dis story 'bout Miss Edith, it did done gorn already an Pa wash meh an ah could remember ah was five but dey had a Bible on ah table by meh grandmother an ah write it down, five-and-a-half years he send to see meh again, 'cause power was now manifested an meh grandmother had to keep it a secret from meh mother, but dey not living nearby, like is a secret to everybody, when ah gorn in Bastor Hall an power take meh is den people know

FH: What power took you, do you know?

MR: Well Shungo, Shungo is first de first two powers dat took meh, one take meh and when ah gorn down an according to what dey did, ah do what Pa well dey had de obeah dey had de manifestation dat came with Shango an

Manja first den he settle those two an after other powers start taking meh again before meh head wash, ah had no peace yuh know an ah hear when dey cyar revenge with Bastor Hall place when Shango take meh an ah didn't know what Mother B did she, 'cause dey know meh, but dey say dat Pa was in de chapel taking a rest an when dey call him and dey tell him a little girl fall but dey didn't know eh meh grandmother always keeping going up by Pa an he told her dat was he giving dis feast in Bastor Hall she must send meh, an she really send meh with some people an power take meh again in de place an den dey didn't know dat power does manifest an nobody say nothing, 'cause I doh think de lady dat does advise my grandmother to go up to him and de other lady I doh know she didn't talk and say dat ah went to get meh head wash or anyting, 'cause yuh know dat people different long time, I doh know what she did she insult Shango in meh head an also meh head throw meh down an she taking . . . an den de lady under de rock she took meh after he call back de power, Shango eh come back Manju take meh up so now ah did get three powers within two and four and five-and-a-half years between Shango, Manja an . . . alright ma say ah small ah had to go to school, dey send meh to school, but ah start to go to school before ah had five years, but dat uses to worry her, so she ask dem as ah does go to church she ask dem to take meh in de school, meh name wasn't on roll and dey start teaching de catechism an ah start to learn it, an before I had six years ah had confirm, yes ah pass an ah confirm, on confirmation day power take meh in de church, ha, ha ha, meh friends an dem say who know ah catch mehself but ah know when ah kneel down in front of de bishop an time he do dat ah didn't know mehself again, an when he had went, I say now after I get big an ah hear dem saying is devil ah say well if is devil why de bishop didn't, yuh know, take away de devil from meh, some of the people laugh ah hear a lady said maybe de bishop was a devil himself, yuh know malicious people nuh in de district an I had a hard time with my people, but when in school if dey only do so an it touch meh from here to here and it gorn an Pa when he check back is another power again I had was seven times yuh know ah God it wasn't nice yuh know, but after yuh had to get sense an every feast dat he had to carry on an it was fall between his feast which is July to August he would carry an I grow up under de mister hand, until dey had ah time dat dey use to call meh back when dey feel de ting an ah feel de vibration ah say use meh words well it was, it just entertain dem an when ah hearing now dey bad talking meh, dey bad talking meh, well ah say is bad talk and dey say look at de little power house, de little power well dat was it, it come to meh like yuh know a big kinda wrong ting, 'cause in dose days an you know now people only running to Orisha people yes, calling it devil but I told some people ef it was devil I done reach where de man did learning meh devil because everyting Pa could of give out it was someting sacred and good yes,

FH: How did he go about teaching you?

MR: Now, well when I travel, head wash, ah travel an according to where how ah travel where ah does bring de vision explain meh what it is, when ah bring de vision explain meh what it is, an probably as ah was so big an dat din't say was on de fifth time dat meh head wash, de fifth time dat a found mehself in a big boat in de sea, dey call it ah ship, but there were nobody in it, I doh see nobody in it, I didn't see nobody an it was travelling from south to north so em when ah look back is only de sea yuh coulda' see, so dey gorn but it gave me one word to say, he say when yuh reach anywhere an ask yuh where yuh going tell dem yuh going on a journey, no dey sen yuh out on a journey an yuh seeking wisdom, knowledge an understanding, understanding of the holy spirit, an dat is all ah coulda' always tell dem, ah whisper, after yuh know ah reach to what ah reach dat ah had to handle people ah get de word yeh, dey didn't give meh dat word in mouth, dey give meh here, send to meh head ah have to wine meh hand over here to meh an he didn't plant ah flat for meh, he say ah had to hand sew it for mehself an yuh know he had Reggie and among dem an all ah dem dat ah give meh first feature, tell dem ah have to sew meh flag because ah have to stand up on meh own feet. So if is one send it right here, an in seventy-two words in language an he never say it for meh, dey had to learn meh, an dat same day when meh flag plant a flag is de flag and den de . . . an dey lay down there yuh know how he use to talk already an ah gorn down an settle so an dis yard did had mud ah dorn down so in de hole an he come over meh an start to pick de words for meh, repeat it and repeat it and when dey did do all of us dey only did get to seven yes, an de next morning after de office dey carry meh back again dey use to tell meh an tell meh he say alright come back, come back again an next ting when he leave ah says peace and everyting finish ah had learnt fifteen words, he tell meh he not giving . . . ah would give, have twenty-one days light make dat . . . pick from a flower mean make it an ting which mean gold make out a an shut out dat light an twenty-one days everything just come to meh, dat man have a place in, ef dey say dat dey have heaven and hell here but ah know he have a peaceful place, ah doh think there is another one like him again.

FH: I don't think so either.

MR: An when ah was dreaming, but not near eh, to a distance, he always showing meh he either down de hill an I on de hill to come down to meet him but am in ah place dat ah could see and den look up an den whatsoever he doing he talking but like I understanding now well dat wha good for dat and dat wha good for dat, ah tell somebody dat dey tell meh is mind over matter ah say well it could be but it not for worse.

FH: So he consecrated your shrine here. When you first started.

MR: Yes, when the need to make the chapel, he come an he consecrate it because all corner of meh chapel have promises an de four corner of dis place here have thunder stone and de centre have thunder stone an I was lucky dat de same thunder stone dat he say he got it from Ma Diamond when he was sick, he was with meh, and he hand meh a good bit when ah give him de feast an when de forty day he had left an tell Roderick, he step son in writing to give me one, three of Shungo drums and de other three was em to give a man dey call Clement from Moruga em not Moruga, inside Gasparillo, inside there. He uses to beat de drums an he was ah kinda of a banback man but his name was Clement, an remember in dis chapel had ah little boat make dat he said dat Ma Diamond came down with, he hand down dat to meh.

FH: The Ooni's visit

MR: In Lopinot was de order from de Ooni when he came so he came down with de map an it was shown to the government an he want an plant ah stone, plant a stone there, ah big stone, but dat morning ah could not have yes, so when de Ooni, because look my chair here still, my chair my children make my chair y'aull should have been on de side of it, ah leave meh chair open, meh name was on it, ah tell dem take it off, just watch when everything finish an take meh chair an carry it back home, ah say I must stay down an she up so, is so with Baptist children an ting an making ah kinda of a pappy show an ting going on, after dat I had something prepare an she didn't know, seven different things an he went to help her, an I, we let dem go an everybody follow an we do so an went to de house de place where he was, he had was to be there, went on de prepare ourself according to orders how we get. An when de Ooni coming in an ah had meh drummers an dem an had meh everything, ah had ah lota pictures yuh know, an I in front an as we coming in so we had to say an everybody an den start haning de tings and giving dem in a calabash an dey taste it just take off dey energy an dey carry on all de night, after dat den dey get to know ting an de next day it had a meeting, no dat same day dey had a meeting when he say "form a council" an let everybody come an ask dem who is dis one, who is dat one who is de other one an let everybody come under one head, one umbrella and let be de head an everybody get together because de man coulda seen his hand know unity an look but is a good ting, when yuh have dis figure, when yuh have respect, when yuh have yuh growth with respect yuh keep dat until yuh die, de give it to meh and ah take it an when dat moment reach and dey heard how someting up in em Matura an dey going lane an dem get a side dey going up Matura an dem is multimillionaire and den dey going to put ting across de road and get people to rub dem, Leone ent grow up so Leone do so an people from Trintoc come right down after Trintoc because de direction yuh didn't read in dat if yuh did read dat is a known he didn't go down Matura from right in Trintoc is right here he came an when he ask an he done cuss out de yard he ask meh if ah have spare Obi ah say yes because the calabash fall because ah know yuh had to have dat. He say ah going to ask three questions, if de Orisha's if here is fit for de Orisha's and dey are here an if I am capable enough to run here and if I am capable enough to bless meh children with de three Obi make six pieces an he touch meh three times an he die, Oh God, de joy in meh so much, ah say Oh God, oh, God oh God oh God ah going down in de ground a loss ah say oh God . . . today de word eh fall ah say ah could dead now, so help meh mother . . . dat was the only ting, ah say dat was de only ting an de answer ah say a could dead now, ah could dead now, ah could dead now. When dey pull meh up an see a full lady she watch meh an de tears come out she eye she say was Obi dat is de ting. Ah say alright an when Leone done talk and everybody talk an everyting dey say well de cars I have de an a car for meh to go all about an Patrick,

Patrick Edwards an de car came an went in de entourage. Dat was a day could never come back here.

As a child at the age of three, Iyalorisha Rodney experienced her first possession and a year later, at age four, again. Her grandmother took her to see Pa Neezer and left her at his place. She cried for her grandmother and they consoled her and said her grandmother would be back. During this emotional outburst, she became possessed again. A woman called "Safa" tied her head and called for Pa Neezer. She can't remember what he did but the following morning the women bathed her. Each morning afterwards she started getting visions. At five years old Pa washed (baptized) her and at five-and-a-half he sent for her as she caught the power regularly. Her grandmother hid the possessions from her mother and kept them a secret. People began to realize her situation when she was in Bastor Hall and publicly became possessed.

The first power she experienced was Shango and Yemanja the second. They called Pa and told him of this little girl who was possessed. They did not know that Mother B and her grandmother had constantly informed Pa of this little girl and her possessions and Pa knew she was there because he asked them to send her to his feast. Pa called back (withdrew) the power. She started to go to school at five-and-a-half. It was a Christian school. They enrolled her and started teaching her catechism and she passed and she was confirmed at age six. On confirmation day the power took her in the church. When she kneeled down in front of the bishop she lost control. Her friends joked about the situation. Later on in life, people in the village referred to the experience as a devil manifestation and said the bishop exorcized it. She had a hard time. She attended feasts every year and they referred to her as "the power house". They ridiculed her as being influenced by the devil and that Pa was creating that influence. She declared that what Pa taught was sacred, was good. She also had a vision of going to the sea and Pa advised her on how to interpret such a vision. He had an indirect way of teaching her and she had to learn a precise language. All this was in the vision. She believes that Pa comes back to teach her ways of leading the Orisha. He must be in heaven.

When she decided to organize her *chapelle*, Pa came and consecrated it, donated thunderstones to the four corners of the *chapelle* including one he received from Ma Diamond (the daughter of an African slave who was Pa Neezer's mentor). Pa also willed her three Shango drums.

The Ooni's visit was a highlight in her life as he recognized her authenticity after she responded to the three questions he posed to her. The Ooni acknowledged the Orisha's presence in her *chapelle*. He touched her three times in a ceremony. . . . He also asked her for three obi seeds which she had. She also had a special chair made for the Ooni that he used during his visit. He also instructed them to form a council or umbrella organization for the religion. While at her shrine she saw several detectives on her property who were accompanying him. During his visit he was supposed to go to several places but he came here instead. The Ooni's visit was an extraordinary and unforgettable experience for her.

The Orisha "Powers" or Deities

In the following section the major deities and their characteristics, implements, days, sacrifices and sacred colours are listed. Since there is a great deal of variation in Orisha theology from group to group, this list records those identifications and characteristics heard most often in my earlier period of fieldwork. This variation may also account for the discrepancies between this list and similar ones constructed for Trinidad. Today there is still some variation among shrines.

Ogun

Christian counterpart: St Michael
Characteristics: God of war and iron; highest deity in the Orisha pantheon since he is the "chief angel". He is so powerful that "he can move mountains".

Ogun is generally the first power to arrive and it is said that no power can arrive before him at a feast. In practice, however, another power can arrive first but the reason is then given that Michael used another power as a messenger, being too busy to come himself.

His behaviour is generally aggressive; he does a good deal of violent dancing, using large steps, with his hands on his hips. Much of his time is spent in diagnosing ailments and solving problems. He uses great quantities of olive oil, which he distributes as blessings or scatters about the *palais*. He most frequently "manifests" on large, stout women.

Implements: Cutlass, sword when angry
Colours: Red, white
Day: Wednesday
Food: Goat, black-eyed peas, rice, corn, rum

Osain

Christian counterpart: St Francis
Characteristics: God of the jungle and bush, a herbalist or "bush doctor". He has three manifestations: Osain Kiribejii, identified as St Francis of Assisi; Osain Demolay, identified as St Francis Xavier; and Osain Metaphi who is known simply as St Francis.

He is a quiet power.

One form of Francis dances bent at the waist, using a slow shuffle step. Another walks on his toes, sometimes with a candle lit at both ends clamped between his teeth. Occasionally he throws himself to the ground and rolls on the earth. He "manifests" on both men and slim young women.

Implements: Pestle (thick vine), "checheray broom", lance, turtle carapace. For Osain Kiribejii: "checheray broom"; Osain Demolay: cross; Osain Metaphi: candle lit at both ends in mouth.
Colour: Yellow
Day: Thursday
Food: Muracoy (land turtle), black-eyed peas and rice

Aireelay (Ajaja)

Christian counterpart: "St" Jonah
Characteristics: "Master of the sea". He has two names because Jonah "died twice". He is revered as a "grim, serious man, no time for play". He paces back and forth with his hands on his hips or behind his back. When he dances, he throws his feet forward and spins on one heel. He is very authoritative and generally delivers a sermon or gives various orders, for example,

to clean the *palais*. He is called by many "the crab". Only three Aireelay "horses" were observed, two men and one woman.

Implements: Bamboo rod called "roseau", dagger, great deal of olive oil
Colours: Blue, mauve belt
Day: Thursday
Food: Guinea bird, black-eyed peas, rice, corn

Shakpana
(Zewo, although the latter is sometimes considered to be the son of Shakpana and identified with St Vincent de Paul)

Christian counterpart: St Jerome
Characteristics: This power "gets rid of evil and disease". He does little dancing; his activity is confined to pacing about swishing his broom. When he "manifests" upon a woman, a red dress is worn. This is tied between the legs to form trousers. He is feared by some people because of his connection with disease, evil and prophecy.

Implement: "Checheray broom"
Colour: Red
Day: None
Food: Cock, pigeon, black-eyed peas, rice, corn

Shango

Christian counterpart: St John the Baptist
Characteristics: The god of lightning and thunder. He does little in the ritual other than dancing actively. He uses large steps and waves his arms, swinging his axe above his head. He is the only power who is "fed". At odd intervals, on Friday night, twenty-four small bits of cotton are rolled to form small balls, put on a plate, drenched with olive oil and lighted. The power then swallows this mixture. Only one specific Shango "horse" performs this feat currently.

Implements: Axe, pestle, cross. For Shango (John the Baptist): axe; Allado (Evangelist): pestle; Amado Shango (John of the Cross): cross.

Colours: White, red
Day: Friday
Food: Sheep, black-eyed peas, rice, corn

Aba Koso

Christian counterpart: St John the Baptist after beheading
Characteristics: The activity of this power is limited to pacing and stamping about with hands on hips. He grunts and groans continually, all the while shaking his head, which is thrown back. The grunting indicates that he has no head and is thus unable to talk. This makes him seem angry and "vexed" and he is often not taken seriously by other people. Only two people, both young men, were observed to be Aba Koso "horses".

Implement: Usually none, sometimes the axe
Colour: Red
Day: Friday
Food: Usually no sacrifice

Aba Lofa or Elofa

Christian counterpart: Eternal Father or "God Himself"
Characteristics: This power was another patron of Pa Neezer and then, as now, was much revered. He has only been seen at Neezer's feasts since he was the only known Aba Lofa "horse" in Trinidad at that time. Occasionally, if at another feast a cattle (bull) has been sacrificed and if the big leader was present, Aba Lofa may "manifest" upon him. I have not heard of any Aba Lofa manifestations in recent times, although Iyalorisha Rodney holds a "cattle feast" every leap year.

This power does not "manifest" suddenly but comes with a slow gradual shaking of the head. This becomes faster and faster, the hands are clasped and eyes closed. As the power comes the "horse" rises but keeps the hands clasped and the eyes closed. The power is an old man and must walk slowly and haltingly, sometimes with a cane. He dresses in white trousers, white shirt, white headband and a white bed sheet that is draped over the shoulders to form a cloak. He dances slowly, manipulating the cloak about him, and holds a freshly killed cattle head on his own head. After a while he holds the cattle head in the crook of his arm and dabs blood on the heads of all people present as a blessing. He also holds a ritual for children, which generally takes place on the third evening. Huge loaves of specially baked bread are brought out of the *chapelle* and are distributed in small pieces by Aba Lofa to all children present.

Implement: Stick or cane, cattle head, three candles, bottle of oil
Colour: White
Day: Monday or Tuesday
Food: Beef or whole cattle, black-eyed peas, rice, corn

Omira

Christian counterpart: St Raphael
Characteristics: This power is sacred to hunters and is more important as a chief archangel than as a hunter. He does little dancing, but generally walks about carrying a wooden gun. He dresses in a pink and lilac dress, carrying a hamsack "for his lunch" over his shoulder and sometimes a "flambeau", a candle, in his hand, since "hunters need a light".

Implements: Gun, candle, hamsack
Colours: Pink and lilac
Day: Wednesday
Food: Fowl, black-eyed peas, rice, corn

Ebejee

Christian counterpart: St Peter
Characteristics: He is a fisherman. As is the case with Raphael, he is more important in Christian terms than as an African deity. He is especially revered by one of the leaders, who calls Peter her chief patron. She is the only individual who manifests this power.

Implements: Keys, dagger, may wear a crown of leaves on head
Colours: Red, yellow, mauve
Day: None
Food: Drake, black-eyed peas, rice, corn

Yemanja (Amanja, Manja)

Christian counterpart: St Anne
Characteristics: Is a water power and lives in the sea. This power is either "saintly" – for example, simply walks about praying and blessing people – or quite actively going through the manoeuvres of rowing a boat. This is done by sitting on the ground and sliding across it while at the same time she carries a calabash of water in one hand and a "pa-gye" or oar with which she imitates the motion of rowing in the other. Yemanja is considered to be one of the most powerful of the female deities.

Implements: Oar, calabash of water
Colours: Blue and white
Day: Thursday
Food: Duck, pullet, peas, rice

Oya

Christian counterpart: St Catherine
Characteristics: She "lives in the air and comes with the breeze". Oya is closely identified with Shango and some individuals speak of them as married. She does a good deal of vigorous dancing, which looks very similar to the dancing of Shango, and occasionally holds her left ear when dancing. This is interpreted as "listening to the breeze".

Implement: Hatchet
Colours: Green, red
Day: Friday
Food: Fowl, pigeon, peas, rice, corn (the only female power who is offered corn, but her active vigorous behaviour resembles that of the masculine powers more than that of the females).

Oshun

Christian counterpart: St Philomen
Characteristics: This deity is a river goddess and "lives in the river". Her dancing is very delicate and often she balances a filled goblet (pottery jug) of water on her head without a head pad and dances with it for as long as thir-

ty minutes without spilling its contents. At special river ceremonies, Oshun wades into the water and offers food to the river. (At one such ceremony the food, which was placed in a calabash, drifted out onto the water and could not be recovered, as it normally is. This was interpreted as the will of Oshun, who was angry at not receiving enough sacrifices.) She is considered by some to be the female counterpart of Aireelay.

Implements: Anchor, goblet
Colours: Blue and white
Day: Thursday
Food: Fowl, pigeon, black-eyed peas, rice

Omela (Mama Latay)

Christian counterpart: Mother of the Earth. This deity is supposed to accompany Ogun-St Michael, and is generally sung to after Ogun. She does not dance but sits on her knees and slides across the floor distributing water in a calabash to the people present and to the four corners of the *palais*. She is supposed to an old, stooped woman.

Implement: Calabash of water
Colour: Brown
Day: Wednesday
Food: Ground provisions (such as potatoes)

Lesser-known Powers

Lesser-known powers or those who rarely "manifest" are listed below:

Bayanni (St Anthony) – implement: three candles, bottle of oil
Oromeelay (St Joseph) – implement: carpenter square
Mayadu (St Theresa) – implement: crucifix, flowers; colour: brown, blue
Da Lua (St Jude); Da Logee (St Simon). These two (Da Lua and Da Logee) are "twins".

Obatala (Mary)
Abatala (Jesus)
Zopah (St Benedict)
Ojah (St Mark)
Ajakba (Mother of All Nations)

Mahabil (St Michael) was recognized by only one Orisha leader, who called him the "Indian King". He was an Indian god who was met by Christ in India and baptized as St Michael. In behaviour he is similar to Ogun, uses the sword or cutlass and dresses similarly. He has an altar and a "tomb" in the establishment of this one leader, but is not recognized outside of her immediate circle.

Today there are a number of shrines in which possession by Indian Hindu deities also takes place.[15] In one such, the goddess Shakti was said to manifest on its leader. In at least one shrine, several new Orisha not traditionally associated with the worship have been added to the ritual. These include Olukun and Egede, whose presence has come about as a result of the increased Yorubanization of the movement.

> ... we gather to sing hymns and ring the bell and shout hallelujah and speak in tongues when the spirit come ...
>
> — *Earl Lovelace,* The Wine of Astonishment

CHAPTER TWO

Spiritual/Shouter Baptism in Trinidad Today

Introduction

SPIRITUAL OR SHOUTER BAPTISM[1] is one of many religions derived from the Protestant stream of Christianity. What makes these religions unique, however, is that their doctrines and ritual observances include elements brought by the early slaves from Africa. Spiritual Baptism, like the Orisha faith, therefore, has African influences, and it is a mixed or syncretic religious form. One of its great strengths is that it is one of the few religions indigenous to the country. All others, with the exception of Orisha, were brought by European colonizers and later by Indian indentured workers.[2] Most of the newer religions found in Trinidad recently were brought by missionaries from abroad, primarily from the United States. In describing the local character and appeal of Spiritual Baptism, the most evocative prose comes from a great work of fiction, Earl Lovelace's *Wine of Astonishment,* whose main characters are a Baptist preacher and his wife Eva. She says, at one point:

> We have this church in the village. We have this church. The walls make out of mud, the roof covered with carrat leaves; a simple hut with no steeple or cross or acolytes or white priests or Latin ceremonies. But is our own. Black people own it . . .
>
> We have this church where we gather to sing hymns and ring the bell and shout hallelujah and speak in tongues when the spirit come; and we carry the Word to the downtrodden and forgotten and the lame and the beaten, and we touch black people soul.[3]

Spiritual or Shouter Baptism is practised not only in Trinidad and Tobago but also in many other islands of the Caribbean, the mainland United States and other areas to which Caribbean people have migrated – Canada and England. It has now become a worldwide faith.

The History of Spiritual/Shouter Baptism in Trinidad and Tobago

Creation and Establishment of the Religion

In Trinidad and Tobago this religion developed in the nineteenth century.[4] When Trinidad became a British possession in 1797, settlers brought not only the Anglican Church but also a number of other non-establishment Protestant denominations.[5] It is highly likely that as English settlers drove to worship in Trinity Cathedral near Woodford Square, their slaves held their own religious services while waiting for them. They may very well have sung the same songs and hymns while injecting more expressive African elements into their worship. These events probably occurred between 1802 and 1834, the year which marked the end of slavery. During this period as well, a group of American Baptists of African descent who had fought on the side of Britain and against the Americans were given grants of land in exchange for their loyalty. These black Americans settled primarily in Naparima, where they formed the so-called company villages named after the military companies in which they had served. Stephen Glazier, a noted authority on Spiritual Baptism, is also of the view that there were connections between the southern United States and the Caribbean – particularly with respect to the important "mournin" ritual – although they are difficult to trace. He cites the influence of the "Merikan Baptists", as the company villagers came to be called.[6] Stewart has also described the similarities between the worship of these "Merikans" and contemporary Spiritual Baptists, noting the importance of dreams and visions in predicting the future, shouting behaviour and the like.[7] Missionaries from the London Baptist societies visiting the area in the early nineteenth century attest to the expressive and emotional nature of the faithful, and it seems highly likely that they were practising a form of religion now known as Spiritual Baptism. Even then, the official London Baptists forced them to stop their practice of "shouting" during services.

Some sources also maintain that the religion originated in St Vincent and was brought by migrants to Trinidad in the nineteenth century. Although Vincentian migrants may indeed have been practising Shouters, or "Shakers" as they are called on St Vincent, historical evidence now seems to support the view that the faith was already well established in Trinidad by the middle of the nineteenth century.[8]

Prohibition

The Spiritual or Shouter Baptist faith and its observances were banned in Trinidad and Tobago for a period of thirty-four years, from 1917 to 1951. The colonial government of the day passed the Shouters Prohibition Ordinance on 16 November 1917. The then attorney general noted in his comments (in *Hansard*) that

> Apparently the Shouters have had a somewhat stormy history from all I have been able to learn regarding them. They seem, if they did not arise there, to have flourished exceedingly in St Vincent, and to have made themselves such an unmitigated nuisance that they had to be legislated out of existence. They then came to Trinidad and continued complaints have been received by the Government some time past as to their practices.

The Legislative Council of St Vincent had passed a prohibitive ordinance in 1912, and that of Trinidad was closely modelled on it. The ordinance prohibited a person from holding flowers or a lighted candle in their hands at a public meeting, ringing a bell or wearing a white head tie, and from any form of shaking of the body.

During the prohibition the Baptists fled into the forests and hills to hold their services. Even here they were not protected. Sister Reyes Hypolite describes how the police came to their service in Sans Souci:

When the police came, they used the word and not a man moved. The police came in ordinary clothes and only two in uniform on the road. Mother saw only them in uniform on the road and she call out the window: "Sister Lopez, police" and one of them not in uniform arrest her and give her three charges: giving a house to keep a Shouters meeting, attending a Shouters meeting and disturbing the police on duty. They took twenty-six of us, they had to make two trips, carry us to Toco the Saturday night. They charge us and send us back a tell us to come up on the Tuesday to attend to court. They charged us with first offence, 10 shillings or 7 days in jail; the mother of the house $21 for three offences and $14 for the second offence or 14 days in jail. Some of us pay and some did not and they went to jail. So, when they arrest me, I was living just there, I went for my child because I can't leave the child alone, they rough me up and tell me, "Get in the van." One of the child aunt was there and she say, "Go on, I will see about the child" and they take us up.

Sister Maundy relates how Elton Griffith, having just come from Grenada

> where he didn't have anything to do with the Baptists was walking in Prince Street and somebody was keeping a meeting, a gentleman, and he met the police arresting the man. And kicking down the bell, the lute and the tyre and he stand and watch. Then he question the police man who tell him that it's against the law. He said from that day, he took up that as his own and to work to free the Baptists.[9]

The stated reason for the ordinance was that the Shouters made too much noise with their loud singing and bell ringing. There were complaints that they disturbed the peace. The worshippers' expressive and emotional behaviour – which included dancing, shaking, falling to the ground, and shouting and grunting – were no doubt considered highly unseemly by the more traditional groups in colonial Trinidad society. The police had been persecuting Baptists for years prior to the ordinance and had even lost a case to them in the courts. Thus the ordinance was enacted because the colonial government of the time deferred to the complaints of property owners, taxpayers and the police. In addition, the established churches also thought that such practices were heathen and anti-Christian, and they were increasingly alarmed at the numbers of worshippers leaving the established churches to join the Baptists. Underlying all of these reasons, however, was the idea that many of these practices derived from an African past. A cultivated Christian society therefore had no room for what were considered to be barbaric rituals. The shame associated with slavery and the so-called uncivilized African heritage of much of the population of Trinidad led many people at the time to try to ban the religion. In general, the colonial ruling class of the time went to great lengths to suppress the culture and traditional religions of the non-white majority. For example, an even earlier ordinance in 1869 cited any "African" form of religion as obeah or black magic, and practitioners were subject to imprisonment and flogging. Playing drums or any other musical instrument between 10 p.m. and 6 a.m. was made illegal, and even bongo and drum dances could not be held without official permission. Although this ordinance was withdrawn, the "music bill" of 1883 prohibited drum playing of any kind.

An article in the *Port of Spain Gazette* provides evidence that the dominant elite of the day were in favour of the ban issued on 10 October 1917. It stated that

> An Ordinance has been introduced into the Legislative Council looking into the elimination of the pseudo-religious body known locally as "Shouters". This is a body that has mistaken noise for enthusiasm, and shouting for religion. It no doubt began in a conscientious way with a desire to worship God, but it has long since degenerated into a burlesque upon religion and a general nuisance to every community where it has squatted down and deceived the feeble-minded.

Shouter Baptism survived and flourished despite efforts to ban it, which included breaking into houses of worship, disruption of public meetings, and incarceration of adherents by law enforcement officers. These attempts merely strengthened the beliefs of the Shouter Baptists.

Throughout the many years of prohibition, calypsonians sang about this religious group. Although some artists recorded Baptist hymns and folk songs, some ridiculed and mocked, the faith, as did The Growling Tiger in a calypso called "What Is the Shouter?" or "Is This Religion?":

> We have the Roman Catholic, Anglican and Salvation
> But what is a Shouter band?
> If it is a religion, do tell me please
> I am tired with the nonsense, give me an ease
> But the Shouters is a husband children and wife,
> and they living miserable a corrupted life,
> If is that they call civilisation,
> it's a disgrace to my native life.[10]

Throughout the 1920s and 1930s the Shouters fought many court battles and tried to counter the general contempt of the public. It was not until the arrival of one Uriah Tubal Butler on the political scene that attitudes towards the Shouter Baptists slowly began to change. Butler was himself a deeply religious man and closely tied to the Spiritual Baptist religion. His public political meetings resembled those of a Baptist gathering because he used candle light, opened each meeting with a prayer or invited a Baptist leader to do so. Butler's close ties with the religion afforded it some legitimacy; he was a prominent politician, founder of the British Empire Workers and Citizens Home Rule Party, who became a spokesperson for labour and called for working-class solidarity. Because of his religious beliefs and practices, he was charged and convicted with sedition by the colonial authorities who also described him as "a religious fanatic and as such a danger to the peace and good order in the colony".[11] This controversy made him an extremely popular figure during the 1930s.

By the 1940s the Baptists had entered the political arena, primarily to fight for the repeal of the ordinance banning their faith, led by Grenada-born Elton George Griffith who was then a member of the Pentecostal Assembly. Motivated by several visions – in one he heard a voice saying "Elton Griffith, I am sending you to set my people free" – Griffith left Grenada and migrated to Trinidad where he joined the Baptists.

The Repeal of the Ordinance

By the 1940s the campaign to repeal the ordinance against the practice of Shouter/Spiritual Baptism gained momentum. In the first place, the many independent Baptist churches organized themselves into the West Indian Evangelical Spiritual Baptist Faith, led by Griffith who was later ordained as its bishop. Also, the country was granted universal suffrage, and for the first time many were given the right to vote.

Under Griffith's leadership members of the Spiritual Baptist faith presented a petition to the Legislative Council in 1940 asking for the repeal of the ordinance. In part, this remarkable petition read:

> We as African descendants crave indulgence of the Honourable Speaker of the House and the Honourable Legislative Councillors to use their good office by assisting us to modify or repeal the "Shouters Ordinance". We consider that this

form of religion or sect, is our ancestral heritage. Owing to this Prohibition Act of Shouters Chapter 4 no. 19 has affected thirty thousand (30,000) members of our faith.

A few years later Albert Gomes appealed to the council to appoint a select committee to inquire into the repeal of the ordinance of 1917. A committee was formed, but it took several years to release its findings that recommended the repeal of the ordinance against the Shouters. In the meantime Griffith and his followers actively lobbied the members of the Legislative Council to support the repeal. By this time the Legislative Council had undergone many changes and was more representative of the population at large. Several of its members had close and intensive relationships with the Shouter Baptist Church. These included Albert Gomes, Uriah Butler, Raymond Quevedo (the calypsonian, Attila the Hun), the Sinanan brothers and Audrey Jeffers. Albert Gomes's constituency contained many Baptists whose votes he courted and because he was such a prominent supporter of the cause, he was appointed to head the select committee. He led the debate in the Legislative Council on the appeal, which was supported by several prominent members of council. The bill to repeal the ordinance was passed on 30 March 1951. A jubilant Archbishop Elton Griffith was carried out of the Legislative Council chamber on the shoulders of his supporters to Woodford Square, where he led a thanksgiving celebration.

The struggles of the Spiritual/Shouter Baptists to achieve their victory have been aptly described as a "struggle of indigenous people against foreign rulers".[12]

Ritual, Beliefs and Practices

The Spiritual Baptists believe[13] that their religion derives from the biblical John the Baptist, and their name comes from the practice of immersing believers in water as a means of baptizing or initiating them into the faith. Their rituals are characterized by mourning, bell ringing, visits from the Holy Spirit and a distinctive form of shouting as a means of expression. The practice of the religion also includes "baptism, proving, mournin"; the phenomenon of possession by the Holy Spirit; the physical manifestation of possession in the shaking, dancing, speaking in tongues; and bringing back spiritual gifts.

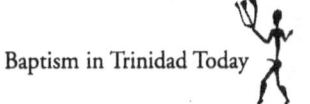

The religion has a complex series of ranked positions. There can be as many as twenty-two named ranks, although the smaller churches recognize fewer of these. The commonly found ranks are those of leader, mother, shepherd, pointer, nurse, prover, captain and teacher. The duties and privileges of these positions vary somewhat, but the first two indicate the highest-ranking male and female members. These positions of the faith are made known to an individual during the process of "mournin", the most important of the Spiritual Baptist rituals.

The mourning ritual involves a period of three to seven or more days where the initiates are placed upon an earthen ground where they lie, sit or kneel; their eyes are covered, and they are given minimal food and water. A member of the church, usually the pointer, officiates at the mourning while the nurse takes care of the physical needs of the initiate. During the "mournin" initiates "travel" spiritually to different places, receive spiritual instruction through visions and dreams, and are told what position in the hierarchy they are to occupy. When the leader decides that the time is up, usually during a Sunday service, the initiates are brought back into the church and share their experiences with the congregation.

From the perspective of the belief system, "mournin" involves symbolic death and resurrection, in that mourners shed their impure lives by "dying" and being resurrected as spiritual and pure beings. In psychobiological terms, the rite of "mournin" actually involves a period of intense physical and sensory deprivation, as initiates are deprived of light and movement and receive minimal sustenance.

Some scholars allege that the ritual can be traced to the rites of some African tribal groups' initiations. They argue that traits such as fasting, not eating salt, a new name, and the colour symbolism of the bands covering the eyes of the initiates suggest African derivation. Others claim that it originates in the Book of Daniel, which states that Daniel mourned for three weeks. In either event, the ritual is the central rite of the Shouter Baptist faith in Trinidad and in all areas of the Caribbean and the southern United States where this religion is practised.

Services are typically held on Sundays and are opened by the leader or mother of the group ringing a brass bell. Candles are also lit, and water and aromatic oils, as well as peas, rice and flour, are sometimes dropped at the four corners of the altar. A liturgy is then recited, followed by hymn singing accompanied by ritual handshaking and the touching of everyone gathered. A sermon is delivered by the leader, followed by more singing and praying. Throughout the service worshippers clap hands, tap their feet and shout out "hallelujah" and other praises to the Lord. Visits by the Holy Spirit upon worshippers may happen anytime during the service. Those visited will begin to sway, hold their heads, shout, speak in tongues, shake and eventually fall to the ground in a state of trance.

Other rituals of the faith include baptism wherein a person is immersed in water at least three times by a church leader, who is then recognized as a spiritual father or mother to the initiate. In fact, membership in the Baptist faith involves the creation of a new "family", bound together by common membership. Initiates become the "children" of the leaders who have baptized them but also brothers and sisters to the persons baptized with them. Other practices include a feast called "thanksgiving" held annually or at special occasions. This rite is normally undertaken for the children of the community and involves the distribution of special foods. Prayer, the singing of hymns and sermons accompany it.

Symbolism plays an important role in the Spiritual Baptist religion. Pictures, engravings and flags may contain one or more symbols including the scale of balance, signifying justice; the balance wheel, depicting righteous living; the cross, meaning deliverance and victory over death; seals, which are closed mysteries; the burning bush, which signifies the Holy Spirit; the star, which means a guide or pointer, and many others.

The bell also plays a very important role in many of the rituals. For example, there is a bell that calls to worship, one that invokes the Holy Spirit, one that signifies consecration and another that means benediction. The bell is tolled during services, sometimes merely for a point of emphasis. Flags are also important items of ritual and display. These include nation flags, protection flags, messenger flags, conqueror flags and others.

Candles are also used, and even the colour of the candle is significant. For example, a white candle signifies purity, truth and righteousness whereas a red one implies love, fire and blood. A blue candle depicts healing and happiness. Other important implements in the ritual include swords and a shepherd's rod. The use of the human voice, however, is unique. Not only is it frequently raised in song but worshippers make a special kind of sound called "doption", from the English "adopt". Instead of using the drum, which was prohibited, the Baptists developed a special sound, sometimes likened to a grunt, made with the tongue in the back of the throat. These drum sounds create several different rhythms. "Doption" can be used to accompany someone speaking or sermonizing, or it is interspersed in a person's own speech when praying out loud or testifying. The practice continues even today and is one of the most specialized forms of music generated by this group, or any other, for that matter.

The Religion Today

In contrast to its earlier despised position, Spiritual Baptism today has been given an important new status by the granting of an annual holiday. The UNC had promised in its electoral campaign to grant a holiday to the Baptists, which the prior government had been reluctant to do. Upon assuming office in 1995 the new government, under the leadership of Prime Minister Basdeo Panday, granted the holiday to be held on 30 March, the date of the repeal of the prohibitive ordinance against the Shouters. In addition to their newly legitimated status, the Baptists, along with several Orisha groups, were also granted twenty-five acres of land in Maloney to be shared among them. Plans for the land include the building of a Shouter Baptist primary school and the construction of a spiritual park.

The religion is growing in membership as new and younger members are joining the faith; some of these are inspired by the African elements in the worship. The faith is now celebrated not only in its traditional venues but also during major public celebrations, such as those held at the grandstand of the Savannah and, recently, on the land at Maloney.

Today Spiritual Baptism and Orisha are vibrant manifestations of the deeply religious nature of Trinidad-and-Tobagonian society. They are especially attractive to younger members who are interested in relating to their African heritage. Even Shouter Baptism, although largely Christian in its main focus on Jesus Christ as the Saviour and its deep belief in the living reality of the Holy Trinity, nevertheless contains elements clearly derived from an earlier origin in Africa. Both contain elements of the African Yoruba religion, but Orisha has maintained more of these than has Shouter Baptism. The most important of these is the belief in spirit possession, in which the Orisha or African deities take over or possess the body of the worshipper.

Similarly, Spiritual and Shouter Baptists believe in a form of trance brought about by the entry of the Holy Spirit into the body of the adherent. In trance or possession, worshippers act according to the wishes of the spirit who has possessed their bodies. In addition, Spiritual Baptists believe in an overtly emotional form of worship that is also thought to be African in origin. Despite some similarities in ritual and observance, the relationship between the two religions of Shouter Baptists and Orisha is ambiguous. There is some overlap between Spiritual/Shouter Baptism and the Orisha worship in Trinidad. Some members practise both religions, and some Baptist leaders also hold Orisha ceremonies. Other members, however, vehemently deny that there is any relation between the two. Both religions are very active in Trinidad and Tobago today. Although it is difficult to ascertain their membership, estimates of the Spiritual Baptist faith range anywhere from about one hundred thousand to two hundred thousand (of a total population of 1.2 million). The numerical strength of the group is complicated by the patterns of religious behaviour in the country. Persons may say they "belong" to as many as four or five different religions because they attend several churches and services. One common expression describing this form of religious behaviour is, "the more roads to Heaven one takes, the better".

Organization of the Faith

The organization of the Spiritual Baptist religion in Trinidad and Tobago is fairly complex. There are three archdioceses in Trinidad. These are the Council of Elders Spiritual Baptist (Shouters) Faith of Trinidad and Tobago, led by government-appointed senator Barbara Burke; the National Evangelical Spiritual Baptist Faith Incorporated, led by Archbishop Clarence Baisden;[14] and the National Congress of Incorporated Baptist Organizations of Trinidad and Tobago, led by Archbishop Murrain. All three were incorporated in 1985. (Recently, a fourth splinter group called the Spiritual Baptist Christians, led by Teacher Hazel Ann Gibbs-De Peza, has formed but apparently remains within the National Congress.) The Council of Elders and Archbishop Baisden's National Evangelical Spiritual Baptists have a very loose "hands of fellowship" relationship, but the National Congress has not been able to work out a satisfactory association with the council. For all intents and purposes, the three groups work independently, and each was given its five-acre lot in Maloney. Each group has plans to develop that land individually and there is currently no attempt to coordinate these efforts.

Each archdiocese is under the leadership of an archbishop and each contains dioceses. The National Council of Elders has two dioceses; the evangelical group, the National Evangelical Spiritual Baptists, has only one diocese but it contains about 130 churches. However, the National Congress is composed of eight different dioceses, and within each one there are many affiliated churches. Thus, for example, the West Indian United Spiritual Baptist Order, led by Archbishop Lancaster, which is a diocese within the National Congress, contains as many as a hundred churches. Anther diocese, the National Ecclesiastical Council of Spiritual Baptist Churches of Trinidad and Tobago, under the leadership of Bishop Taylor, contains at least fifty-five churches. Thus, there are literally hundreds of churches affiliated with the three archdioceses. As well, there are unaffiliated churches that function entirely on their own. The archbishop in charge of the National Congress therefore estimates that there are as many as two hundred thousand Spiritual Baptists in the country.[15]

The splits in the religion occurred some years ago. The then Archbishop Elton Griffith, leader of the National Evangelical Spiritual Baptist Council, wanted a leading role in the formation of the congress. His move was resisted by other groups coming together to form the congress, in an effort to create an umbrella group to administer and modernize the infrastructure of the religion. Accordingly, the evangelical group retracted its membership and began operations on its own. The National Council of Elders was formed under the leadership of Senator and Archbishop Barbara Burke as a third group.

Factionalism is encouraged by the ways in which the religion is organized. Spiritual Baptism, like the Orisha movement, is indigenous to the country and it lacks the international infrastructure of other religions. Its worship began with any individual who claimed to have a call to the ministry and established a church. All that was necessary was to secure a building and attract followers. The result was that hundreds of independent churches were established, and it was only within the last dozen years or so that any attempt at centralization has begun.

The resulting "disunity" has remained. Senator Barbara Burke was baptized by the late Archbishop Elton Griffith and remained part of his evangelical group (National Evangelical Spiritual Baptists) until she formed her own diocese. Archbishops Randoo and Douglas, two leaders today, were also initially part of the National Evangelical Spiritual Baptists. This group broke away from the National Council of Elders in 1998 and held its own celebrations on the national holiday, as did the National Congress. The total split among the three groups was allegedly stimulated by accusations of financial mismanagement on the part of the Council of Elders, led by Senator Burke.

The religion today is marked by a considerable amount of what one respondent described thus: "they are always squabbling, fighting, arguing". There is also criticism among some members of the faith that the congress "is all individual archbishops; how can you have a religion with so many leaders? We need one leader." This respondent also said she was "fed up with [the] 'I am the boss, I am, I am' attitudes of all those archbishops". She was not alone in expressing the view that the religion is characterized by leaders who are interested in the power that comes with authority and titles. This sentiment was echoed by a nurse writing to the letters section of *Newsday*[16] in response to a letter written earlier by a Spiritual Baptist archbishop, who complained that the songs, symbols and even "the bells and the candles" of the Spiritual Baptist faith were being appropriated by a group of nurses protesting during a job action. However, Spiritual Baptists are not represented around the conference table for "talks and mediation". The writer asks, "Who's capable of representing the Spiritual Baptists?" She notes, "There are so many leaders who believe that they are the boss . . . each one of these is a boss in their own right, no one is backing down, so there's no unity within themselves, then who can you send?" She notes also that many of the demonstrating nurses were, in fact, members of the Spiritual Baptist faith, and any impropriety on their part was the result of the teaching they received. What is interesting in these comments is that the discourse of disunity and the so-called bossism of Spiritual Baptist leaders is so pronounced that it even reaches the letters pages of a newspaper.

Several of the leaders interviewed wanted to stress that the archbishops are, in the main, educated theologians. Many of them hold certificates from Bible colleges and theological centres in the Caribbean and abroad. One Spiritual Baptist archbishop is the secretary of the Inter-Religious Organization (IRO), a body on which all religions (except the Orisha religion, until very recently) are represented and which acts or lobbies for the religious institutions of the society. It should not be thought, respondents were quick to stress, that Spiritual Baptist leaders were without theological training. The majority of members are, however, relatively uneducated, poor and without means or resources of their own. They are not overly concerned about the lack of organization within the religion nor the competition among its leadership. They are, in the main, primarily interested in the religion because of the spiritual comfort it provides. Like the Orisha group, Spiritual Baptism can claim a substantial number of notable members, again especially from the artistic community. Singing Sandra, the country's prize-winning calypsonian, is an active member of a Spiritual Baptist church, as are a number of other calypsonians and popular singers. The faith also claims the support of a number of middle-class businesspeople, most of whom were drawn to it because the religion and/or one of its members provided special assistance in a time of need.

Another example of disunity is that members of the three groups, while recognizing their common Baptist orientation, strongly differentiate themselves from each other. Archbishop and Senator Barbara Burke, for example, always notes that her groups are Shouters because "we shout". Reverend Gibbs-De Peza maintains that the difference is that Spiritual Baptists belong to the Christian sector whereas Shouter Baptists are African influenced and worship African deities. These constructions do not necessarily conform to reality, as both groups "shout" during their ceremonies and both use the bell, use the drum and catch spirit in much the same manner. For purposes of their own identification, differentiation appears necessary, but to the observer the beliefs and practices appear to be generally similar enough to classify them together. Many of the leaders maintain that there is only one set of Baptist beliefs, practices and doctrines, but that the religion is split into several competing groups led by competing leaders. There is also common recognition of the need to come together, at least for political purposes, and to some extent this is being done. The differences in the personal style of leadership, however, appear to preclude unification at this time. All leaders agree that unity, or the lack of it, is the central problem with the Spiritual Baptist religion. This issue also surfaced in 1993, as evidenced by the fact that a committee – the Special Committee on the Unification of Spiritual Baptists – was formed by the Office of the Prime Minister, then held by

Patrick Manning. This apparently came about as the National Congress registered and incorporated its group and an effort was made to bring the National Evangelical Spiritual Baptists and the congress together. In fact, in a letter signed by the late Archbishop Elaine Griffith of the National Evangelical Spiritual Baptists, the prime minister is thanked for his efforts to "assist in the unification of all Spiritual Baptists in Trinidad and Tobago".[17] The groups are also frequently exhorted by the prime minister and the leader of the opposition in this regard.

In addition to leadership competition, another major point of dissension relates to the position of women in the hierarchy of the religion. The majority of the leaders, and especially those within the National Congress, do not agree to women holding positions of bishop or archbishop despite the fact that, at the local church level, women play a very important role. About 85 per cent of the membership in this religion are women. Moreover, women occupy many of the positions in the church such as mother, teacher, nurse and so on. The mother is often the leader of the church and, in all regards, women are the major participants at all levels of the church organization. Women in the Spiritual or Shouter Baptist faith have paid a significant role in the development of the movement. They do almost everything, from cleaning and decorating the altar for church services to seeing to the candidates for baptism. Archbishop Driscilla Paul, Gertrude Mundy, Bishop Eudora Thomas and Elaine Griffith, wife of deceased Archbishop Elton George Griffith, were among the pioneering women in the faith. At the higher leadership levels, however, very few women are accepted. Teacher Hazel, as she is called, said the nurturing role of women is very evident in Spiritual Baptist churches:

> The mother in the church takes care of children, the nurse sees after the pilgrims and the candidates for baptism, for mourning. The mother sets the table for thanksgiving, does the cooking, sets the altar for service. There are all kinds of motherly activities, so that you find it becomes much easier for women to gravitate to that kind of activity. Still, within some Spiritual Baptist churches there is a glass ceiling. Women can reach as far as mother superior, but they are not allowed to be consecrated bishops and archbishops.[18]

The main group that does not agree with the prohibition against women leaders is the National Council of Elders, whose leader is not only a woman but also a government-appointed member of the Senate. One of its most prominent spokespersons, a woman who is regularly featured in the media for her outspoken and forthright views, is Archbishop Monica Randoo. She says:

> A man can't watch me, Sister Monica, and tell me I can't be Archbishop . . . I can be anything that God wants me to be. . . . You go to any church, name it now and you will see the women there. They are the bastions, but what has happened they are not being recognized in this society. My view is that the man-made dogmas have filtered in our minds and settled there like plaque! But it could be drilled out after a time by the dentist drill: their word – the piercing word of the women. There are going to be women at every age and era that are going to drill it, and it is going to be eradicated.[19]

The National Congress has, at present, a woman as its second vice-president and she will, at their next election, become its first vice-president. While the National Evangelical group does not appear to have a highly positioned woman, its general secretary is female.

It is also worth noting that the unease with female leaders does not apply to the diaspora. The present male archbishop, Clarence Baisden, enthroned Archbishop Deloris Severight in her position as leader of the evangelical group in Toronto a few years ago. The late Archbishop Elton Griffith was a proponent of equality between the sexes in the church. Citing the example of Mary anointing the feet of Jesus, the archbishop argued that if a woman was worthy enough to anoint the feet of the Lord, she was also capable of serving at the high altar. His own wife followed him as archbishop of his diocese.

Baptists who reject female leaders cite the Bible as their source, claiming that after the overall authority of God, there is man, followed by woman. Several leaders claim that they are trying to become more liberal in this regard and are actively seeking dialogue on the subject. "It is only through dialogue that the majority can be changed," maintained the leader of the National Congress.[20]

Although the Baptist groups have made great strides in gaining acceptance in the country, there are still areas of concern. For example, one of their archbishops has recently made representation to government to have discriminatory legislation removed from the statutes. There are two statutes that are offensive not only to the African religions but also to all religious groups. Both statues were cited in the Parliament during the debate on changing the Public Holiday Act in 1995, and even then their removal was requested. Five years later a Spiritual Baptist has taken up this cause again. The focus of their complaint is with Section 43 of the Summary Act of No. 31 of 1921, which reads:

> Any person who, by the practice of obeah or by any occult means or by any assumption of supernatural power or knowledge, intimidates or attempts to intimidate any person, obtains or endeavours to obtain any chattel, money or valuable security from any other person, or pretends to discover any treasure or any lost or stolen goods, or the person who stole the same, or to inflict any disease, loss, damage or personal injury to or upon any other person or *to restore any other person to health*, and any person who procures, counsels, induces, or persuades or endeavours to persuade any other person to commit any such offence, is liable to imprisonment for six months, and, subject to the Corporal Punishment Acts . . .

The statute goes against almost all religions, since most indulge in some form of healing practice. Even the very act of prayer is often used for healing purposes. However, when such healing practices are used by a traditional church, they become acceptable. This point was made dramatically in a speech to the Senate on 4 July 1995, in which Senator Mejias said,

> When my grandmother used to take me to the Catholic Church in Mount St Benedict and to buy scapular to put around my neck as a child, and tabeche to put around my hand, that was not obeah. But when a person goes into a Baptist church and takes a bath and they put a banner on him and some beads around his neck, that is the practice of obeah.

What this observation reveals is that the use of various charms and amulets by an accepted church goes unchallenged, but similar devices in the Baptist faith are considered to be heathen and black magic. This is a strong indication of differential treatment accorded to non-denominational as compared to traditional Christian groups.

The second example prohibits both the playing of musical instruments, such as drums between 10 p.m. and 6 a.m. and any assemblage for the dancing of the "bungo" [*sic*] or Bongo. Clearly this statute is directed against African religions that use the drums and specifically the Orisha religion, some of whose deities dance a bongo-like dance.[21] (Recently several members of the Orisha religion have protested against this statute.)

Although these statutes are no longer implemented, their very presence on the legislative books still suggests the earlier rejection of African religions. In fact, the claim that healing involves the practice of obeah affects just about every religion in the country. Moreover, it is clearly indicative of the fear and apprehension with which such practices were regarded during colonial times and, to some extent, even today.

Various members of the faith still claim that they are discriminated against because of their religious practices. Reverend Gibbs-De Peza maintained in a speech held at the public library one day before the holiday celebrations that "being a Spiritual Baptist is a struggle and continues to be a struggle". She noted that even at her workplace "the first day I went to school as a teacher with a headtie on my head . . . teachers who had been my friends shunned me".

Another indication of the still prevailing negative attitudes towards African religions was reported in the *Trinidad Guardian* of 15 April 2000. A Baptist woman waiting to appear before a magistrate's court in Port of Spain "caught power", according to the report, which is worth quoting:

> With eyes closed, the woman, wearing a white head wrap and an orange coloured dress, got off the bench and began jumping up and down, jiggling her body. At the time, she was with three other Baptist women, one of whom knelt down and used the index finger of her left hand to mark a strange sign on the top of the stairway. At first, the sounds of "Oh God! Oh God!" was heard, but after, nothing the woman said made sense. Eyewitnesses, who immediately fled the scene, said the Baptist woman was "speaking in tongues". One police officer who witnessed the five minute scenario said there was a lot of evil spirits around the place. "She must be catch one of them," he said matter-of-factly, adding, "or one must be catch she."

What is immediately apparent in this report is that people are still afraid of the religion, since they quickly fled the areas. In the description of the witnesses, one of the women was seen to make a strange sign; it might well have been the sign of the cross! Moreover, the eyewitness maintained that there were a lot of evil spirits around and immediately arrived at the conclusion that the woman was possessed by one of them. That a good spirit might have possessed the woman was never even entertained. Thus, Baptism is still, in some quarters, automatically equated with evil.

In a moving tribute to her Spiritual Baptist grandmother published in the *Express* of 3 April 2000, Afiya Butler described how her proud grandmother wore white dresses and head ties and regularly attended services at the Baptist church. The writer was much influenced by her during her childhood but as the grandmother died, her faith diminished. She notes:

> I began to grow ashamed of the Baptist heritage I had claimed so proudly before. If a friend asked me if I were a Baptist I would deny it. When I was told I looked like one, I was angry and insulted. Now I am angry only with myself . . . I felt that denying my past as a Baptist was the only way I could move up socially. [Eight years later] I had made a mistake in my choices. I was and still am a Baptist in my heart.

For this young woman to have been able to write this story and have it published in one of the country's leading newspapers was a sign of legitimation. In another example, following a lecture about Spiritual Baptism a young girl thanked the speaker: "The girl, a Pentecostal, said the lecture helped to counter the brainwashing she underwent, which led her to believe Baptists were devil-worshippers. She said for the first time in her life, she could see Baptists are good and would strive to accept them for who they are."[22]

The lecture has been given by Reverend Gibbs-De Peza, who noted that her religion has made strides but has not yet gained ready acceptance within the society. Perceptions of Baptists as poor, uneducated, backward Africans still exist within the mainstream. She also said that many people confused Baptism with Orisha and that the two are not the same, since the latter is derived from Africa whereas Baptism is a Christian faith.

The present government of the country has supported the Spiritual Shouter Baptists. While the official view of the government is that the holiday was granted because of the need to create equality between this religion and others in the country, a more cynical view is expressed by substantial numbers of people. According to this perspective, the present UNC government is trying to pry votes away from the People's National Movement (PNM), who have traditionally claimed the electoral support of the Spiritual Baptists. In any event, the public holiday has given this group a prominence in the public discourse that they have never had before. To a considerable extent, the Spiritual Baptist religion has achieved a level of respectability rivalling that of conventional denominational Christian faiths.

> It is indeed my conviction that the recognition of African religion is the ultimate step in the reclamation of self for the diaspora African.
> – *Eintou Pearl Springer*

CHAPTER THREE

The Formal Processes of Political Legitimation

PAST AND PRESENT GOVERNMENTS of Trinidad and Tobago have played a role in validating and legitimizing the African-derived religions that had always existed on the margins rather than in the mainstream of religious institutions of the country.

Government Actions

- Repeal of the Shouter Prohibition Act, 1951.
- Registration and incorporation of the two Orisha groups (in 1981 and 1990) and several Baptist religions (in 1985). These mechanisms have given the groups corporate status.
- Visit of the Ooni of Ife in 1989; the prime minister and many government officials attend a massive celebration at Jean Pierre; the Ooni visits shrines, consecrates a leader and declares himself pleased with the practice of the Orisha religion in Trinidad.
- Enthronement of Molly Ahye as head of Opa Shango in 1991; many members of government and notable members of society attend the

president's reception held at his house; the event is televised and given substantial other media coverage.
- PNM government gives the Orisha religion a public festival day of celebration in 1995; UNC grants the Spiritual/Shouter Baptists a national holiday on 30 March of every year and continues the Orisha public festival day.
- Both religions given land at Maloney – twenty-five acres shared among five groups; deeds of ownership to the land given in 2000.
- Passage of the Orisha Marriage Act in 1999.
- Iyalorisha Melvina Rodney given a Hummingbird National Award at the Independence Day celebrations in 2000.
- Regulations to the marriage act are written; first Orisha marriage officer granted a licence in March 2001.

These religions are now, or soon will be, equal to the many other religions practised in Trinidad and Togago.

At another and more public level, one of the most interesting developments has been the way in which Orisha and the Baptists have come out of what might be described as underground and almost secret forms of worship to overt, large-scale public celebrations of their religion. The many commemorations of the Baptist holiday, three in 1999 and 2000 in different locations, and the observance of a Family Day at Lopinot for the Orisha religion are some examples. These events attract hundreds of participants and many spectators who come merely to see what is happening and to lend their support. They also attract substantial print and electronic media coverage.

Of particular importance to the present discussion, however, is that the events are attended by the prime minister and members of his cabinet and are used as occasions for making major policy statements, usually in the form of promises, to those assembled. They have therefore become the vehicle or medium used by the government to further its political purposes by attempting to attract the political and electoral support of the largely Afro-Trinidadian membership of these religions. At the same time, however, these legislative acts have benefited the two communities significantly, in terms of both material and social acceptance. The very public nature of these occasions, helped by media coverage, plays an important role in the legitimation process.

Spiritual Baptist National Holiday Celebrations

Celebrations of 30 March 1996

In what is described as "Glory Day"[1] the Spiritual and Shouter Baptist community of Trinidad and Tobago celebrated its long awaited Liberation Day holiday. The meeting took place at the National Stadium and, apparently, all three of the major dioceses of the religion were there together. The proceedings began at about 10:30 a.m. with prayers, hymns and greetings from foreign members and leaders. Greetings and blessings were also delivered from the Baha'i and the Orisha faiths. Patrick Manning attended and was originally seated in the box reserved for VIPs, but was later asked to sit on the dais with the dignitaries. He received a standing ovation from the audience, which showed appreciation by repeatedly chanting his name. He did not stay, leaving shortly before the prime minister arrived. Basdeo Panday was led to his assigned seat by several Baptist elders, given a candle and asked to light the main torch or flambeau as part of a presentation "entitled Light the circle of Love and Unity heralded by a fanfare of bells and followed by energetic clapping, singing and dancing". A speech was delivered by Molly Ahye from the Orisha movement in which she praised the women and mothers of the Spiritual Baptist faith who kept it alive. Senator Barbara Burke and Senator Junior Barrack also made speeches, followed by a song from a guest artist.

In speaking at a press conference held one day before the celebrations, Senator Barbara Burke thanked the prime minister for his participation: "I want to thank Prime Minister Basdeo Panday and wish him health, strength and long life. His heart and love was so much with the Spiritual Shouter Baptist community. All we can say is 'thank you' to him."

She then clearly and publicly introduced a political discourse by linking political affiliation and ethnicity: "We came to our own, the PNM, the African government and our own received us not. They did not see fit to give us dignity and status in Trinidad and Tobago. But the scripture is fulfilled now."[2]

Although the leader of the opposition, Patrick Manning, attended, he did not address the gathering. Mr Panday noted in his address:

> For too long the Spiritual Baptists have been used as a political football. Hopefully these days are gone . . . this government has not come to divide but to

Figure 1 Prime Minister Panday surrounded by Baptist dignitaries, including Senator Burke (in red), participating in a candle ceremony at the Spiritual Baptist national holiday celebration, Queen's Park Savannah, 1996

unite . . . [granting the holiday] was in keeping with Government's quest for national unity. . . . We have also insisted that we shall make every effort to leave behind the politics of exclusion, marginalisation and alienation and to promote participation and active improvement for all.

Celebrations of 30 March 1997

Divisions in the Spiritual Baptist community had become evident by the following year when two celebrations took place. The Spiritual Baptist Shouter Liberation Day was celebrated at Woodford Square in the heart of Port of Spain and was conducted by the National Evangelical Spiritual Baptists, led by Archbishop Clarence Baisden. In the meantime, the Council of Elders of the Spiritual Baptist Shouters Faith led by Archbishop and Senator Barbara Burke celebrated in the grandstand of the Queen's Park Savannah along with the National Congress.

There were approximately three hundred persons present at Woodford Square, but several hundred more were in the grandstand. Both events included drumming, songs by a variety of choirs, hymn singing and sermonizing. Several older members of the faith, called "patriarchs", were honoured at the grandstand. At Woodford Square the celebration was much the same, but it included a lengthy and in-depth speech on the relationship of the faith to the African heritage. Drawing upon his extensive knowledge of African history, Archbishop Baisden gave an informed lecture that emphasized the placement of the Spiritual Baptist faith squarely in the African tradition.

The continued politicization of the Liberation Day holiday was again strongly evident, because the feature event at both venues was the attendance of the prime minister at one and the president at the other. It would appear that the government took pains to ensure that the political presence would be strongly represented, since the two first officers of the country shared the duties. Prime Minister Basdeo Panday, accompanied by members of his government, attended the grandstand, where he gave a speech praising the Baptists for continuing their struggle "in the face of unrelenting harassment". He noted that although the ordinance prohibiting their worship was repealed by the then government in 1951, it was his government that had granted "Shouter Baptists a symbol of national recognition over adversity" in the form of a national holiday. With both Easter and the Hindu Phagwa festival being held during the same time period, he noted that religion should be a unifying force in society and suggested that national unity meant more than politicians coming together. For his government it meant "a united force in our battle against unemployment and poverty and drugs and crime". The speech praised the Baptist struggle, while at the same time drawing attention to the role that the UNC government had played in bringing the religion to this point. Thus he was able to communicate a strong political message: that it was his government that had granted the holiday and that it is his government that stands for the fight against the social ills of society. The prime minister was greeted by applause and ululation upon his arrival, and particularly at the conclusion of his speech.

At Woodford Square His Excellency A.N.R. Robinson, president of the Republic of Trinidad and Tobago, was given a rousing welcome and called a "son" of the Spiritual Baptist faith. During the introduction Archbishop Monica Randoo, who called herself his "mother", delivered a strong political message; she said that Robinson's presidency was a cause for celebration

Figure 2 President A.N.R. Robinson flanked by Archbishop Randoo, Archbishop Clarence Baisden and Senator Barbara Burke at the Spiritual Baptist national holiday celebration, Woodford Square, 1997

because it finally cemented the nationhood of Trinidad and Tobago.[3] She described him as a god-fearing man and a friend of the faith. The president was given a plaque to signify his support of the faith. He, in a very short address, thanked the congregations and urged them to continue their spiritual messages to the country. Commenting on the fact of the two celebrations, another speaker urged the group to greater unity and an end to racial divisions.

Celebrations of 1998

Because of the several and distinct dioceses in the religion, two major celebrations took place in 1998. One observance, organized by the National Evangelical Spiritual Baptists, took place in the grandstand of the Savannah[4] and was attended by about four hundred members of the faith and a small number of onlookers. The second, organized by Senator Barbara Burke's group, the Council of Elders of the Shouter Baptists, was held on the land granted to them in Maloney. This is an area on the Beetham Highway located across the road from the government-subsidized housing development at Maloney. Several temporary tents were erected to house the speakers and members, and a public address system and water system were installed especially for the occasion. At both events the agenda included opening prayers, welcome addresses, sermons by visiting members of the faith, addresses by visitors, hymn singing – especially by the many choirs that exist in both groups – announcements and the like. What was extremely interesting, however, was the very obvious political tone that permeated the celebrations. In fact, the appearance and speech of the prime minister and, often, the leader of the opposition were the highlights of the day's agenda.

There were common themes addressed by both groups. The Baptists emphasized the transnational character of their religion by having representatives of their religion from other areas in the Caribbean, Canada, the United States and the United Kingdom. Both groups emphasized unity. In fact, Prime Minister Panday stressed the need for unity in the nation at large as well as within the religion. It is worth noting that as this plural society is split between two ethnic groups, the African religions are decided among two Orisha groups and at least three Spiritual Baptist groups. As a consequence, the theme of unity in these religions becomes a metaphor for national unity.

Minister Daphne Phillips made unity her main focus in her speech at the Savannah, arguing that religious people should unite, as should all people in Trinidad and Tobago. In a show of unity, Archbishop Randoo of the Shouters group appeared at the celebration of the other group at the Savannah, holding a lit green candle symbolizing togetherness.

Political themes were also in evidence at the Savannah celebration, where one of the speakers predicted that a future prime minister would come from the Baptist ranks, a comment that was met with loud cheers. Other speakers called for more representation of Baptists on government agencies and boards.

The prime minister and some of his ministers, including Kamla Persad Bissessar who is of Indian heritage, arrived in Maloney during the mid-afternoon. At the Savannah two government ministers were present, including one of African and one of Indian heritage. The attention to ethnicity in the representation of members of government illustrates the importance of ethnic politics in this plural society.

The leader of the opposition, Patrick Manning, visited Maloney but not the Savannah. At Maloney, his activities included shaking hands and saying a prayer. His small participation was met with substantial applause.

Figure 3 Leader of the opposition Patrick Manning (now prime minister) seated with Baptist dignitaries preparing a Bible reading at the Spiritual Baptist national holiday celebration, Maloney, 1998. (Wearing a white mitre is visiting Archbishop Dolores Severeight of Canada.)

The prime minister was introduced and referred to by Archbishop Randoo as a "Son of a Shouter" and a man from God. She also acknowledged his part in the legislation of the religious holiday. He was also presented with a scroll making him an honorary member of the faith by Archbishop Senator Burke, in the following speech:

> Honourable Prime Minister, Honourable Basdeo Panday and to the Chairman thank you, our visiting Archbishops from Barbados, Canada and the Caribbean, you wonderful people, our Minister of Culture, our Minister of Public Administration, God bless the people, the Honourable Minister John Humphrey, our beloved Sat Balkaransingh, may God extend long life, health and strength to these wonderful people. In my hands is a scroll, and I will read the contents of the scroll.
>
> The Church of the Spiritual Metaphane Incorporated and the Council of Elders of Spiritual Baptists Shouter faith be it known that on Monday 30th March 1998 we did bestow upon our beloved brother, the Right Honourable Basdeo Panday, as an Honourable Member of the Order of the Spiritual Baptist

Shouter faith, we sincerely hope and pray that our beloved brother would recognize and protect by all enabling him to enjoy the rights and privileges as a member of this Order of the Spiritual Baptist Shouter faith in testimony herein now with our hand and seal, Senator Archbishop.

The prime minister responded as follows:

Thank you Archbishop, I must be the luckiest man in the world, I was born in the home of a Hindu, I went to a Christian college, I got married to a Muslim woman and today I have been consecrated into the Baptist Shouter faith. I am the luckiest man in the world . . . Today, our people of African descent are preserved of any aspect of their ancestors material and spiritual culture in Trinidad and Tobago and it is because of the institution of the Spiritual Baptist Church whose members centred their social activities around religious and secular festivities and practised and understood the beauty and sense of African tradition fused with Christian teachings . . .

I am particularly pleased that my government has seen it fit to identify with the Baptist community in naming March the 30th a national holiday in the cause of religious freedom and tolerance and in the need to extend equality and justice to a once alienated and abandoned sector of our society. Today I join with you and raise a shout of my own "Mataphane", Mataphane is an African word that means let us be together with one another together.

The overt political nature of this and other celebratory meetings was obvious. The press played up the prime minister's honorary status as a Spiritual Baptist. One newspaper, the *Independent*, used it as the basis for its "man in the street" feature. The question "What do you think of Prime Minister Panday being made an honorary Baptist?" was reportedly posed to a cross-section of people by ethnicity and gender. Responses included:

"It's up to the Shouter Baptists to choose who they want to make an honorary Baptist."

"It is like I am in authority and I want to prove to you that I can be in anything. Something isn't right here. But every man has his own thing."

"It doesn't make any sense. That is stupidness – he is already practising a religion."

"It's something that goes with the territory. It does not mean as much to him as it does to them. He accepted it as he is the Prime Minister not because it means something to him. Maybe if it were a Hindu or Muslim."

"That's just another political thing. I don't see the reason for it."

"I don't think he should. I just don't think so."

"It's just a political gimmick as a gift from Barbara Burke for being appointed to the UNC. It's just an exchange."

"That is very controversial in relation to his religion and that's not because he is the Prime Minister."

Judging by these responses, admittedly a selected and limited sample, the move was not especially popular with the "person in the street". On the other hand, it would have been even more inappropriate were the prime minister to have declined the honour.

Spiritual Baptist Celebrations, 1999

In 1999 further dissension in the Spiritual Baptist faith was evident as three separate groups sponsored public celebrations, a fact that was noted by both the prime minister and Patrick Manning, who urged the groups towards greater unity. At Maloney the prime minister, members of his government and Mr Manning spent at least one hour. In a strong show of support, Mr Panday and his group managed to visit all three celebrations. The National Evangelical Spiritual Baptists celebrated at City Hall and their official host was the mayor of Port of Spain, John Rahel.

During his address, Mr Panday handed over a "memorandum of understanding" giving each group five acres of land at Maloney. He outlined some of his government's important legislation, including the Equal Opportunity Bill and the Orisha Marriage Act, and called these "acts of affirmation". The prime minister was extravagant in his praise of Senator Archbishop Barbara Burke, calling her very dedicated and citing her "great powers of persuasion". He also strongly implied that she was responsible for the legislation of the national holiday and the granting of the land.

Of special interest in these celebrations was the continued presence of the leader of the opposition, who was greeted warmly at these events. His speech made reference to the theme of unity by noting that when he was in office he had made numerous attempts to unify the Spiritual Baptist movement without any success. He likened their divisions to the Irish situation with its Catholic and Protestant splits and warned that there was a strong possibility of it happening again. He called for "unity among you, after all, there is only

Figure 4 Senator Barbara Burke, Prime Minister Panday and Minister of Culture Daphne Phillips at the Spiritual Baptist national holiday celebration, Maloney, 1999

one God and one Shouter Baptist faith". Minister Daphne Phillips called attention to the gender issue by praising this group, the Shouters, for having women in top positions, noting that there is no gender issue here as in many other religions.

The prime minister's introduction as the "man who took us to another phase of our history" was interrupted by the announcement of the winning cricket score in the test match pitting the West Indians against the Australians, "Praise Jesus and praise Lara!"[5] The prime minister took up this theme by referring to the West Indian cricket victory and praising their own Prince Lara. Referring to his status as an honourable member of the faith, Mr Panday noted, "I come as your brother." And, while noting the problem of unity, he made light of it by calling himself "thrice blessed" for giving the feature address at three celebrations. He described it as "joyful" diversity. He noted that although there is tension in a plural society such as Trinidad, "we live in a blessed land".

The print media followed these celebrations in great detail, but the 1999 events were considered so newsworthy that there was full television coverage of the prime minister's visit to at least two of the meetings. The newspapers published many stories and photographs in the weeks following the celebrations.

Celebrations of 2000–2001

In the year 2000 the various Baptist groups held two major celebrations: the Shouters convened in Maloney as was customary and the National Evangelical Spiritual Baptist Faith met at City Hall. Both events were well attended by ministers of government, the leader of the opposition and the prime minister. In 2002 the prime minister was able to deliver the actual deeds to the lands at Maloney to the various groups. As in previous years during the Baptist holiday celebrations and at meetings of the Orisha faith at Lopinot, the prime minister's presence was greatly appreciated.

The 2002 Baptist celebrations were marked by a minor controversy, duly reported in detail in the press, that bears directly on one of the central themes of this book. The controversy gave an ample demonstration of how these religious groups and their public celebrations have become politicized. It provides a demonstration of how the ruling UNC government, constructed as "Indian", worked to gather more support from these groups that have been, and likely still are, strong PNM supporters.

One of the government members accompanying the prime minister was the minister of education, Kamla Persad-Bissessar, an ethnic Indian. She addressed the crowd as "my brothers and sisters in the faith", explaining that she could say this since she had been baptized in the faith as a child. She also appeared wearing a white robe and head tie, the traditional garb of Spiritual Shouter Baptist women. Her claim to be a Baptist met with widespread skepticism, as she is known to be Hindu. Shortly after the Baptist celebrations this same minister fell ill and had to be hospitalized. About a week later, an opposition member of the house made a speech during a meeting held for a by-election. The member noted that Minister Persad-Bissessar's recent illness might well have been caused by her lying about being a Baptist and that she had, in fact, received a "spirit lash" that was responsible for making her ill.[6] He was immediately reprimanded by archbishops of the Spiritual Baptist religion, including their appointed senator, for having made a derogatory statement about the Baptist faith. The senator vigorously denied mentioning the term "spirit lash", saying that it was a member of his audience who had made that comment. He did, however, apologize to the members of the religion. The story does not end there. In defence of the minister, a pastor of the Spiritual Baptist church maintained, in an article in the *Express* of 8 April, that her father did indeed baptize Minister Persad-Bissessar when she was a teenager and that her entire family had been baptized. In the meantime, the prime minister joined the fray when, at a political meeting in Arima, he lambasted the opposition member who had allegedly made the original remark about Minister Persad-Bissessar "playing" Baptist. Panday is quoted as saying, "He made the most insulting and derogatory remarks about the Baptists. We have been trying to end 500 years of discrimination."[7]

The incident of the alleged "spirit lash" was not restricted to the politicians. Members of the general public and especially those who lecture and debate at the "University of Woodford Square"[8] took up the issue by arguing over whether or not an apology was necessary. However this event also allowed some people to criticize Archbishop and Senator Barbara Burke openly. Comments made about the spirit lash issue include:[9]

> "Archbishop Burke must apologise to the Spiritual Baptist community for attempting to use it for UNC's political gains . . . The Senator is playing too much politics with de Baptist religion."
>
> "Barbara Burke is looking for too much bacchanal with de religion. Burke feel because she is ah archbishop, she speaking for all Baptists but she wrong."
>
> "Barbara Burke could be president of de Elders Council or not, she can't influence we Baptist people to vote for de UNC. Is only politics and nothing spiritual does come out her mouth."
>
> "That is why plenty Baptist don't even bother to listen to her these days."

There is strong sentiment among people who are affiliated with the other Baptist groups that Burke is a political liability to the UNC. They applauded the appointment of a Baptist to the Senate as good political strategy but feel that the government made the wrong choice in Archbishop Burke. It is alleged that the government has regretted her appointment for many years and would like to replace her with another Baptist, but find difficulty in doing so.[10] Meanwhile, a poll released in April 2000 to survey the electorate about their voting intentions in the next general election, to be held sometime in 2000, showed that only 13 per cent of Baptists would vote for the UNC, they were "shouted down" by an overwhelming 59 per cent who said they would vote for the PNM.[11] Interestingly enough, these results were headlined by a newspaper that proclaimed in large, bold headlines, "Baptists shout down UNC". If these results held on election day, the many efforts made by the government and its Baptist appointed senator to capture votes among this constituency achieved little result.[12]

At the celebration meetings of the Baptists in 2000 the prime minister introduced each of the ministers who had accompanied him and especially those who had come out of opposition ranks. He told the congregation that it was his government and not the former PNM government who had granted both the national holiday and the lands at Maloney. He also appealed directly for their support by saying jokingly that he hoped to be in office in thirty years when the lease for their land would be renewed.

In the meantime, opposition leader Patrick Manning also milked the crowd, beginning his appearance by singing a popular hymn, "What Do You Think about Jesus?" – to which the crowd energetically responded, "He's all right". By singing this hymn, Manning clearly identified himself as a Christian, versus the prime minister's Hindu faith, and sought to invoke identification with the Christian Baptists. The opposition leader received a more enthusiastic response from the audience than did the prime minister or any of his ministers. This might suggest that the group still maintains its support of the PNM government, despite the benefits granted to their religion by the "Indian" government of the UNC.

There are other examples of both the government and the opposition party playing politics with these religious groups. For example, at the opening of an African Methodist Episcopal church reported on 29 March, the prime minister's speech recounted how much his government had done for the Spiritual Baptist and Orisha religions. He specifically named all five groups who had received land at Maloney. At a political meeting for a by-election on 31 March 2000, the prime minister again named the five groups who had received land. He also joked with the crowd, referring to Dr Eric Williams who, in 1981, promised the Baptists a holiday but died before this could happen. Then the Chambers government continued the promise but the prime minister also died. Skipping rapidly over the National Alliance for Reconstruction government of President A.N.R. Robinson, Panday continued by saying that Manning had also promised the Baptist holiday but "then he died politically".[13]

In another major demonstration of the intermingling of politics and religion, the opposition party, the PNM, held a Spiritual Baptist service to commemorate the holiday at their political headquarters, Balisier House, on the day preceding the holiday.

The press clearly believes that a considerable amount of "politicking" is taking place at these religious events. In reporting the celebrations the *Trinidad Express* carried the front page headline: "Manning upstages Panday at Baptist Celebrations" (31 March 2000), and the caption for an article on the following page read, "Shouters give Manning standing ovations". In it, opposition leader Manning's speech to the celebration at City Hall is recounted in some detail. It notes that he was showered with "thunderous applause and standing ovations several times. . . . When Manning was introduced . . . the crowd stood up, cheering boisterously," Again, Mr Manning seemed to invoke his own Christianity at the expense of the prime minister's Hinduism, beginning his speech by singing, "I am delivered, praise the Lord." The article continues with "To screaming cheers, Manning continued: And today I come to you as a child of God in the name of Jesus Christ."[14]

The media provided coverage of all of the celebrations, and in 2001 the celebrations also provided material for several cartoons. The "spirit lash" cartoon refers to Patrick Manning, who had mentioned at Maloney that he would pray for the prime minister (see Figure 5). At the same ceremony, the prime minister was made an honorary Baptist. The cartoon suggests that not only does Panday control the government but he could, as a Baptist, now also dispense a supernaturally motivated physical blow to the leader of the opposition. The "honorary pupil" cartoon pokes fun at the difficulty Mr Panday would experience, were he to become a pupil again (see Figure 6).

Private sector companies also took the occasion of the celebration to use Baptist themes in their advertisements. The Colonial Life Insurance Company (CLICO) took out an advertisement in the newspapers showing a Baptist woman with her hands raised, singing "Ring de Bell for Freedom, Ring the Bell for Justice", from a song composed by soca singer, Brother Resistance. The caption reads: "Clico joins with the Spiritual Baptists of our nation, and indeed with all our peoples in the enjoyment of our religious freedom."

Figure 5 "Spirit lash" cartoon

Figure 6 "Honorary pupil" cartoon

Politicization Processes

Case Study: The Parliamentary Debates on the Granting of the National Holiday

The following case study illustrates the highly political nature of the national holiday granted to the Spiritual Baptists, and is based on the debates in the Senate and the House of Representatives on the granting of public holidays to groups such as the Spiritual Baptists, the Orisha religion and others. These debates were prompted by these groups requesting official holiday status. They were also stimulated by the lobbying for a holiday to celebrate the arrival of indentured Indians to the country in 1845. The matter became polarized because it was quickly construed as an issue of ethnic divisiveness.[15] The government of the day, the PNM, established a bipartisan joint committee of the House and Senate to consider the "entire question of public holidays and to report by March 31, 1995".

After some delay, the committee reported in July of that year. In view of the inflammatory nature of the issue, it was unable to reach a consensus and two reports, one representing the majority and the other the minority, were tabled in Parliament. The two reports coincide with the political affiliation of the committee members, in that the government members agreed to the majority report which recommended that no official public holidays be given to the African religions but rather both would be honoured with public festival days. All the opposition members agreed with the minority report. The majority report recommended a holiday on 30 May commemorating the arrival of indentured Indians to Trinidad in 1845, to be designated Arrival Day. The minority report called for the granting of national holiday status to both African groups and the name "Indian Arrival Day" to the Indian communities. Political party affiliations were strictly adhered to in the subsequent vote. All present PNM government members voted against the first amendment that called for the acceptance of the minority report, whereas all opposition members voted in favour of it. When the principle motion to accept the majority report was called, all government members voted in favour of it while all opposition members present abstained from the vote. This contentious issue created a considerable amount of public discussion. The PNM's attempt at a conciliatory majority report led to many criticisms, even by those who are normally PNM supporters. And a noted university professor said that "Arrival Day is a devious, ambivalent PNM response to requests for a clearly justified 'Indian Arrival Day'".[16]

History and Debates in Parliament

Both the Spiritual Baptists and the Orisha religion had for many years agitated for recognition of their faiths in the form of a national public holiday. Even during the days of the PNM government of Dr Eric Williams, the Baptists had asked for a public holiday. On 30 March 1976, during the tenure of the Williams government, the Baptists celebrated the repeal of the ordinance against them at Woodford Square. The event was attended by Dr Williams, who promised the group a national day. According to Senator Gray-Burke,[17] there was widespread optimism that this would be granted. But shortly afterwards, the prime minister passed away. His successor George Chambers offered 1 August as the day, but this was refused because it was not the day of the repeal. The next prime minister, A.N.R. Robinson, attended the Liberation celebrations the following year and stated that "next year the almanac will carry March 30 as a public holiday". Later, in 1988, Patrick Manning visited the National Evangelical Archdiocese. Senator Burke commented, "It was to solicit votes for the up-coming election. I recall him saying 'when I am in power my government will grant a public holiday'." Several members of the Spiritual Baptist groups were there and they displayed "our dissatisfaction on issues affecting us. He was present; he was accustomed to coming there and was a close associate to the Spiritual Baptist community". The following year Manning again attended a Baptist celebration. In 1990 another celebration was being planned and Senator Burke and her close associate, Archbishop Monica Randoo, visited Mr Manning's office to invite him to attend. In the discussion he declared:

> "I would be the next Prime Minister." We were thrilled, because he had confidence in himself and Baptist people are positive people. I recall it as if it happened yesterday. We began saying to him that our Father of the Nation [Dr Williams] demised. Mr Chambers and also Mr Robinson did not give it. His words were: "When I become Prime Minister the first thing I would do is give the Spiritual Baptist community the public holiday. I know of their struggle . . ." The PNM government won the election. Archbishop Burke and Archbishop Monica Randoo were always waiting and listening to hear the day announced.[18]

The senator goes on to discuss her grief and disappointment: "a government I had fought for through blood and sand . . . we put them there and cannot receive anything at all from them". Subsequently the senator met with Mr Basdeo Panday, then still in opposition but having declared his support for the public holiday during the debate in the House of Representatives and he noted that the Baptist community was not represented in Parliament although they have supported "a particular political party for thirty-nine years". He offered her a position as an opposition senator, which she gladly accepted because it gave her an opportunity to "come face to face with broken promises which have been the history of the relationship between past governments, the present government and the Spiritual Baptist community". She concludes her contribution to the debate by thanking the then honourable leader of the opposition, saying, "We know how to show gratitude and are overwhelmed by your demonstration of keeping the vigil for those who have been alienated and humiliated for so long."[19]

What is particularly noteworthy, and especially in the context of the increasing political legitimation of these African religions, is the overt political nature of the senator's comments. There is very little of the religious or spiritual in her speech. The discourse reveals several levels of meaning. In the first place, it is primarily a political statement in which the history of broken promises by former governments is revealed. The main point being made is that the PNM, which has the traditional support of the Spiritual Baptist community, has let them down in not keeping to their promise of granting the holiday. The senator is even willing to forego the governments of Eric Williams, Chambers and A.N.R. Robinson, but it is the allegedly overt promise made by the then leader of the opposition of the PNM that has her most upset. Even though that government was still in office for some time before the next election, the following year (1996) brought the UNC and its leader, Basdeo Panday, to office. The senator is clearly indicating her willingness to change her political allegiance and perhaps those of her community whom she can influence. By accepting the opposition senatorial appointment and then publicly thanking Panday for it, she signalled her change of political alliance. The timing of her contribution to the debate is also significant. Her speech in the Senate was delivered two days after Mr Panday, then leader of the opposition, clearly stated his intention to grant a public holiday to the Baptists on 30 March if and when he came to power.

Mr Manning's main point on the issue of public holidays[20] was that there were already too many holidays and the strategy for the country should be to reduce their number, not increase them. He believed that granting both groups a public festival day instead of creating a public holiday would provide sufficient recognition to these groups. He also wanted to ward off other groups coming forward with their requests for a public holiday. (During the debate it was revealed that there had already been eleven requests from other groups, many of which wanted various festival days of Hinduism such as Phagwa recognized as national days.) He believes that the present government will face problems with the Orisha religion, which was not granted a holiday. (This has apparently not happened, despite the group's continued interest in having a holiday.) Manning also reasoned that the granting of such a holiday creates further divisiveness in an already ethnically divided society. Granting the Indian community a holiday called "Indian Arrival Day", rather than "Arrival Day" as his government wanted, as well as giving the Afro-Trinidadian community the Spiritual Baptist holiday, would reinforce division in the country. This could be avoided by leaving out the label "Indian" in Arrival Day and leaving the Baptists and the Orisha with public festival days.

According to Mr Manning, the holiday further divided the Spiritual Baptist community itself. He brought together seven out of eight Spiritual Baptist groups and created the Association of Independent Ministries, catering to them, Pentecostalists and other non-aligned religious groups. He maintains that the present government of the UNC showed favouritism to one group by naming a senator from one group. This, he maintains, was using a divide-and-rule policy that is very evident today, as the Spiritual Baptists are more factionalized than ever. His evidence for this was the number of different groups celebrating the holiday. His government's granting of public festival days, plus naming the other holiday "Arrival Day", was in the spirit of multiculturalism, whereas present government policies are aimed at racial polarization that, according to him, is increasing in the country. He did not address the promise he allegedly made to Senator Burke and her colleagues.

During the course of the debate, some of his then members commented on other benefits offered to the religious communities, namely land and the possibility of building a cathedral dedicated to Spiritual Baptism. It was not clear whether the government was intending to fully or only partially fund these initiatives. While Mr Manning is on record, both in personal interviews and in the press, with respect to the several reasons why his government chose not to grant a holiday, it is also known that he was very much against the removal of the Easter Monday holiday to make room for the Baptist holiday without sacrificing another work day. His reasons appear to be based on his own sense of Christianity. "The festival day is really Easter, and by removing Easter Monday as a holiday, it in fact cancels the implication of Easter Sunday – a holiday for Christian faiths."[21]

The displeasure created by the PNM's refusal to grant a holiday to the Orisha religion was demonstrated in the broadside reproduced in Figure 7 and distributed during the Lord Shango celebrations held in 1998. Its author is not known.

Senator Mejias spoke in the debate on behalf of the Orisha religion. Unlike the overt politicization of Senator Burke, Mejias placed his comments within the discourse of African-centred ideology, claiming that "our voices seem never to be heard with the same credibility or authority as the voices of others". He notes that honoured and respected voices coming from the universities and elsewhere speak "on behalf . . . of the African man [who] could not speak for himself, so someone always has to speak for him, whether their work was correct or incorrect, bias or unbiased, damaging in context to the African man or neutral". Using an article about Shango (Orisha) as his reference, the senator pointed out that depriving an African of his identity and "adopting him as a Son of God through European Christian doctrines and beliefs commonly called Scripture, so that he can have salvation through an European government is an insult". Using very strong language he continued:

> To refuse the indigenous religion of the Yorubas, the Orisha worshippers a national public holiday to honour the deity Lord Shango that is the strength of the black African people . . . is regarded as an act of racism, and religious bigotry, directed against the indigenous descendants of African people in this diaspora.[22]

Mejias is expressing a very strong anticolonialist discourse since he maintains that the Orisha religion would have been the dominant one in this country were it not for the "slave master concept of religion", in which "children of the Orishas [were dispersed] into European major state religions which essentially destroyed the African forms".

ATTENTION

Manning and All PNM Members of Parliament are against THE ORISHA and LORD SHANGO:

- All PNM Members of Parliament voted against LORD SHANGO DAY

- All PNM Members of Parliament voted against the Spiritual Baptist Deliverance Day

They are denying the AFRICANS.
We want our day.
Wake up AFRICANS!!
Wake up NOW!!

Figure 7 Broadside protesting PNM policy

Further on in his address he notes that the Orisha religion is based on prayers and invocations but no preaching because "dance is our major expression of the will". The music of the drums is not incidental or for pleasure; it is integral to the worship. Such practices were considered "heathenish, devilish and non Christian". This senator, then, unlike the previous one, also delivers a politicized address but one that emphasizes the discourse of the need to revitalize Africanness in Trinidad and Tobago, because of the destruction wrought upon the peoples and cultures of Africans in this part of the world first by slave masters and then by colonials. In both instances African culture and religion were partially destroyed. The point of the holidays, then, is to legitimize these religions.

The debate on the public holidays report occupied considerable time in both the House and the Senate. In defence of the holidays, Senator Junior Barack, speaking on 4 May 1995, puts the matter in perspective:

> It is a place to start because for the first time we would be saying that we recognize something which is inherently African by putting it on the national stage. It may not mean a change in the physical lifestyle of individuals in the sense that they might not change from one religious perspective to another, but the fact will be that they are recognized and we have removed the identity problem.

This senator concludes his address by bringing the issue of politics squarely into the debate when he states that

> the purpose of the public holidays committee was not about that. It was not about dealing with the African and wider community and settling problems within that. It was primarily political, to deal with the issue of granting Indian Arrival Day.

There is speculation among the members of the House of Parliament and elsewhere in the society that the whole issue of the granting of the Spiritual Baptist Holiday was intimately related to the quest by the Indian community to honour their arrival to the country. As noted earlier, the African religious communities had lobbied for their own holidays for many years, as had Indians who wanted to celebrate their arrival to the country. However, the need for the debate on the holiday issue was motivated by the Indians' demand to celebrate their arrival in the country,[23] and to commemorate the one hundred and fiftieth anniversary of their arrival on 30 May 1845 as indentured workers. Rather than act unilaterally, and favour one ethnic group over the other, the then PNM government appointed a parliamentary committee to investigate the entire issue of public holidays. In view of the ethnic politics that are pervasive in this plural society, no government could give a holiday to one group without, at the same time, so honouring the other. However, the then PNM government sought to effect a compromise, which was to offer 30 May as "Arrival Day" without specifying whose arrival, and to designate two days as public festivals for the Baptists and Orisha. It would appear that the 30 May Arrival Day holiday was granted specifically for the year 1995 to honour the one hundred and fiftieth year of East Indians coming to Trinidad. (It was also thought that Republic Day honouring the country as a whole was not sufficiently celebrated, and that a new programme of thanksgiving and rededication was required.) In that way, it was thought that no group would be either significantly honoured or offended. The theory was that "arrival" would celebrate the arrival of the many ethnic groups into the country. It could therefore refer not only to the arrival of Indians but also to all other groups as well, and would thus function as a all-purpose multicultural holiday. The problem with this, as critics were quick to point out, was that 30 May does indeed mark the arrival of the first group of Indians to the country. As Mr Panday, then in opposition, declared:

> If you mean that it shall be a day on which everybody shall celebrate their arrival – why are you forcing the Chinese to celebrate on May 30th? They probably came on the first. Do they want the Portuguese to celebrate arrival day on May 30th? . . . so that the Indians have not got their holiday on May 30 as Indian Arrival Day . . . they are afraid to use the word. Is it because they think they could hoodwink somebody? Do they think that by leaving out the word they can go and tell the other sections of the population "you see, we are not really giving them any holiday, you know. Let them think they are getting a holiday, but they did not get any." That is playing with race![24]

The government position was that Arrival Day was supported precisely for the same reason, that is, that emphasizing the differences among the ethnic groups would lead to further disharmony. The neutral "arrival" without the ethnic designation would therefore signify harmony rather than the promotion of ethnic diversity. Moreover, the Indian community should be satisfied because their particular arrival day was chosen as the holiday. And no group would welcome the addition of at least eight more holidays to celebrate the arrival of all the other ethnic groups in the diverse society.

Another opposition member made very fine linguistic differentiations when he agreed that the chosen date had special significance for East Indians but it also had significance for the remainder of the population. Although they did not come to Trinidad on that day, they are asked to "emphasize with a historical event in the life of Trinidad and Tobago . . . it is Indian Arrival day but it has significance for the whole society". He then furthers the ethnic nature of this debate by recalling that Emancipation Day (celebrating the abolition of slavery on 1 August 1834) was not called African Emancipation Day but "everybody understands that that day celebrates African Emancipation Day". He criticizes the government for having omitted the ethnic designation by saying that, had the word "African" been included, "then we would have arrived as a society and as a country. But the superficiality with which they want to deal with this problem shows their insecurity in dealing with these problems in an open and candid manner." The long debate concluded with the majority report of the government being approved, but no further legislative action was taken.

On 30 May 1995 Indian Arrival Day was celebrated as a public holiday to honour the arrival of Indians to the country. It was declared a public holiday for that day only by a presidential order. Afro-Trinidadians participated in substantial numbers in the celebrations that took place throughout the country but centred in the "Indian" regions. Mr Panday stated that he was happy to see that the event had such national appeal and showed that "people of all races were beginning to appreciate and learn from each other's culture".[25]

By the end of 1995 the PNM government was defeated and the UNC, led by Basdeo Panday, was elected into power. In one of his very first actions in Parliament, on 26 January 1996, Mr Panday called for the establishment of a public holiday for the Spiritual Shouter Baptists to be held on 30 March, and of the granting of land to them for the purposes of erecting a school and other facilities. The legislation that followed, on 16 February 1996, order #32, brought the Spiritual Baptist Liberation Day into being and, in order to create room for it, Whit Monday was removed from the holiday calendar.[26] On the same date, Indian Arrival Day was made into a public national holiday.

Thus, it seems apparent that the granting of the Baptist holiday, while motivated by the desire to bring about religious equity in the country, was also related to the ethnically divided nature of this society. By granting an African group a national holiday, the UNC was also able to restore the ethnic designation "Indian" to Arrival Day, thereby unequivocally marking it as an ethnic holiday honouring the East Indian–derived community.

The debates about the new public holiday took place some years ago. That it is still a contentious issue to some is reflected by a feature piece in the *Trinidad Guardian* on 11 April 2000. Under the headline "Hullabaloo hollow over Baptist Day", the writer maintains that a public holiday was given to a "group of Christians" numbering twenty thousand, if so many. She also disputes the name change of Arrival Day to Indian Arrival Day, saying that the latter represents "all of us" instead of just "one of us". She argues that the Baptists are Christians and there are already several Christian holidays celebrated throughout the year. In the most telling argument in this piece, the writer challenges the African nature of the religion by noting that "some people continue to promote a major falsehood that these offshoots are African religions, as their location in the African spiritual park would suggest". On the other hand she also challenges the name of the holiday, noting that were it called "traditional religions day, it would have served the Orisha faith and the Amerindian religion as well". This opinion piece, written and published years after the events took place, provides yet further evidence that the granting of a Baptist holiday and the creation of a specific Indian Arrival Day remain contested issues in this society so sensitive to ethnic politics.

The Orisha Marriage Act

One of the announcements made by the prime minister when he first began creating legislation specifically designed to bring the African religions into the mainstream was the development of a marriage act that would allow Orisha priests to perform rites of marriage, death and any other rituals requiring the services of a legitimized priest. This had long been requested by Orisha members, who wished to marry under their rites rather than accept a civil ceremony or a marriage performed in a traditional church.

The demand was so strong that, instead of including this provision in the general marriage legislation that regulates such practices and that is under review, the government decided to create a new act designed specifically for Orisha devotees. Entitled the Orisha Marriage Act, 1999, it came into law that year. Its purpose is to give legal status to marriages performed according to Orisha rites. It grants licences to marriage officers who "shall be priests or priestesses of the Orisha faith". As with any legislation, however, the act also requires regulations as set out by the Ministry of the Attorney General, and although the act itself was swiftly put into effect, its accompanying regulations were still not made public months after the bill was enacted. One of the contentious issues that delayed the issuance of regulations was the controversy around the designation of marriage officers. The act merely states that "any Orisha priest or priestess who desires to be licensed as a marriage officer shall make an application in writing to the Minister". In view of some of the contested claims to leadership in the Orisha faith, still a highly individuated religion, anyone might qualify under these loose guidelines. Some Orisha members fear that unqualified and untried "priests" will set themselves up as marriage officers, thus tainting the spiritual nature of these rites. Some leaders claim that an Orisha marriage officer should have been an Orisha priest for some years and also should lead a shrine properly certified and registered with the Council of Orisha Elders.

Finally, the Orisha Marriage Act and its regulations were put into effect by the granting of a marriage licence to an Orisha priest and elder, Baba Songodele Adeleke Kunle, in March 2001. The event was reported in both major newspapers and was accompanied by a photograph showing Attorney General Lawrence Ramesh Maharaj presenting the licence to the priest. Members of the faith, including Iyalorisha Melvina Rodney, Eintou Pearl Springer and Patricia McCleod (Iya Sangowummi) and others, gathered in a semicircle during the presentation. The event also included an Orisha drummer, and the members present chanted several Orisha songs.

Changing the Summary Offences Act

One final governmental intervention sought for years by both the Spiritual Baptist and Orisha communities is the removal of antiquated and repressive legislation still on the books. Dating from 1921, the act prevents the use of drums at night, faith and spiritual healing, and the practice of obeah. At a meeting in August 2000 held in honour of Emancipation Day, the prime minister again promised that his government was working to remove these old laws. He noted that

> the AG will complete the necessary work for the introduction of laws to repeal those sections of the Summary Offences Act which historically have institutionalised discrimination against the Orisha faith and which historically has [sic] institutionalised discrimination against members of the Spiritual Baptist faith.[27]

Once this legislation has been removed, government intervention in the management of the African religions should have been completed. At the time of this writing, the necessary legislation was before Parliament. It also remains to be seen if the government will take any action against squatters who have moved onto the lands at Maloney. These lands are to be used as an African Spiritual Park by the Baptist and Orisha groups; they are thus far unusable due to the presence of substantial numbers of squatters.

Another noteworthy event took place early in 2000. Community groups are encouraged to submit names of potential Hummingbird Award recipients to the government. The Council of Elders of the Orisha Faith put forward the name of Iyalorisha Rodney, and she was selected for a silver Hummingbird Award that was given to her at a ceremony at the president's house. The council was extremely gratified that she was chosen, and took this award to their leader as a signal of their acceptance not only by government but also by society in general.

The televised ceremony took place at the president's house before an audience of carefully invited guests. It was a very formal and dignified event, with the president and the prime minister and their wives seated at a dais at the front of the large ballroom. The president's aide-de-camp read out the name of each recipient, as the television announcer gave a brief description of the contributions that led each person to receive the country's highest honour. In this way, the viewer was informed briefly about the achievement of each recipient. However, when Iyalorisha Rodney was called by the aide as "Melvina Rodney, high priestess", the television announcer merely echoed the same announcement, omitting any biographical detail. She was not announced by her title, "Iyalorisha", nor was the religion of which she is "high priestess" identified.[28] The event was televised in its entirety throughout the country. Some viewers might therefore have wondered why this woman was receiving an award. Moreover, one questions why her African-

based religion was not identified. Perhaps some decision maker, in either the president's office or the television station, thought that it would not be appropriate in contemporary society to admit that not only was African religion being practised but that its highest leader was selected to be honoured.

> Ifa is the source. Ifa to the Yoruba is what the Koran is to the Muslims, the Bible is to the Christian, or the Torah to the Jews, you know, and many of the retentions or continuity came directly out of Ifa.
> – *Patricia McCleod (Sangowummi)*

CHAPTER FOUR

The Orisha Religion from Sacred to Secular
The Evolution of the Shango Cult into the Orisha Movement

The Visit of the Ooni of Ife

THE MOST SIGNIFICANT EVENT in the restructuring and secularization of the Orisha religion took place in 1989 when the Ooni of Ife visited Trinidad.[1] The Ooni, Oba Okunade Sijunade Olubuse II, is the acknowledged spiritual leader of the Orisha religion both in Nigeria and throughout the world wherever the religion is practised. He came at the invitation of the government to participate in Emancipation Day celebrations. On his arrival, the Ooni was officially met by members of government, including several ministers. Many events were planned in his honour. The Ooni travelled to many areas of the country, visiting not only Orisha shrines but also many other sites. He laid a stone at the historical site on Lopinot Road, located off the Eastern Main Road, which is believed to be ancestral land in which African slaves were buried centuries ago. The stone honoured a well-known Babalawo, Isaac "Sheppy" Lindsay, who died before the Ooni's visit. He also visited the shrine of Iyalorisha Melvina Rodney, spiritual leader of the Orisha religion in Trinidad. Of this visit, Iyalorisha Rodney says:

> Oh God, it was something . . . the best day of my whole life . . . I couldn't believe he actually here. I had my children build a chair [a substantial wooden throne-like chair covered in carvings] for he. He does really come. When I see the man, I fall to the ground, touch my head to the ground [as she speaks, she demonstrates this by actually falling to the ground. She is eighty-four.] He raise me up, bless me head. I take him to my *chapelle*. As he walk in, I fall to the ground again and say bless me, bless me. He raise me up again and look at everything in my *chapelle*. Later, I give him tea . . . . He sit in the chair. He bless my whole yard. Oh God, Oh God, it was a day . . . . Like it was yesterday.[2]

Iyalorisha Rodney says that the Ooni consecrated her shrine and anointed her as the spiritual head of the Orisha religion in Trinidad and Tobago. Although this is generally accepted by the majority of the present membership, it is contested by a few people in other factions.[3]

Because his visit was official, a massive celebration took place in the Jean Pierre Complex, a large sporting arena near Port of Spain. The event was marked by the presence of the then prime minister, the president of the republic and many other members of government. They all sat along with the Ooni and his Nigerian entourage on a raised dais shielded by umbrellas. The complex was decorated with flags and bunting and there was entertainment in the form of drumming, singing and parading. Several leading entertainers, especially those with Orisha commitments, performed. David Rudder, for example, was presented with a necklace for his performance.

The event was staged by Molly Ahye, the leader of the other Orisha group, Opa Shango; Ahye's background includes dance and choreography. She arranged for a procession of Orisha icons to be brought into the ceremonial area. During one of her visits to Nigeria, Ahye obtained a staff of Obatala, one of the principal Orishas. She says that she did not trust anyone with it so gave it to her son to carry. Her son is an active Orisha worshipper and many powers manifest on him. Midway along the processional he "caught power", with Obatala beginning as an old man with faltering steps. As his steps appeared to lead him in the wrong direction, Ahye called him,

"Papa, it up there you have to go", and as she said this he became the young Obatala, taking huge strides. He marched towards the dais and addressed the dignitaries. In so doing, he appeared to be affirming his mother's role as a legitimate Orisha priestess. This event was televised and at this point the television commentator, who was not sure of what was happening, announced that Molly Ahye used to be a dancer and choreographer and that the appearance of Obatala was a staged event. The possession experience of the young man as Obatala was, however, reported in the newspaper.[4]

In addition to the public celebrations that honoured his visit, the Ooni played a strong role in advocating for a united administrative structure for the religion. He suggested that a National Council of Elders be formed, consisting of the major shrine heads in the country. This was subsequently done. Despite earlier attempts at secularization and centralization, this visit marks the real starting point in the process of building an administrative infrastructure for the highly individualistic Orisha religion.

The Incorporation of the Orisha groups

There are two Orisha groups in Trinidad and Tobago today. One of these is the Egbe Orisa Ile Wa ("The Religion of Our Land"), led by Iyalorisha Melvina Rodney whose shrine is in Marabella, near San Fernando. This group was registered as a religion in 1981 and officially incorporated in 1991. Iyalorisha Rodney is the spiritual heir to Pa Neezer. She says that Neezer anointed her three days before he died during one of her last visits to him in hospital. She is his spiritual child, and her ritual adheres very closely to the manner in which Pa Neezer conducted his feasts. Her *chapelle*, which contains many chromolithographs of saints and the implements of the Orisha, is closely modelled on those of Neezer's time. I first met her in 1956 at Pa Neezer's feasts, where she often worked in the kitchen. At that time she was still in the background and did not often manifest possessions publicly, but clearly she had been his disciple for a long time. Iyalorisha Rodney was, and still is, widely considered the leader of the Orisha religion in Trinidad, and this was legitimized by the Ooni's consecration.

The other group is the Opa Shango, which was incorporated in 1990. Its leader is Molly Ahye, who succeeded Mother Gretel, a respected Orisha leader, in that position. This group also includes Babalorisha Clarence Forde and the late Aldwyn Scott, both of whom supported the enthronement of Molly Ahye as its head. One major difference between this group and the Egbe Orisa is that Molly Ahye does not have an Orisha compound, does not conduct *Ebos* and does not appear to have any real group membership. Clarence Forde, on the other hand, is a very active Orisha leader who participates in many celebrations and *Ebos,* as was the late Aldwyn Scott. Forde's backing of Opa Shango appears to be somewhat nominal, and he supported Ahye's official leadership because he has known Molly Ahye since she was a child. He was also a friend of her mother, who was an active Orisha worshipper. He is familiar with her outstanding career in dance and research, and values her education highly. He believes that she has been fighting for the Orisha religion for a long time.

Molly Ahye is a member of the middle class. She holds a doctoral degree from an American university and is well known as a folklorist, former dancer and now as an African historian. She has close links with Africa and visits there often. Babalorisha Forde recognizes, however, that the choice of Molly Ahye was not popular with other elders and members of the religions. Ahye has spent time in Nigeria and the Republic of Benin and has close ties to the African forms of Orisha, especially in Ifa. She claims that she arranged for the Ooni of Ife to come to Trinidad and Tobago, but when he came, "he created confusion here".[5] She maintains that he has no authority to anoint leaders and that each shrine must be respected and treated equally. She also questions his dominion or authority over people and events in other countries, and feels the Nigerians are trying to use and exploit the New World religions because the people in Trinidad need the affirmation and legitimation that the Ooni and the Nigerians can confer. She thinks that the other Orisha group latched on to the Ooni for their own benefit in an effort to shut her out. Clearly, there is some tension between Molly Ahye's Opa Shango and the main Orisha group, the Egbe Orisa Ile Wa, although Babalorisha Clarence Forde is eminently successful in bridging the gap between both groups. He is also a respected elder in the Council of Elders, and while Ahye's name has appeared on some of the council's literature, she does not attend their meetings or participate in any of their events.

Ahye and Babalorisha Forde established the Opa Orisha Shango in order to create an umbrella organization. The organization was formed in 1981 with the cooperation of only one "house" or *Ile,* that of Forde. The Opa

Shango was registered with Parliament in 1991, and soon thereafter, Molly Ahye was enthroned as its leader in a public ceremony. She wanted to establish organizational rules and a structure, but the traditional people resisted her efforts. Apparently, at this point, the transnational character of the Orisha religion began to have an impact on the local scene in Trinidad. When Ahye met with some resistance locally, she turned to Marta Vega, a scholar of Puerto Rican origin working in the United States and head of an organization in New York called the Caribbean Cultural Committee. Vega was excited by the Orisha religion and wanted to include it in her cultural display. Molly Ahye developed a water ceremony to express and symbolize the culture of the Orisha religion.

In 1980 a cultural festival in New York was dedicated to the Orisha religion and apparently, at that time also, an international Orisha body, the World Orisha Congress, was formed. It focused on Cuba, Brazil and Nigeria. In 1983 its first conference was held in Nigeria. According to Ahye, the conference and the organization were undermined by the Nigerians, who wanted to lead the group because they felt they were the "authentic Africans". The supporters of Marta Vega left the international body as a result but the remaining members, including Trinidad and Tobago, continued to hold conferences. In 1998 they met in San Francisco with a delegation of Trinidadians, including Patricia McCleod, Eintou Springer, Rawle Gibbons and Iyalorisha Joan Cyrus. The decision to host the next conference in Trinidad and Tobago was made there and the Trinidad delegates were made responsible for the local arrangements.

The other main Orisha group in Trinidad is the Egbe Orisa Ile Wa, whose spiritual leader is the renowned elder, Mother Iyalorisha Melvina Rodney. Her *Ile* is located in Marabella. She has one of the largest followings in the country and claims hundreds of spiritual children and grandchildren. She is revered as a true "old head" and most of the notable members of the Orisha faith, who have only in recent times made their commitment public, are children of her shrine. Mother Rodney, born and christened as a Roman Catholic, began manifesting Orisha powers as a very young child. Her first possession took place in Baster Hall near Couva, home of a famous Orisha leader, Mother B. The famous "king" of the religion, Pa Neezer, was also present and he confirmed her Orisha power and initiated her. Now in her mid-eighties, Iyalorisha Rodney is still the mainstay of the Orisha religion.

She holds an *Ebo* every year and also participates in the Family Day celebrations held annually at Lopinot. (See chapter 1 for a case study on Iyalorisha Rodney.)

Thus, there are two Orisha groups in name, but the Egbe Orisa really constitutes the heart of the religion. It is widely believed by members of the Egbe Orisa that the basic difference between the two groups is social class. Molly Ahye represents the brown-skinned, middle-class segment of Trinidadian society, while Iyalorisha Rodney and most of her members are working class or "poor black people". Iyalorisha Rodney's shrine, for example, is extremely simple, and her house is rundown and in need of repair. She sometimes sponsors $15-a-plate barbecues to support the shrine. In earlier times the government seemed to favour the Opa Shango at the expense of the Egbe Orisa. One example of this disparity is the inauguration, or enthronement, of Molly Ahye as head at a public ceremony followed by a reception at the president's house.

Early in 2000 the two groups merged, and currently Iyalorisha Melvina Rodney and Babalorisha Clarence Forde are the leaders of the combined Orisha religion in Trinidad, now both under the guidance of the National Council of Orisha Elders. The two groups were brought together through the efforts of several negotiators including the present chairman of the National Council of Orisha Elders, Babalorisha Sam "Baja" Phills, who played a major role in the merger. Opa Shango's former head, Molly Ahye, apparently is no longer actively involved in the leadership. Although there has been some tension between the two groups in the past and particularly between Molly Ahye and Iyalorisha Rodney, the two women and, by extension, their two groups, have started to settle their differences. During the emancipation ceremonies held on 1 August 2000 several people received awards, including Iyalorisha Rodney and Molly Ahye. Moreover, as the deed to their lands at Maloney were handed over by the government, Ahye and Babalorisha Sam Phills, Eintou Springer and other members of the Council of Elders were present. Tribute was paid to Molly Ahye for her support and involvement in the maintenance of the Orisha religion in Trinidad and Tobago.

The Formation of the Council of Elders

During the parliamentary debates on changing the public holidays to accommodate the wishes of the African religious groups, Senator E. Mejias recounted how the National Council of Orisha Elders was formed.[6] The Ooni and his high priest, Dr Illuemi, met with members of the Orisha faith including Iyalorisha Melvina Rodney and several other members of the faith, including the senator. According to his account, the Ooni suggested that ten persons were to be selected to form a council of Orisha elders. Elder Jeffrey Beddeau and Babalorisha Clarence Forde were delegated to select eight other persons to form a council of twelve and to report to the Ooni. These twelve persons were then brought before him, and he chose Iyalorisha Rodney as the chief priestess. Molly Ahye was secretary and Jeffrey Beddeau was selected deputy secretary. These twelve constituted the "lawfully appointed and installed" Orisha Council as of 6 August 1988.

Sometime in 1994 another meeting was convened in order to rejuvenate the council, which had not worked well. The council was pruned to seven members. Later an administrative committee was formed to conduct the business of the Orisha religion. Most of the elders were on the committee.

In 1998 a major development took place with the establishment of a formally incorporated Council of Elders. The council held an annual convention that included an overview of the year's events and a discussion of new ideas and plans. Decisions affecting the religion as a whole were made by the council. As of this writing, the council includes Mother Rodney and Babalorisha Forde, Sister Gonzales, Babalorisha Arthur Monseque and Iya Eudora Thomas. Its chair is Babalorisha Sam Phills. In addition to its directors, the council includes two coordinators for the city of Port of Spain and five district coordinators representing other areas of the country, including Tobago. Its executive committee consists of a general secretary, a public relations officer and an administrator. The council's formal programme of activities includes economic development, educational development and publications. Each programme is assigned to an administrative officer.

The council's primary tasks were to plan the programme of activities for its annual Family Day celebration and any other public events planned. Members of the council, including both administrative officers and elders, provided the liaison between the religion as a whole and the government. Thus, for example, two meetings were planned for February 2000. One was a visit to the president of the country to apprise him of developments and to lobby for the continuing removal of negative legislation against African religions. A group of five members drawn from the council were selected to meet with the president. The other meeting was a site visit to inspect the Lopinot sacred lands and the acreage at Maloney. Present activities of the council include the development of regulations to accompany the Orisha Marriage Act, and fundraising strategies to begin to develop the lands at Maloney. One recent activity of the council has been to certify the authenticity of the many Orisha shrines throughout the country. Each shrine was visited a few years ago on behalf of the council in order to develop a list of shrines and their addresses. In 2000 the council created a certificate of registration in the name of the shrine leader, signed by Babalorisha Sam Phills, as chairman of the Council of Elders, and Iyalorisha Rodney to certify that it has been approved. It read:

> Certificate of Registration, Council of Orisha Elders of Trinidad and Tobago, This Certifies that _____ of _____ is registered with the Council of Orisha Elders and is granted all the rights and privileges pertaining there to. Given this day _____
>
> (signed) Sam Phills, Chair; Clarence Forde, Melvina Rodney, Spiritual Heads.

Some shrine heads display this certificate prominently in the compound. Twenty-two shrines, including the strongest and most active, have applied for and received the certificate. Such centralized authority had never before occurred in the faith, largely because there has not been an administrative structure until recently.

The council has also made strong representations to government urging for the removal of sections 17 and 43 of the Summary Complaints Act, chapter 21, 1921, that constrain the free expression of African-derived religions. One of the most aggravating sections is 59.1 that states,

> The Governor may . . . prohibit during periods specified . . . or any of the following things in any street, highway or public place: a) the carrying of any lighted torch; b) the beating of any drum, the blowing of any horn or the use of any other noisy instruments; c) any dance or procession . . . etc.

One of the sections also orders that any form of drum beating requires a licence from the police. Although this and other prohibitions are generally ignored, some shrine heads still apply for the licence. Both the Orisha movement and the Spiritual Baptists want these offensive statutes abolished. The

Council of Elders takes every opportunity to request these changes, and a group held discussions with the Ministry of the Attorney General for their removal. An act to repeal these statues is currently being considered by Parliament.

The general mandate of the Council of Elders of the Orisha Religion appears to be to meet the need for recognition as the Orisha religion has had to deal with the stigma against it for too long and "we now need to work to take our rightful place in society, we want arrival, like Indian Arrival Day".[7]

The Contested Issue of Orisha Membership in the Inter-Religious Organization

As part of the secularization process, the Orisha movement has attempted to access the mainstream of the country's religious structure. One continuing area of contestation is the refusal of the Inter-Religious Organization (IRO) to admit them to its membership. The IRO is an umbrella group that brings together representatives of the main religions in the country. It was formed about thirty years ago by four religious leaders representing the Roman Catholic and Anglican Churches and the Hindu and Muslim religions. Other religious groups are now also members. It is government supported, and one of its main functions is to provide leaders and prayers for the opening of official functions, of which the opening of Parliament is one of the most significant. According to the representation made by the Orisha, the IRO is seen as a powerful body to which members of government and politicians turn for advice. Without representation in that organization, members of a religion are never invited to functions or to lead prayers, and cannot receive ecclesiastical grants and other benefits.

This issue entered the public discourse in September 2000. The Sanatan Dharma Maha Saba, one of the country's leading Hindu organizations, celebrated a Hindu festival, Utsav, in honour of the Hindu deity Ganesh, and invited members of the Orisha and Muslim faiths to attend in a display of inter-religious and inter-ethnic cooperation. This meeting was called "a show of non-Christian unity" and both Sat Maharaj, the Maha Saba's director and Eintou Pearl Springer, spokeswoman for the Orisha religion spoke of the importance of "non-Christian religions joining forces in the face of continuing non-Christian disrespect".

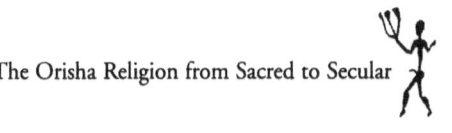

In attendance were chairman and Babalorisha Sam Phills of the National Council of Orisha Elders and Eintou Pearl Springer. Sat Maharaj, the Maha Saba leader, said in a public speech that unless the IRO invited the Orisha and other faiths that had applied for membership, the Maha Saba would create its own inter-religious organization. This was welcomed by Springer, who spoke about the role that spirituality could play in bringing about inter-ethnic harmony in society. Maharaj's threat was immediately countered by a variety of spokespersons or affiliate members of the IRO. During a televised broadcast on 4 September 2000, Dr Ibrahim Mansoor said that the Orisha had not been rejected and that discussions were currently underway. Archbishop Amilius Marrain, a Spiritual Baptist whose religion is registered with the IRO, was quoted as saying that "none of us [religious leaders] are intimidated by threats to our lives or positions".[8] The archbishop "categorically denied prejudice on the part of the IRO". He also explained the application process by saying that a five-member interview panel usually reviewed requests for membership but that the process had been slowed by one of its members being abroad while another, Archbishop Pantin of the Roman Catholic Church, had recently died.

The controversy continued to occupy the attention of the media. Sat Maharaj and Eintou Springer were guests on a morning television programme the following day. Mr Maharaj quoted a letter that he had received from the late Archbishop Pantin in 1987 referring to the admission request of the Amadiya Islamic group, in which he said that other Muslim groups would not sit at the same table with them. Mr Maharaj noted that the organization is

> not a private club only for the privileged [but the IRO] was to embrace the various religious groups of the land and give them a common meeting point. The government is moving to ensure equality . . . why at the level of the IRO can't we have the same level of religious equity.[9]

Springer stated in the discussion that she had written to the late Archbishop Pantin in 1995 applying to the IRO. There was no response to her letter. Exactly one year later, during a television interview, the archbishop said that the Orisha request was "under consideration". Springer then wrote to the newspapers, enclosing her original letter to the archbishop, to complain about the treatment the Orisha faith had received at the hands of the IRO. Springer maintained that she was glad to hear that there was no prejudice against the Orisha – which the archbishop had also said in the interview with her – but that her religion stemmed from one of the oldest in the world, the Yoruba faith, and was deserving of the respect and recognition of the society. Then, with a broad smile on her face, she said she was led to call upon "Brother Sat Maharaj who fought so assiduously for recognition of his traditional religion now that he is happily ensconced in the religious hierarchy". The host announcer then shifted the discussion to questions about whom Springer represents and the role of factionalism in the Orisha religion. Springer vigorously challenged this "unnecessary and irrelevant" comment, saying that every religious group has different groupings within it and why is it, she questioned, that African religions are always castigated for their so-called factions. Maharaj also took up this issue, pointing out that there are many Hindu and Muslim groups and at least 150 different Christian groups in Trinidad. When he was asked why the Maha Saba had entered into this discourse, he noted that it was because all efforts of the Orisha and other contested groups to get into the IRO had failed. In discussing some of the reasons for the rejection of the Amadiya, and especially because other Muslims would walk away – "If you come in, we go out" – he said, "This is blackmail . . . that is Mafia leadership." Springer also took the opportunity to state that the Orisha were fighting to have offensive statutes removed from the legislative books, and the IRO as the body protecting religious rights should have been involved in the battle against the "criminalization of African religion and instead it has concurred with the criminalization by keeping us out of the IRO". And when the host suggested that the Orisha already had a voice in society, Springer replied, "We raise our voices but we don't have a voice!"

What appears to be the end of the controversy, at least as far as public discourse is concerned, is the publication of an article in the *Trinidad Express* of 6 September 2000. It cited the monthly meeting of sixteen members of the IRO on 5 September, in which no decision on Orisha membership had been made. Instead, according to the group's first vice president, "We have to dialogue with them", and to that purpose a meeting was scheduled between the organization and a delegation of Orisha members for the following month. Present at the meeting was Orisha council chairman and Babalorisha Sam Phills, who said that he wanted to talk to them because he was upset with comments made in the press. The vice president said that this meeting had nothing to do with the threats made by Sat Maharaj to create a new organization. In an attempt to explain why the Orisha faith had not been invited to join, the vice president said when they had applied for membership earlier "they were not yet incorporated and they didn't have everything in place yet so we asked them – you have some homework to do – put things in place and then come back to us".[10] This explanation seems to be somewhat specious, since both Orisha groups were incorporated years before they applied to the IRO. The Orisha faith was finally welcomed into IRO membership in 2001.

What is quite apparent in this controversy is that both Sat Maharaj of the Maha Saba and the Orisha movement as represented by the Council of Elders were joining in a collaborative effort, cutting across ethnic and religious lines, in order to further objectives to which both groups aspire. The Orisha desire full participation and the secular recognition that comes with belonging to a national organization. The Maha Saba, on the other hand, wants to be seen as a champion of ethno-religious cooperation in a society that has traditionally been divided along these lines. As well, it gives both groups an opportunity to rail against traditional Christian hegemony. (Although some members of the IRO represent Hindus and Muslims, some of the more non-traditional groupings within these religions also faced some difficulty in gaining membership to the national organization.) This issue presents an excellent example of how some religious groups are trying to bridge the ethnic barriers that exist in the country but also, more importantly for our purposes, it shows that the Orisha movement is reaching out to other religions in its attempts to secularize aspects of the religion.

There is a national discourse for unity that pervades the public speeches of spokespersons, and especially that of the politicians who find it difficult and frustrating to deal with more than one group. Although the plea for unity is perhaps more strongly directed against the even more factionalized Spiritual Baptist groups, the Orisha faith too has been subjected to this discourse.[11]

African Religions in the Schools

There is very little instruction given in the public school system about the doctrines and beliefs of the African religions in Trinidad and Tobago. One result of that omission has been the attempt by the religions to provide instruction in schools of their own creation. This part of the over-all secularization dynamic affecting the Orisha faith demonstrates that the older forms of communication are now being amplified and enhanced by formal education.

Both the Spiritual Baptists and the Orisha movement have plans to build schools on their property in Maloney. One diocese within the Baptist community has already begun the process by laying the groundwork for a school. Both religions require substantial funding to develop these plans.

One group has already achieved the goal of a school but it is a private school founded by Patricia McCleod and assisted by some retired academics and other persons with educational backgrounds. The Osun Abiadama Day School or Centre for Life Long Learning now has an enrolment of over one hundred students. It is fully accredited by the Ministry of Education and caters to all levels, from kindergarten through primary and to secondary levels of education. Its curriculum offers all the traditional subjects taught in the public system, but it also includes instruction in the Yoruba and Swahili languages, "religious instruction" and "comparative religion". The philosophy of the school is Afro-centred, and its religious instruction strongly emphasizes the Orisha religion in Trinidad and the African Yoruba religious traditions. Among other educational objectives, it includes a strong focus on African values: "To teach the greatness and uniqueness of the African race by disciplines used in today's world; To teach and practise those values and principles which have made Africans great . . .; To teach African children that they are equal to all. . . ."

The Orisha religion is also taught to an adult class that meets in the school. Babalorisha Sam Phills and Professor Funso Aiyejina (of the University of the West Indies) are the instructors trying to teach Orisha leaders and members more about the beliefs and practices of the Yoruba tradition. The objective is to raise their level of understanding of their African heritage. A similar adult class held at Babalorisha Clarence Forde's shrine in Tacarigua is offered on Saturday mornings, also by Professor Aiyejina.

In a more traditional way, knowledge of the Orisha faith is transmitted primarily through the instruction given by the shrine leaders to their spiritual children. A great part of this instruction consists of newer members relating their dreams and visions to their shrine head, who then makes an interpretation. Some also use divination to provide answers to their members.

The New Membership: Cultural, Political and Social Notables

Another part of the secularization of the Orisha religion includes a growth in the membership of "notables". These are people who have a public profile; whose participation is noted by the media; who are cited, quoted and respected. These people are not traditional Orisha worshippers; that is, they are not at present working class, poor or underprivileged, although many of them come from humble beginnings. They are now largely middle class and have professional occupations. Some of these high profile people, many of whom secretly supported Orisha even in earlier times, have now publicly expressed their belief in and commitment to the development of Orisha.

It is perhaps no surprise that the majority of these notables come from the artistic community of Trinidad and Tobago. Artists are very often at the forefront of social change and, by their very definition, are modernizers and revolutionaries. They include painters, musicians, calypsonians, writers and poets. Among these famous people are the country's best-known painter, Leroy Clarke and the less well known, but very talented, Makumba Kunle; David Rudder, arguably the best calypsonian and soca artist of modern times; Ella Andall, a folkloric and calypso singer of extraordinary ability; Brother Resistance, a rapso artist; and calypsonians Lord Nelson, Composer and Sugar Aloes. One of the country's best musicians and composers, Andre Tanker, is a supporter who regularly plays with some Orisha drummers. Writers such as Earl Lovelace, winner of many national and international awards for his fiction, attend Orisha and Spiritual Baptist events. The poet and playwright Eintou Pearl Springer is one of the administrative mainstays of the Orisha religion. Professor Rawle Gibbons, a theatre director, playwright and former director of the Creative Arts Centre, plays an important role in the administration of the Orisha religion. There are others, too numerous to mention.

Some well-known business entrepreneurs are also connected to the Orisha religion. Chee Mook, a bakery of long standing in downtown Port of Spain, sometimes supplies bread products to the Family Day celebrations of the

Orisha faith. Isaac McCleod, a well known and wealthy quantity surveyor and developer, his wife Patricia McCleod and their children are devotees and sponsors of Orisha events. Others who have made their commitment public include management consultants working for government or private firms, human resource managers, engineers and other professionals. In addition, politicians, administrators and high-level professionals are involved.

There is an entire new class of membership composed of middle-class professionals who are either devotees themselves or who publicly support and affirm the validity of these religions. Their very presence lends legitimation to these religions. The major change here is not only because of the eminence of these new members but also because of the public nature of their commitment. For some, adherence becomes a public celebration. This can be contrasted to former times, when both religions were marginalized. Their very Africanness was despised and rejected. And, although middle-class people would seek the counsel of Orisha "bush doctors" and Spiritual Baptist healers, they did so in the secrecy of the night and never publicly acknowledged, sometimes even to their own family members, their visits to such practitioners.

Among the individuals who are either full participants of the Orisha religion or simply supporters of it is Leroy Clarke who, though not a practising Orisha in the sense of attending *Ebos,* has a deep-seated faith in the religion and acknowledges it as an important source for his creative expression. Eintou Pearl Springer's story illustrates the role of politics, identity and religion that her Orisha faith brings together. Brother Oludari is an innovator, in that he is attempting to bring back many original Yoruba traditions. Although he and his shrine operate outside of the mainstream of the Orisha networks, his ideology is strongly rooted in the religion. Lastly, Patricia McCleod has found her personal spirituality in the worship of Orisha. Her story emphasizes the practice of the religion in its purest Yoruba sense, in that she has been initiated at Ife and follows many of the tenets of traditional Yoruba Orisha worship. With the exception of Patricia McCleod, the people featured here are primarily motivated by the need to reaffirm African identity through the Orisha religion. McCleod follows a primarily spiritual path.

Case Studies

Leroy Clarke

Leroy Clarke is Trinidad's best-known painter. He sells many of his pictures and appears to earn a comfortable living from his art. He is a man in his early sixties who maintains a substantial public profile. He attends many political and cultural events, always dressed in African-designed robes. He is very critical of the state of Trinidadian society, claiming that it is a false and artificial one that has sold its cultural birthright to the American way of life.

He was born Anglican, which he admits "never fascinated me". He grew up in a working-class neighbourhood in Gonzalez in upper Belmont, where many "Shango and Shouter people live . . . a very African area". As a young man, he saw beyond Roman Catholic and Anglican Churches and he was bewitched by things African. At his birth, a "seer" woman told his mother that "he don't belong to you". He was fond of a particular Shouter woman, a mother of her church who treated him as her son. She told him that he would find his way.

In his early thirties he "entered" Orisha while abroad in New York. A woman who had a "house" (*ile*) in Brooklyn initiated him. His deities are Yemanja and Ogun. Clarke says that he has a deep maternal instinct and a great passion for life – his two deities treat these two forces. The "Woman" in his work, in his paintings, is Clarke himself or that side of him that is feminine. Ogun, Yemanja and other deities feature prominently in some of his paintings, but they are his visions of them and not necessarily identifiable. He says that his art is deeply affected by Orisha and Africanness. He appears at Orisha events, such as at Lopinot where he donated a large painting to the movement, but he does not frequent feasts or *Ebos*.

Art is his language of being – a way of validating himself and expressing himself. Orisha is part of that language of being and becoming and of creating oneself. Religion is a quality of environment, and the language of his environment is being African. "I selected Orisha, I am a devout African, I dwell in an African house" that was blessed in an Orisha ceremony.

For Leroy Clarke, being an Orisha devotee, although he does not appear to go to feasts or become possessed by the deities, means expressing and living an African dynamic of life. He is not so much African in a politicized sense, but rather uses his African identity as a means of relating to his spiritual inner self.

In August 2000 Clarke was selected as one of sixteen artists working in the Yoruba African diaspora to create original paintings for an exhibition mounted by the Ifa-Yoruba Contemporary Arts Trust of London. The trust is dedicated to the celebration of Yoruba art throughout the world. What is especially interesting and relevant about this honour – especially since Clarke's work is already shown all over the world – is that he was selected through the process of divination (Ifa). Divination not only selected the artists but also gave them the *Odu* – the sacred verses that form the basis of Yoruba religion and world view – on which to base their paintings. Clarke's *Odu* was the sixteenth of the sixteen and that signifies good fortune and greatness. Of his painting celebrating this *Odu*, Clarke says:

> Other times there were barriers of nothing . . . yet at other times, regeneration where eternities are the multiplications of forest and sky and an endless flow of springs and waterfalls and seas of birds and fish in a breathtaking interchange of scales and feathers.[12]

Eintou Pearl Springer

Eintou Pearl Springer is the director of the Heritage Library in downtown Port of Spain. She is in her early fifties. She is currently unmarried, although she has a number of children from previous marriages. She is also a grandmother. She holds a bachelor's degree and a master's degree in library and information sciences from an English university.

She comes from working-class origins and had somewhat of a turbulent youth. She was born into a staunch Roman Catholic family in Cantaro, in the Santa Cruz valley above Port of Spain. She comes from a very mixed background; one of her grandfathers was the son of an African slave in St Vincent and her mother's people are of African, Carib and Venezuelan origins. She believes that the nationalistic fervour that swept the country in 1956 undermined the power of the Catholic Church. One of her earliest memories is seeing the then archbishop of the Roman Catholic Church, Count Finbar Ryan, "he of noble lineage, railing against Dr Eric Williams, saying to the congregation that it would be a sin to vote for this man who dared challenge the power of the Church of Christ".[13]

However, Williams's government was voted in, although it did not bring about the significant changes that she had dreamed about. In her own powerful words, she says:

> I along with many thousands of educated and uneducated young Africans let the society know in no uncertain terms the rage and terror we felt at our aborted hopes and dreams. For us, education had not been the panacea promised in 1956 . . . we had been given a black government . . . but his was a government with no consciousness or sense of black pride that could root us as young Africans into a sense of ourselves. They could give us no direction, no values. In fact, education came as a double curse. It dragged us away from the traditional values rooted in village and family and gave us instead hopes that within the context of society that could not be realized. Our faces were absent from television. We were not represented among the ranks of bank workers. Private enterprise was virtually closed to us. We were absorbed in the fallacy of rainbowness from which the colour black was conspicuously absent. In 1970, our first act of defiance, our first blow for liberation, was to enter the Roman Catholic Cathedral and drape the images in black. In our youth, we did not fully understand the depth of that symbolism. All we knew was that anger and frustration reached boiling point. The God we served, in His Whiteness seemed to mock us . . . And the poets and musicians blossomed and trumpeted our pain, determination and our links with our history. And the political directorate was forced to listen and make concessions. But the movement failed; failed because it did not root itself in the spiritual needs of the Africans in the society, and consequently soon lost direction. In the aftermath of the failure of the National Joint Action Committee [the nucleus of the Black Power movement in Trinidad] many of us came to the traditional African religion as an act of political and ideological self expression.[14]

She got involved in Orisha through Afrocentricity and, although not religious as such or even very spiritual, she believes Orisha is a living link to the African past. She reveres the Ooni of Ife because he is the head of the religion. She is the spiritual daughter of Iyalorisha Rodney, with whom she has a very close relationship: "We speak every day on the telephone and I consult her on everything I do."

In addition to being a librarian, Eintou Springer is also a published poet, writer, theatrical producer and actor. She has several volumes of poetry to her credit. She is involved in educational theatre and travels all over to perform one of her plays, accompanied by singing and drumming, about domestic violence against women. Like her "religious" commitments, her artistic products are all strongly political. She calls herself a "political animal", and says everything she does has a political function.

Springer defines herself primarily as an African artist. Her view of the world is entirely Afrocentric. She plays a crucial role with the National Council of Orisha Elders, where her official title is public relations officer. Moreover, she writes the briefs and attends the meetings with officials of government as the Orisha movement is negotiating its new status in the society. Springer is the most vocal and certainly the most active of the spokespersons for the group.

Oludari Massetungi

Oludari is the leader of an Orisha shrine in Petit Valley. He is approximately fifty years old. He lives very simply in a small house behind his shrine and owns very few material possessions. He does not have a telephone or car but receives e-mail messages and has a Web site, all of which are maintained by one or two of his followers. Like Eintou Springer, Oludari is a child of the 1970s Black Power revolution in Trinidad. He differs from her in that he is deeply involved and firmly positioned in the Yoruba religion. He is a devotee and practising leader, and the practice of the religion is at the heart of what he does. Brother Oludari is viewed as a major agent of social change because he constantly incorporates new Yoruba elements into his worship. At the same time, however, he is equally Afrocentric, and he believes that African religion, values and norms should regulate the way of life in Trinidad. He is only too aware of the role of politics and the asymmetrical power relations in society, especially in Trinidad, and the importance they hold in modern life.

Oludari views his personal life in Orisha and the Ethiopian Orthodox Church as follows:

> In 1970 when there was global change taking place in the world in terms of social perspective, in terms of man's re-definition of himself and an attempt to relate with balance to the cosmic powers and intelligences in the universe, so we had things like "flower power", . . . while in the Caribbean you had the black power movement and so I was out of secondary school at the time and that in fact is upon me, and so I responded via this way, that was one government re-involve-

The Orisha Religion from Sacred to Secular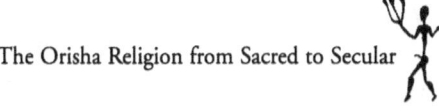

ment, but at another level it was during that time drums was predominant, I studied under the best Orisha priestess in Trinidad and Tobago as far as I am concerned, Iyalorisha Orisha Louisa Catherine Toussaint, she would have been perhaps junior to Babalorisha Orisha Ebenezer Elliot but certainly contemporary in his time.

I studied with her and quite a lot of the things that she told me over the years I have been able to verify that it is so and in fact many people from Nigeria were extremely surprised to see that that kind of information had remained in Trinidad and Tobago. So I must say I was very, very fortunate, I studied under her for about fifteen years . . . .

The Ethiopian Orthodox, yes, it's a Christian church and in fact you know though we have moved away from Roman Catholicism but as Professor Josef ben Jochanen has pointed out Islam, Judaism, Christianity all have their roots in African sacred science, if the kind of leaner way in which we think the universe developed and that things may have issued from one central point, if that is so then all the present evidence point to and suggest that Africa would have been the home of modern day religion, so Christianity is not a alien concept to us, it's not something we necessarily fight is perhaps some of the religious symbolism in Christianity relates directly to Yoruba sacred science. However what we perhaps fight against is the Eurocentric perspective that is now in the Christian forms that we have, we have to look at the culture form . . . trust in one supreme intelligence, do good to your fellow human beings, do not lie, do not steal, all those are good principles, you know, so we have nothing against those principles, as I say, if we recall our own recent history here persons, captives entering here under the Cedula had to become Christians, we had to profess Christianity so this was, this mood was now forced upon us and if we say that 1834/1838 provided us with freedom I suspect that the emancipation proclamation does not just stop at labour, and so we are saying that if we were free from then, then we ought to have been free to practise our religion as it ought to have been practised and in fact my own position and my own organization's position here in this country perhaps at one point in time we may have been considered hard liners and we may have actually pushed, but we are not against anybody who want to practise Yoruba sacred science the way that they feel. We are also not against any practising Christians or any other religion.

Brother Oludari has a profound understanding of the role of religion and spirituality and the relationship between the natural and supernatural worlds. Because he firmly believes that Africa was the birthplace not only of humankind but also of religion, he is able to provide an important rationalization for those who prefer to retain Christian syncretic elements. In believing that Africa is the birthplace not only of humankind but also of many of its cultural forms, Oludari is able to practise Orisha in his Africanized manner while accepting that others will keep to its Christian tenets. He, Springer, Sister Valerie, Patricia McCleod and a few others are the nucleus of the "innovators".

Patricia McCleod (Sangowummi)

Patricia McCleod's story is especially interesting because she came from a middle-class background. Her family both feared and rejected the Orisha tradition. She traces her path from her earliest contact with the "Shango" religion to her position as one of the most informed scholars and practitioners of the Yoruba religious tradition in Trinidad today.

PM: How I got involved into the Orisha tradition and sometimes I go back to different points and maybe since I was small, a little girl, maybe I was leading in that direction, now this is a wonder-whizz story because it didn't start off as a little girl me going directly into the Orisha tradition. I remembered my mother's sister, my aunt, aunt Nellie lived at St Francois Valley Road, I had never heard about Orisha, Shango or even Spiritual Baptist. What I knew was that my family was Anglican and I don't even think at the age of, probably I was about three or four, that it mattered, I don't even think that Anglican mattered to me, but I remembered that when my mother left my sister and myself one day, I heard drumming up on the hill and I was wondering where this drumming was coming from and when I realized it was up the hill although I was curious enough to want to go to the drumming because it actually called me . . . well I went for some water and you know Pat, I told Pat to stay inside and when I came back I meet Pat running up the hill by those Shango people, . . . I know my mother was so petrified I think she almost give me another licking that I had gone to these Shango people . . . being a good Anglican and being a good Christian at that because I remember that we would go to church on a Sunday morning, on a Sunday night and in between because we would go to Pentecostal churches, we would go to Nazerine Churches because my mother did feel that the more you went to church she felt that it was better for you as a good Christian . . .

So when I was through with my studies in England I came back here just in 1970 and just as I came back there was the revolution, the Black Power uprising and I jump into it but I walk with the marches and so and then in the ending I used to go up Gloster Lodge Road to the lectures with NJAC [the National Joint Action Committee – the local Black Power group] had gone, from that I decided that I can't just stay on the fringes I had to do something, so I founded an organization called the African Association of Trinidad and Tobago and the reason why I did that is that most people even though they would say they were pan-Africanist they were afraid to associate themselves with African, the word African and if you had an association that called itself the African association and you came to the association that means first you would be honouring your roots as African to be able to identify with the philosophy of the association. So as we come along, there was no spiritual base to this at all, it was just a pure pan-African base with lectures and programmes we try to organize and so. But what happened every time at certain times of the year we used to have a family day and a dinner and what we tried to do we would try to get somebody to come in to do the prayers and bless the day and that sort of thing and after looking we could not find anybody else except the Orisha, we couldn't find because the association was so left to what was African that even if we took the Spiritual Baptist, even though we had Spiritual Baptist members, Spiritual Baptist first consider themselves Christian so we didn't even want to go that way so we had to go straight to the Orishas and that was the first time that I ever heard the term Orisha. So we used to ask Isaac Lindsay who was from south – Fyzabad – and he said all you know what all you asking but we will come anyhow and he will come and they will do what they call a clearing and so and do the rituals for the thing. So they became like part of us because every time we had something that we need a blessing that we would ask them.

African association went ahead with its work. We had launched African history month which we launch in November and some friends of mine came back. Dr Fitz Baptiste from the University and his wife, they had just come back from Nigeria and they had been guest of the Ooni for dinner and they were saying what we were going to do for the next Emancipation Day and if they think that we should bring the Ooni of Ife. He wanted to come . . . if we get all the other African groups together and actually that is how COATT came about and we met at UWI [the University of the West Indies] and it had nothing to do with the Orisha at that point, all we were thinking of bringing down the Ooni who is a king from Africa. When the Orisha community heard that the Ooni was coming, the Ooni to the Orisha community is like the Pope to the Catholic community, so they started now it had many skirmishes they say who give us the authority to bring down the Ooni, which was nonsense, but I mean we could have brought him if the man wanted to come,

FH: When was this?

PM: This was twelve years ago, going on twelve years ago and I think I still have one of the programmes when he came. And they were saying that the Ooni cannot come here and the Orisha community not involved, but we had no idea then at all about Orisha, we were a set of academics who were just bringing him down on a pan-African thing. So after we wrote the Ooni and thing and the Ooni confirmed and say well yes . . . then the Orisha people came into the thing and they planned the kind of reception he have and so and then I started to get more familiar because outside of Isaac Lindsay now I meeting other Orisha groups and the first Orisha group I met prior to Ooni coming was Iyalorisha Melvina Rodney, right because I had already met Babalorisha Isaac Lindsay and I still kept aloof from the tradition, I know it existed if I wanted any prayers done or whatever it is for the association I would call Isaac Lindsay but I never took part in any of the Orisha yards or anything like that. But I remember once at a meeting, I say well I really never go myself you know, she say so what religion are you, I say I am no religion but quite frankly if I have to go back to religion, I will go to a traditional African religion.

And that time the minister was Margaret Hector and she called me and she said, "Mother say she wants to see you, she is having something at her shrine", so I say, "Mother?" She say yes, Bishop Eudora Thomas, and then she came the week after the Monday after the conference and she said, I would like to see you, I want to invite you specially to my feast, so I was a little bit confused because I thought she was Bishop Eudora Thomas, she was a Spiritual Baptist and here now by that time I started to learn enough about the Orisha to know that I didn't think that Baptist had feast. So anyhow, I went up to the thing, she invited myself, Mr P and a friend of mine and we all went up as guests and she said, "I do both you know, I do both",

I did the Baptist and I did the Orisha because I alone remain up there and it was like a good forty-five minutes when I just see after they make a circle they call me and all the people start taking off my shoes which to me I was kind a little bit upset because to me I didn't have a say in the matter and they brought me into the circle, when they brought me into the circle now when they brought me in the circle they pushed me down to kneel down and they took the Lota and so on and they started to touching my head and my shoulders and my chest and my back and so and what ever . . . to me like I was there for hours but maybe it was just a few minutes right so by the time all the time was so happy and was singing that this thing had happened to me and so and by the time I got up I went back I put on my shoes and I told Mr P and they that I was leaving and as I was going back up I remembered that earlier that day I had a pain in my back and I realized that when I got back up to go up the pain had gone and when they say well okay if you want to go we will go, when we were walking down the hill I say well what ever it is they do I don't understand it but whatever it is my pain has gone and they started to laugh so I had lost the pain.

But Sister Valerie now she was the insistent one so on the Monday afternoon she came and she pick me up she say you going to do what the power tell you to do so I said yes and I started to give her the story and so and that was my formal introduction into the tradition and that is how I ended up at Kenny Cyrus [a well-known Orisha shrine in Enterprise] and from there I brought in all my children and so, but when I look back I realize that there were little things that were leading me into that direction, particularly after my initiation, when I was initiated in Nigeria and on the third day of my reading they started to tell me things of my father's family which has been with me for the longest while and even Papa because a lot of the things that he had tell me and he still with me all the time, so I realize that I was leading and having thought it out saying that if I have to go to any kind of religion it going to be an African religion and that also sealed my faith because it know, what they say, you put mouth on yourself, they say you put mouth on your self so that is the story of how I started practising as an Orisha . . . .

What happened as I did not know anything about the Orisha tradition I went into Kenny Cyrus with open arms and they . . . I gave all that I had to give and I was very receptive to whatever there was, but there were things that I still was not very happy with, for instance like if we have what I would call an initiation what they would call it baptism which a baptism is a Judeo-Christian kind of thing, and if they had a kind of initiation they would still use the Bible as the book of truth and you know, and it always bothered me because to me something was inconsistent about that and my history . . . probably because I came into the tradition as a pan-Africanist and probably I didn't go to the tradition because something was wrong with my foot or I didn't have a job or any of those things I saw the tradition from a different level, so I went into . . . So we always had arguments about that.

FH: You mean with Joan and the people in the shrine?

PM: Then I started buying any thing that I can put my hand on that said Orisha but the first book I bought which probably has lead me on this pathway and different things along the line is that I was in London and I went to a bookstore in Covent Gardens, I have it here that is the first book that I had and when I read it was so different and the whole concept was so different from what we did here and I asked Mother Joan and Sister Valerie about it and they tell me don't bother with the book, who write that book? We go still see the Orisha and to me that wasn't satisfactory is not a matter of seeing or not seeing the Orisha, even though I don't see the Orisha manifest upon somebody I know their essence is here and I experienced them in everything that I do you know, and we couldn't see eye to eye because they couldn't understand that the tradition or if they did they didn't think it was necessary to streamline, to me the theology and the philosophical trimmings of the Yoruba tradition to me that was very important, to me the cosmological view of how the Yoruba people see the world to me that was extremely important and to just go to a shrine and sing and dance and so and if something wrong with your foot you go and call the energies if you don't have a job and so to me the tradition is such a beautiful tradition is beyond and much deeper than that, they don't have a world view on how they see the tradition, they don't understand the tradition religious structure, they don't understand how they themselves this body is an equator, is a factor in the equator of the wider universe, right, and I'm not saying that, criticizing them for it, it doesn't suit me, we brought it up and it was bringing an argument and contention and I just had to leave because it did not make sense to me. Once I had a copy of Ifa in my hand, the sacred oracles and once I started understanding who I am in terms of the universe I couldn't worship in that situation again. For instance, like they would use olive oil and I feel that your tradition must sustain you physically, spiritually, emotionally, economically, if you use olive oil in your tradition, and olive does not grow here either that means that you are enriching another group of people outside of your own people. So I use palm oil, it is very difficult to get but I make the effort and I try to get palm oil. I love olive oil, I don't know any oil that taste as nice as olive oil, I cook with it, I eat it, I put garlic in it and herbs and cook meh bread in it an so but when coming to things of the tradition I use palm oil and I try to go back because what I realize if they practise the religion as how it should be practised and not just mixing of Indian spirit and Chinese spirits and all these other draw from it. So I see the tradition in a totally different way, when you came this morning this is a paper I am writing to present to UNESCO next week and they are talking about the retention which I say continuities of the Yoruba tradition in Trinidad and Tobago.

So what I was saying is Ifa is the source, Ifa to the Yoruba is what the Koran is to the Muslims, the Bible is to the Christian, or the Torah to the Jews, you know, and many of the retentions or continuity came directly out of Ifa.

I really don't believe that the Orisha and the Catholic saints are one from what is my understanding of Orisha as primordial energies and what I understand as a Catholic saints of somebody who manifest and do it must be a different kind of energy for me Oshun could never be St Philomen, Oya could never be St Ann, and people marry them and there is where I depart I am not getting into argument with people if that is what they believe but what I do I try to keep the tradition as traditional as possible where I know the structure where I know we have our sacred oracles to guide us and so, so you may find if you want me to give you the tradition how I see it here from a Trinidadian perspective I would not want to unless is a academic exercise to deal with it because this is why I left that situation and this is one of the reasons why I got initiated in Nigeria and even outside of Nigeria even though that you find that you in the Santeria there makes the saints but there is still a structure for the African part of the tradition.

If lineage is important because lineage is very much part of the tradition because for instance I am of Oshun lineage but the Orisha on my head is Shango because of what my role and my function is on this part of the world before I travel back right, so it took the Ase of Shango to do what I had to do but if I say this to a Trinidadian they would watch me like what are you saying, you know and the point about it is that they will go on again to tell me that I'm wrong, then they would say let me tell you something not even the Nigerians know it you know, they would say that, they say the Nigerians don't know it the Nigerians come here and join the tradition here 'cause the Nigerians don't know it, not realizing that the Nigerians themselves have suffered just as we have and most of them are Christians, the Christians one who come here and join the tradition don't know it but the tradition is still very much alive and structured and well organized. They have societies and all that in Nigeria and that is the only way that they were able to have the world congress because of the level of people who are still involved in the tradition who know it how it should be and do it.

So from a Trinidad perspective I can tell you what I plan to do with our community, we have formed a small community called Ile Shango/Oshun Melosha. That is a teaching Ile and we teach about the tradition from a holistic kind of situation we teach about the cosmos, we teach about how it affects you, we teach how you see it, how you worship, the rituals of worship, how you become. What is a devotee, what is a priest, what is the function of a priest, because a priest have different functions. What determines who you are and what you do is Ifa so once the divination system is placed and you divine Ifa is the one who guides and tell us . . . we always say that you know where you want to go but Ifa is the road map. We have a small group of about fifteen or so.

If I were to look at the Orisha tradition how it is practised in Trinidad and Tobago today, I would have to say it is very materialistic but I don't know if it address all the other concerns that I am interested in, I don't know how they see themselves in line with the universe, I don't know how they see themselves interacting with the different energies, I don't know . . . to me most times when they talk to me they talk about Orisha as though Orisha is man or woman and you know, I could understand that . . . putting that human aspect on the Orisha for people to understand and relate to them at certain levels but I think for the hierarchy that whole spiritual heights of understanding the energies and how they play and how they form and understanding the relationship to the ancestors, understanding that our . . . we don't have schools in place.

I have just attempted to put a school which I am trying to build a broader school in Santa Cruz that would kinda address some of the things that I talking about, what is required for you to become a devotee, what is required of you to become a priest, what is required for you to become a herbalist, which is very much part of the tradition, if you don't understand the herbs and you don't understand what is out there, what you know. There are so many things and I'm not criticizing the fact that it is not in place because I understood what they went through and like . . . people like Sam, and Iya and all of them the fact that I am here today is because that they have kept the tradition in whatever form so I am not knocking it, what I am saying is that we have come to a point where we have to for the continuity, for the understanding of our own children and to save our own children we have to put some structures in place and this is the point where I am at because when I was initiated, my Eta was about putting, projecting the tradition that in particular putting Shango as a priestess of Shango on the ground and when they say that that means to enforce it strongly and you know, solidly let people understand what the religion is all about, what the way of life is all about rather than we get involved in just the protection part of it, of the rituals because if we understood the whole concept of spirituality and language of the universe and how we talk to the universe many times we may not have to rely on the rituals as heavily as we do now you know. So is from that perspective I'm coming from.

I went to the tradition just because I was guided there and felt that I should be in an African tradition that probably came out of some ancestral memory or some ancestor push me that way but most middle-class Africans find the tradition because something was wrong with them, they either had couldn't find a job, they either was ill, some thing was not right like some problem and they would have gone there after all else had failed, after the Catholic priest or whatever, all else had failed. And they would have gone there most times sneaking into the night because they would have felt embarrassed if anybody had seen them there and these people were there to take them and clean them up and put them back on their path so a lot of them who come to the religion come in at the ritual side knowing that they get clean up and to them . . . like a problem solving thing, and then they leave, and even those who don't leave who stay at the level of the ritual side because of security so if you back hurt you ring up your spiritual mother and you tell her you know meh back hurt me, if you had a dream you ring up your spiritual mother and you tell her you know you had a dream, if you want to go for a job you ring up your spiritual mother and tell her you know you want to go for a job so even at that level and I am not saying because I myself is a priestess I am saying that there is no role for the priestess but what I'm saying is that because the structure and the understanding of the tradition is not entrenched and in place people feel insecure if they spiritual mother don't put they hand on everything whereas Ori play a big part in this tradition, your Ori is you highest Orisha and if you cannot communicate with your Ori and be blessed by your Ori then you can't be blessed by no other Orisha you see so these are the kinds of things that I would like people to understand and for us to try to put certain things and another thing that I am afraid of is that I am happy that the Orisha tradition and they are happy the Orisha Elders of Council that they are coming together in a certain kind of unprecedented way but within that there is also a place that you can fall of because they have been coming so kind of Westernized that they will leave some of the traditions behind for instance we were talking about the marriage act and so and they were saying that they would be the ones, the council this is, would be the ones to approve of who going to be marriage officers because they feel that some people have no integrity and so when you look at the economic situation of the African people both here and in the Yoruba land and when you look at what a tradition supposed to do for you, for instance, like all the Yoruba people in Trinidad and in the Santeria too, but the Santeria have made their claim because they say they access African gods but under a Catholic system so you have no problem with that but if I were to say that if people in Trinidad do that under a Catholic/Hindu any kind of system they will get upset with me and say no they are Orisha which to me is not really true right, so I even have although I will not be Santeria but I have some respect for the Santeria because they have stated what they are, they access African gods under a Catholic system so their saints are in place but in Trinidad I am not sure what I really don't know, I can't come to terms, I am not comfortable with the saints.

McCleod is at the forefront of re-establishing the pure, authentic Yoruba tradition as learned at Ifa. She has been initiated there, has studied the sacred *Odus*, and is extremely knowledgeable about the original religion. She is careful in not being critical of the practice nor the practitioners in Trinidad because they have maintained the religion, but she feels strongly that it must be brought back to its original source.

> What we hope to achieve is an appreciation by African people of their own heritage and their own past.
>
> – *Oludari Massetungi*

CHAPTER FIVE

Contested Theologies in the Orisha Religion
Discourses of Authenticity and Inauthenticity

The Authenticity Debate in Trinidad

IN SOME GROUPS IN Trinidad today "authentic" is simply constructed as African or Yoruba, whereas the many syncretisms, mainly of a Christian nature, that have evolved within these religions are described as "inauthentic". Less sophisticated members believe that the authentic tradition, as they define it, is still practised in Nigeria but reports from that country indicate otherwise. Christian elements constructed as "inauthentic" in some circles are being omitted from the ritual. The older and the more traditionally inclined worshippers are resisting these radical ideas, thereby creating dissension among members.

Many modern members of the Orisha religion believe that the original syncretism with Christianity is itself inauthentic because Christianity was only used to mask or disguise the traditional forms of Yoruba Orisha worship in earlier times.[1] Most believers in the faith today subscribe to the disguise theory because it coincides more with their political orientation.

Disputing the disguise theory, others have proposed that syncretisms taken from Christianity, Hinduism and other religious forms merged naturally with the African forms of worship. According to this view, African slaves in Trinidad were exposed not only to the Yoruba religion that they brought with them, but also to the Christianity that was imposed on them, and that gradually, over time, the two merged. (In a similar fashion, some aspects of Hinduism brought in by the later arriving Indian indentured population also gradually merged with Orisha.)

Much of the contemporary literature on the role of colonial hegemony supports the latter view. For example, the Comaroffs' work in South Africa shows how the foreign colonizer and the colonized were engaged in a mutually interactive relationship in which a considerable amount of cultural exchange took place.[2] Theorists such as Homi Bhabha maintain that all forms of interactive culture are in a state of hybridity and subject to contestation and change.[3] It is therefore quite likely that the syncretisms that took place between the two religious systems happened naturally over time.

The debate on authenticity also relates to the thorny issue of syncretism, discussed in the next chapter, which some scholars and quite a number of believers feel created the inauthenticity in their religious forms. The process of syncretism is largely in scholarly disrepute today, and has been rejected as part of the hegemonic controlling processes of slavery and neo-colonialism.[4] A religion must, according to this view, rid itself of the imposed, syncretic, inauthentic elements in its ritual and belief system. This debate rages fiercely among Orisha worshippers. Charles Stewart and Rosalind Shaw have argued for the retention of syncretism as an analytical construct because it has been shown that there are "two opposed rhetorics: syncretism as tolerance and syncretism as hierarchical encompassment".[5] They note, for example, that the syncretisms in Nigeria between Yoruba Orisa cults and Islam have more to do with the rivalry and competition between two empires than between global and local forms. Syncretism, according to this latter perspective, can be an example of tolerance as much as oppression. Most Orisha innovators in Trinidad tend, however, to cling to the older view that syncretisms are examples of Eurocentric slave and colonial oppressive hegemonies that must be removed from the religion.

In addition to the debate on contested authenticity, defined in terms of African (Yoruba) religion versus Christianity in Trinidad, the movement is also being influenced by developments taking place in the United States, where the Orisha religion is one of the fastest growing religious movements among African Americans. As a result of increased contact between African American and migrant Caribbean Orisha worshippers, new arenas of debate are opening. For example, it is now claimed that the truly authentic Orisha worship is one in which worshippers have learned the religion straight from African sources without the need for Christian intervention, as occurred in the colonized Caribbean. This movement towards the authentic source took place as African Americans took issue with the Cuban practice of Santeria, in which Christianity is given equal pride of place with the Yoruba faith.

In African American houses where Orisha is practised it is claimed that the tradition is more complete in Nigeria than in the diaspora because, through travel to the Caribbean and South America, it became somewhat fragmented. This was allegedly due to the fact that there were insufficient numbers of worshippers to fully sustain the religion. In some African American religious houses where the "African [that is, Nigerian] way" of performing rituals and African patterns of divination is closely followed, the liturgical melodies sung at drum and dance celebrations are largely Yoruba inspired. Cuba is the only diasporic society that has retained Ifa, but frequently Cuban *babalawos* (diviners) only know the gist of the sacred texts or *Odus,* and not in any great detail. According to some, therefore, the Cuban and other diasporic practices are missing pieces of this important oral tradition.[6] In addition, the Catholic saints with whom the Orishas are syncretized are rejected by African American adherents who do not recognize their legitimacy. This matter is linked to other concerns about race and culture. Some African Americans have found the Cuban version of Orisha (sometimes called *lucumi,* the designation for Yoruba slaves in Cuba, meaning "friend" or "fellow tribesman" in Yoruba) unacceptable and have begun to develop an African American version of Orisha that looks towards Africa and, more specifically, Nigeria for its spiritual sustenance.[7] Notwithstanding the fact that the source from which Americans have learned the religion has itself undergone changes, their claim for authenticity is loudly proclaimed.[8]

The issue of authenticity takes on yet a more ambiguous meaning when one realizes that Orisha worship among the Yoruba people in Nigeria today has changed even more dramatically than in the diasporic survivals. The most obvious trend in Yoruba religion is the decline of the traditional religion that has had to confront the strength of both Islam and Christianity. By the early part of the nineteenth century, Islam had spread widely in Yoruba areas of Nigeria. The middle of the nineteenth century saw the beginnings of missionary activity by Christians. The region became increasingly colonized and it is alleged that, by the census of 1952, more than four-fifths of the population of the Yoruba provinces were said to be either Christian or Muslim.[9]

In fact, modern African nations are deeply influenced by Western philosophies and traditions. Many African leaders were educated in the West, and the political ideals of socialism and Marxism that some of them brought back with them are Western creations. And as a noted African philosopher, V. Mudimbe, observes: "Modern African thought seems somehow to be basically a product of the West." He believes that the conceptual framework underlying African thought is "both a mirror and a consequence of the experience of European hegemony", and, citing Gramsci, explains this as "the dominance of one social bloc over another, not simply by means of force or wealth, but by a social authority whose ultimate sanction and expression is a profound cultural supremacy". Mudimbe sees this hegemonic supremacy in the "increasing gap between the social classes, and within each class, of the conflict between those who are culturally Westernised Africans and others".[10]

Today the majority of Yoruba are Christian or Muslim, but individuals have clung to more traditional beliefs. An Ifa diviner, or *babalawo*, is still used for help and counsel, although Christian and Muslim sect leaders are also consulted.[11] In a startling reversal that provides further evidence of the need to question the authenticity of the source, Peter Sutherland examines the emergence of a revitalization of original religion in Benin, where a Vodun festival has been created.[12] He describes how a new Vodun festival in Whydah, celebrating the memory of African slaves, started in 1992. The creators of the festival sought to gain government recognition for the country's majority religion and to integrate its indigenous cultural traditions into the development of modern national identity in Benin. The festival celebrates "rhetorical doubling" – of ancestors and brothers, of spirits and bodies, of return and no return, remembering and forgetting, sadness and joy. It throws a new light on the concept of roots in diaspora discourse and, in an interesting reversal, the traditionalist faction of Vodun practitioners are attempting to refashion their public identity in Africa by reference to their practices in the Americas. The festival reinvents the Atlantic passage as two-way traffic, because the festival calls upon the spirits of the slaves from the Americas to return, even in human form. Sutherland notes, "The festival challenges the long-standing oppression of Vodun and its practitioners by the state and Christianity." In this reconstituted festival in Benin, Christianity is seen as modern whereas Vodun is equated with underdevelopment and tradition. Sutherland notes that "Whydah's festival's championing of Vodun traditions clearly distinguishes itself as an indigenous counterdiscourse of modernity based on black solidarity". The festival defines a discourse of African-based modernity. The government is being pressured to accept Vodun as the major religion and shift emphasis away from Christianity.

The syncretic nature of contemporary African belief systems is wonderfully described in this extract from Ghanian philosopher Kwame Anthony Appiah's semi-autobiographical book, *In My Father's House*. He describes his sister's wedding:

> English prayer book, "Dearly Beloved . . . we are gathered here in the sight of God." In the front row sat the King of Asante, his wife, the queen mother, and the King's son . . . . Afterwards we went back to the private residence of the King, and there we had a party, with the queen mother's drummers playing . . . . But not long after we began, the Catholic archbishop of Kumasi (remember this is after a *Methodist* ceremony) said prayers, and this was followed (and remember this was a *Catholic* archbishop) by the pouring of libations to my family ancestors . . . . The words addressed to those ancestors were couched in the same idiom as the words of [a traditional ceremony witnessed in 1920]. And the King of Asante is an Anglican and a member of the English bar; his son . . . has a PhD from Tufts; and the bride and groom met at Sussex University in England . . . a medical sociologist and a Nigerian merchant banker.[13]

Appiah and his family, as modern Africans, see no contradiction among the elements of this no-doubt remarkable "syncretism".

The contested arena of authenticity around Orisha worship in America revolves around Nigeria as the source, the Caribbean as an area of retention and survival – however imperfect – and the African American forms that claim greater authenticity because they have gone to the original source. In Trinidad, the issue of authenticity versus syncretism was recently articulated by Patricia McCleod in a paper presented to the Sixth World Orisha Congress. She noted that "the time has come when we must analyse what we now have, where we were before, where we would like the tradition to take us, and to understand its source".[14]

She then quoted an American Orisha priest who stated that

> the Yoruba religion is different in the Old World of Nigeria-West Africa, than in the New World of the Americas. The difference is that the basic fundamental concepts have been *largely misinterpreted in the New World. The mysticism has been overshadowed by the occultism. Basic mis-conceptions result from this.* In the Old World it has not been forgotten that the aim of the mystic or priestly orders is not to dwell upon occult powers but to seek the divine essence . . . Yoruba is a divine journey to the inner self and to God-Consciousness. [Italics mine.]

McCleod went on to state that in earlier times it might not have been possible to reintegrate the ideas "from the source into the practice", but today the old excuses no longer work. She posed the challenge of the inauthenticity debate in clear terms by asking:

> Do we want a Yoruba tradition or a New World Order with African traditional inputs? Do we want to continue in a dual system of Orisa, influenced by everything else? Depending on the answers we maybe forced to *reclaim it or rename* it as some others in the region have done.[15]

She closed her paper by noting that because Trinidad is a plural society, both racial mixing and cultural crossovers are experienced in calypso, music, foods and other aspects of culture, but that "neither Christian, Hindu or Muslim communities have accepted African deities". Thus, while the African religion may have been forced to syncretize with Christianity and more recently has also accepted elements of Hinduism in its ritual, the reverse crossover has not occurred.

The Attempt at Authenticity in Trinidad: The Africanization of the Orisha Religion

The issue of authenticity and how it plays out in the Trinidadian form of the Orisha worship by describing the dynamic of Africanization of the religion is an important one. One of the main strategies used by innovating Orisha practitioners in Trinidad is to introduce, reintroduce or simply reinvent their construction of African, that is, Nigerian Yoruba forms of religious expression and culture. Current Orisha practitioners, especially the small group of innovators trying to Africanize the religion, do not define the terms of their discourse. They simply make the changes they believe are African rather than Christian and attempt to insert these into ritual practices. There is no attempt at problematizing "African", and they do not deal with the issue of Christian and Muslim proselytizing and conversion in African societies that have themselves produced a syncretic hybrid. Some Orisha practitioners in Nigeria, and even at Ifa, rely on earlier ethnographic descriptions to bring their contemporary ritual back to its earlier and more authentic forms. Professor Abimbola, who has written extensively on the Yoruba *Odus* or sacred texts, himself admitted at the World Congress in Trinidad that he regularly visited Brazil to be in touch with their more authentic practices. These thorny issues of what is African about current African practices are ignored and unimportant to the devotees in Trinidad. Africa has, in a sense, become an imagined community where everything authentic, good and uncontaminated by Christianity can be found. Becoming more Africanized or Yorubanized therefore means merely using more Yoruba language and prayers, substituting what is currently construed as "African dress" for ordinary clothes, and other behavioural changes. The single most important change, however, is the attempt to eliminate Christian elements in the ritual, and that has, thus far, had only limited success.

Language Changes

Language provides a major vehicle through which behaviour, both real and symbolic, can be changed. Learning how to speak a greeting in another language or to sing in that language is a key indicator of symbolic commitment to the language and what it has historically or emotionally meant to a people. In using the vocabulary of a language, significance beyond the mere meaning of a word is communicated. It reflects a symbolic attachment to the heritage to which it belongs. Thus, modern Orisha worshippers have taken it upon themselves to learn as much of the Yoruba language as is necessary or convenient to their lives and, more importantly, to the enactment of the ritual performance. Linguistic performance is therefore an important indicator of commitment to Orisha. One important change involves the substitution of Yoruba for English terms. This has taken place mainly in the use of words to identify or designate specific events and activities. There has, for example, been a conscious attempt to replace English words with Yoruba ones to describe aspects of the ceremony. Outside the ceremonial context, some modern Orisha worshippers sometimes use the Yoruba word *alafia* (peace) as a form of greeting upon meeting or even when answering the telephone.

One of the most obvious changes is the name by which the religion is known. Earlier, "Shango" or "Shango Cult" was its usual designation, although some of the highly placed leaders of the time did refer to it as the "Orisha work". "Shango" was used by local Trinidadians to refer to the religion when they discussed it. It was also the name used by some calypsonians. "Shango" was the designation used by early scholars, such as Herskovits and Simpson, but it is unclear at this point whether they learned the name from respondents or defined it themselves. They did, however, describe the religion as a "cult", which then, as now, was a misnomer, since even then Orisha contained all the elements of a religion. Today the terms "Orisha movement" and "Orisha religion" are widely used and accepted.[16]

Leaders and those with authority within the movement are now known by Yoruba titles. These include *mongba, iyalorisha, babalao, baba, babalorisha*. These are mainly honorifics and are used to designate position and prestige. These titles, with the exception of *mongba*, usually designated as *mamba* in earlier times, were infrequently bestowed. A most striking example of the use of Yoruba titles was the designation given to the president of the Republic of Trinidad and Tobago, the Honourable A.N.R. Robinson. The title Chief Olukun Igbaro was conferred upon him by the Ooni of Ife, during the Ooni's visit to Trinidad in 1989. Not only was the president designated as an honorary Yoruba chief but the name selected – Olukun – is that of an important Yoruba Orisa.

Younger and more modern Orisha worshippers use the term "shrine" to describe sites where leaders hold their ceremony instead of the older generic *palais*, which designated not only the ceremonial area where the main religious activity takes place but also a leader's compound. The irony of using a term derived from Christianity while, at the same time, attempting to cleanse the religion of its Christian syncretic elements merely indicates the flux that the group is undergoing. However, the more innovative leaders now use the Yoruba *Ile,* meaning "house". The term *Ebo,* meaning literally "sacrifice", is now used instead of feast or ceremony. Another popular linguistic convention now used by many of the modern people is the Yoruba *ashe* or *ase* to end a phrase or an address to an audience, or even an e-mail. The idea behind this appears to stem from the belief that the power or *ashe* to deal and interact with the world comes from the Orisha. The concept of power itself is defined in African terms, and its use symbolically notes the affirmation of African identity.[17]

Another major language development is the increased use of Yoruba text, especially in songs. Today several leaders and a number of African groups give classes in Yoruba and young people are actually studying the language. At some of the more Africanized shrines, photocopied pages of songs in Yoruba are distributed so that members can sing the actual chants. In former times the singing of a large majority of participants consisted of some remembered Yoruba words, many French patois words combined with nonsense syllables and pure sounds such as "ah, ah, oh, oh". While the older members still sing the songs in this manner since they have learned them through imitation of sound rather than from the printed page, newer members have actually learned more of the Yoruba words. Some of the *mongbas* and *iyas* who give *Ebos* now also include some Yoruba prayers along with Catholic ones. Thus, the Yoruba language, long forgotten, is making headway with younger members of the faith and at some *Ebos,* one can actually hear the language spoken, chanted and sung.

Warner-Lewis, who has studied the retention of the Yoruba language in Trinidad, notes that although the use of the language "has shrunk to a few prayers, lexical items embedded in English and French Creole language matrices" it is in the Orisha chants that most of the linguistic retentions occur. The chants were and still are being sung by rote, and it is usually only the leaders who know the Yoruba meanings. What is significant today is that new and younger members are making a self-conscious effort to learn at least Yoruba religious terminology.[18]

Another major initiative is the teaching of Yoruba forms of Orisha to adult members of the faith. Members who are interested in learning more about the Yoruba theology, practice and the traditions of *Ifa* (divination) can now attend classes on these subjects. One such class is taught at a traditional Orisha shrine – that of Baba Forde in Tacarigua – by Professor Funso Aiyejina, who is a Nigerian. Another class is affiliated with the Osun Abiadama School, a private school established by Patricia McCleod, where an adult class is taught by several of the elders, including the chair of the council, Babalorisha Sam Phills.

The importance of the Yoruba language is also demonstrated in Kamari Clarke's work on Oyotunji, the Yoruba village constructed in South Carolina, where it is used as a primary agent of establishing Yoruba authenticity among African Americans who are attempting to reclaim their African Yoruba identity. Clarke describes the group's travel to Nigeria and their almost self-conscious use of the language as they proceed through airport formalities.[19] The use of the Yoruba language has become a primary signifier of "belonging" to the Yoruba nation. While the use of the language by Orisha members in Trinidad is not for the purpose of establishing transnational identity, it is nevertheless increasingly becoming a signifier of being, at least in part, African in identity.

Dress

The membership of the religion used to consist almost entirely of the working class and the poor in the Afro-Trinidadian community. Few people had significant funds to spend on clothing. As a result, most Orisha worshippers would come to a feast dressed in very ordinary clothes. The men wore old pants and a shirt, and the women usually wore white skirts and simple tops. The head ties and sashes used to "tie up a power" were ordinary lengths of cloth, sometimes not even hemmed.

Today African dress is *de rigeur* at an Orisha *Ebo*. The women come in very elaborate dresses featuring vivid African designs, usually mid-calf or floor length. The dresses are often draped in the manner of African dress. The old head ties have been replaced by very intricately tied, sewn head coverings that can hardly be described as "ties" and are more deserving of the name "headpieces". At public meetings, the female elders are dressed in strong-coloured, bright patterned cloth, sometimes decorated with braiding, sequins and sparkles. The male elders also dress in traditional Nigerian men's wear when they attend public meetings. These include very elaborate tunics over trousers and intricate hats. At *Ebos* women wear African clothes but men, unless they are leaders, tend to wear more traditional European outfits.

At some *Ebos*, the women all come in colour-coordinated African dress. The most common colours observed were white, pink and red. The shrine *mongba* will have had a dream in which a particular Orisha makes this request. The colour selected usually is the sacred colour of that deity. Groups of worshippers also attend public events such as the Family Day celebrations wearing colour-coordinated dress to indicate that they are part of a particular shrine. Once possession takes place, the headpieces are usually replaced by ordinary sashes. The dresses sometimes become stained when individuals fall to the ground but as one female elder told me, "the clothes always cotton – easy to wash".

Changes in Cosmology

The Africanization or Yorubanization process, as it is being instituted by the innovators, involves changing the religion from a relatively simplistic set of rituals designed to help people in times of illness or when they need spiritual guidance to a more sophisticated cosmological system. What is really happening is that the religion is becoming more mature or complex by moving the emphasis away from simple ritual to a cosmology where the deities are understood to be in the atmosphere where they can be contacted. They must also be propitiated and their help can then be sought. The contact between deity and worshipper becomes more metaphysical and less behaviouristic. The gods are there, but one need not entertain them in one's body. Spirit possession – the most extreme form of making direct contact with the supernatural – is no longer as necessary for the religion to be maintained. The tools of divination today have assumed even more significance than in former times and are used to make contact with the deity, using a more ephemeral form of contact. Perhaps that is the real reason why there are fewer possessions or manifestations taking place at feasts or *Ebos*. People feel that they have a better link to the deity through more sophisticated methods of contact and through the greater use of divination.

The increased importance assigned to the ancestors, in keeping with traditional Yoruba belief, is also a step towards enhancing the complexity of the religious practices. Rituals and festivals devoted to the *Egungun* (ancestors) are now being introduced and are likely to increase in the future. More people now recognize that the first level of spirits are one's own ancestors and, after they have been propitiated and their advice sought, the worshipper can reach higher levels of the supernatural. The increasing roles of festivals, those to Olukun, Oshun and the recently reintroduced rain festival, are also indicators of this intensification. There is now a deeper and more intense understanding of the Orisha cosmology and their role in the universe. Of course, the majority of worshippers, and especially the older ones, follow the more traditional practices. However, the newer innovators in the religion are extending its boundaries far beyond what was envisioned by the early descendants of slaves who managed to remember and retain some of their practices, adulterated by time and the hegemonic influence of Christianity.

Public Events: Sacred and Secular

One of the first organizations in Trinidad and Tobago to celebrate the African heritage was the Egbe Onisin Eledumare that began in 1971, closely following on the Black Power movement in 1970. It describes itself as an "African Spiritual organization" that respects all African sacred science systems. Baba Oludari, its leader (whom I have interviewed and quoted extensively in this chapter), states that their objective is

> re-educating the African person . . . we bring information to an African person whether they are Catholic, Anglican or whatever that this is what African secret science is all about. What we hope to achieve is an appreciation by African people of their own heritage and their own past . . . you don't have to become an Orisha devotee but this is what your ancestors did, this is what African sacred science is all about.

From its inception it has promoted the Orisha religion and it is headquartered in an Orisha compound that includes all the necessary accoutrements. Visitors to the compound are welcomed by a member and asked to stand by the shrine of Eshu, located at the entrance to the compound, while a short prayer is said to this deity, worshipped as the guardian of the gates. The prayer is meant to purify the visitor and to secure Eshu's blessings for the visitor.

Baba Oludari celebrates a number of Yoruba events in addition to the traditional Orisha feasts and ceremonies. At this strongly Africanized shrine, the calendar year begins with the celebration of the Yam festival, following the Yoruba thanksgiving tradition. A yam is planted and when it is ready, a

Figure 8 Water festival to Oshun, August 2000

special festival honouring the earth and its bounty is undertaken. Later in the calendar year some of the Orisha deities are honoured outside of their traditional *Ebos*. For example, the group celebrates Shango Day with public meetings, drumming and parades. In its year-2000 celebrations, members of the indigenous Carib community joined in the commemoration of Shango Day held at the corner of Lopinot Road and Eastern Main Road, Arouca. Grain, fruit and honey were offered to Shango, god of thunder, and the spirits of the land were honoured in the ceremony.

The group also celebrates the deity Olukun, the Yoruba deity of the ocean, by holding a festival in his honour that culminates in a boat trip up the Caroni swamp in central Trinidad. In 2000 the festival lasted for an entire week that included a variety of ceremonies prior to the trip to the swamp. Baba Oludari noted that there are usually manifestations of power that take place during these festival events, and care has to be taken while on a boat that no accidents or mishaps occur. The powers are urged therefore to keep calm. Later this group, or organization as Oludari calls it, using a secular term, celebrates the spring equinox. This usually involves taking the children of the group to some natural spot so that they can begin to relate to animals and nature. In addition, the group celebrates an annual feast that takes place sometime between November and February.

The doctrine of this shrine, taken in large part from Yoruba traditions, also strongly emphasizes the relationship of people to nature. And, although animal sacrifice is an important element in the Yoruba Orisha religion, Brother Oludari and his members are trying to move away from blood sacrifice and use only plant products such as fruits and seeds for their sacrifice. He explains that seeds contain a great deal of power and energy and are therefore especially useful for sacrificial purposes. Another reason to eliminate blood sacrifices or to do them only for the membership is that they plan to make videos to send to schools, universities and other groups. The filming of an animal sacrifice might make the videos unpalatable to some viewers.

On a more secular note, this organization also celebrates the birthday of Marcus Garvey and the events marking Emancipation Day in Trinidad. The group places great emphasis on communication, publishing a magazine called *Ifa Speaks* that contains articles about Orisha and other African events. They have recently added a Web site to their dissemination strategy. One of their main objectives now is to prepare a series of radio broadcasts called "Introducing the Religion". They hope to produce videotapes for sale. They have also hosted two conferences on the Orisha religion; one in 1987, held at Valsayn Teachers' College and one in 1995 at the Royal Palm Hotel. Although they had hoped to have tapes of the conferences, they have not been able to secure help in transcribing the tapes.

Ancestor Worship and the Egungun Festival

Part of the Africanization process involves the learning of West African traditional beliefs. The veneration and worship of the ancestors is a strong feature of most West African religions. Ancestors are broadly defined as including one's own but also historical figures and famous people. The worship of ancestors was not formally retained among New World African-derived peoples, but the belief is making some headway not only in Orisha communities in Trinidad but also among those in the United States and other parts of the diaspora. Ancestor worship was considered by Christian denominations

Figure 9 Prime Minister Panday surrounded by Orisha elders blessing the ancestral memorial at Lopinot, Orisha Family Day 1999

to be part of the religion of savages and, along with drumming and other aspects of African traditional culture, was strongly frowned upon.

Today these prohibitions no longer exist and the belief in ancestors is common among worshippers. Most public events begin with prayers and libations to the ancestors. At the Lopinot Family Day in 1999 even the prime minister participated in the pouring of the libation over designated ancestor stones. While such formal occasions call for acknowledgement of the ancestors, some modern worshippers will also invoke the "blessings of the ancestors" when they wish to favour a person with special treatment.

Reverence for the "elder" is part of the African tradition of respecting the wisdom and experience of older persons. Today, the senior Orisha leaders are called "elders". Even ordinary persons of age are addressed as "elder" and it is a mark of respect to acknowledge, or make some reference to, "elders" present when addressing a group. Not only are persons in positions of authority acknowledged but the presence of elders, regardless of who they are, is recognized.

One of the most intriguing changes in ritual and ceremonial aspects has been the introduction of the Yoruba Egungun festivals. This festival honours dead ancestors and consists of costumed dancers, wearing traditional masks, who represent the ancestors. The "ancestors" enter into the space of the living, dance, counsel and generally interact with the new generation of worshippers. Divination, libations and drumming accompany the ceremony.[20] This festival of the dead was unknown to the Orisha worship in Trinidad until 1994, when an African-oriented *Ile* or shrine was formed in Princes Town.

The formation of this *Ile* provides an interesting example of the transnational movement of the Orisha religion. It began when a meeting was held between an Orisha leader in New York and a member of the faith in Trinidad. At this meeting they agreed that "there was a need to take steps to enhance and uplift the African tradition if we as a people are to stem the tide of moral and spiritual decay within the African Community".[21] An *Ile* was formed by Valerie Stephenson Lee Chee, consisting of initiated members who were to act as teachers, bringing aspects of the Yoruba religion to Trinidad and other areas of the Caribbean. As one of its first functions, they created the Egungun Society of Trinidad and Tobago in August 1994. The society was founded by an Iyalorisha from the United States in collaboration with Stephenson Lee Chee and a few others. Thirteen people, including the former, were initiated "into the mysteries of Egungun". A year later another festival was held and the membership increased to twenty-five. The group went into hibernation the following year, when the American Iyalorisha returned to the United States. Another contact was made with Babalawo Ifayomi from New York, who visited in 1995 and a connection with his *Ile* "Orisa Sango" was established. His book, *The Lost Orisha*,[22] was launched in Trinidad in 1996. The group held several seminars on aspects of the African faith, accompanied by *Ebos* and the building of a shrine. The membership increased and several now practise the Yoruba religion "in keeping with traditional guidelines".[23] In 1998 the group severed its relationship to the American *Ile* and a local *Ile* called Enia Wa was formed in Princes Town. The group have maintained the traditions to the best of their ability and have celebrated "all major festivals and feast observances of the Orisa", including Oya Day, Gelede, Ibora, Sango, Yemoja, Obatala and the Egungun festival.

The ancestor festival of Egungun has increased in importance, as it has now been observed at several public occasions. The Egungun masqueraders were presented at the Family Day celebration at Lopinot in March of 1999.

Accompanied by drums, a procession of masked dancers entered into the open space in front of the dais and danced for about twenty minutes. They were vigorously applauded by the assemblage. To date the Egungun festival has been celebrated at this *Ile* but not elsewhere in the country.

African elements are strongly encouraged at the shrine or *Ile* of Brother Oludari. One innovation is the festival honouring the deity Olukun. When asked why this festival was introduced, the leader talked about man's relationship to nature; it seems that the person-nature relationship, so characteristic of Yoruba religion, is being introduced here. Brother Oludari stated that

> Olukun is a mentor for the entire planet so basically what we do at the Olukun festival is to afford our island state the opportunity for healing. We have misused and abused our coastal and fringe lands for quite a long time . . . we just have to go down the road here, less than 15 minutes drive and see all those housing projects situated on wet lands . . . there are environmental laws and nobody obeys them. If some little person go and build some shacks somewhere in the swamps police may raid them but these entire housing projects all up on the Northern Coast . . . people planning to put down hotels and golf courses but there is a lot of research to show that the run off from the chemicals that would be used to maintain that place destroy the marine and aquatic life . . . I'm not seeing anything being done about it so in our own perspective we feel that if humans damage their environment at least one means of making repair to gather is through the ritual and in our way that's what we are doing.

While the effectiveness of ritual process is frequently debated, Brother Oludari sees clear evidence of its efficacy. He says that some years ago the Scarlet Ibis, the national bird and symbol of this island nation, had left its traditional roosting place in the Caroni Swamp in central Trinidad. But

> from the time we made our festival preparations, they started returning but since they are again being poached, they might leave again, but at least if it was one time we had a visible evidence of having done something and get a result that was very good.

Both the introduction of the Olukun festival and its meaning as interpreted by this shrine relate not only to the Africanizing ritual in general ways but also to actually making a definitive cosmological statement about the relationship of people to the forces of nature, closely following upon traditional Yoruba religion. In looking at the history of religion in human soci-

Contested Theologies in the Orisha Religion

eties, it is obvious that many are pantheistic, featuring a large constellation of deities who function to control and manage the forces of nature. The principal reason in a social evolutionary sense for the development of pantheistic religions was because humankind could not by itself control the harsh elements of nature. Early people were at the mercy of wind, thunderstorms, floods and other natural disasters. Deities and spirits were identified with these forces and it was believed that by propitiating and invoking these deities, nature's cataclysms could be controlled. In these religions, of which the Yoruba Orisha is one, deities were assigned specific responsibility over elements of nature such as wind, water, fire, animal and vegetable life.

As societies evolved and technology became more developed the direct relationship between nature and humankind took on more symbolic meanings. Many of the deities and their rituals became traditional elements in the symbol system of the religion. In the case of Orisha worship in the New World not only time, but also the additional factor of the enforced transplantation of African peoples, must be considered, so that it becomes even more obvious that the deities no longer need to work on the elements of nature with which they were associated in earlier times. Thus, the worshipper today no longer asks Oya to control the wind or Shango to control thunder. Their role and function in the cosmogony has become symbolic. Their advice and counsel is sought not because they have expertise over the elements but because they are supernatural deities who can help make life for human beings easier and more successful. What Oludari is promoting, however, is a return to that former direct relationship between people and the environment in which they live and which they now pollute. The original work of the Orisha is invoked in order to help clean up the natural world that human beings have soiled. In so doing, this shrine is reverting to the primordial bases of religious forms.

Secular Meetings: Family Day

The Africanization process also means moving the religion into the public arena. One of the most dramatic changes in the ceremonial life of the Orisha religion is that a division is now made between the sacred – the *Ebos* and other ceremonial events such as the river ceremony dedicated to the deity Oshun, the celebration of Lord Shango Day, the recently revived forest ceremony – and the public or secular festivities, such as the Family Day now held annually at Lopinot.

With the creation of Family Day, the Orisha religion moved into a new phase of its development. Family Day celebrations are a common occurrence among the many other religions practised in Trinidad. They are essentially meant to bring together biological and sometimes spiritual family worshippers in an atmosphere of fun and gaiety. The day reinforces family values as well as the traditional belief system of the religion. The Family Day celebration at Lopinot has established itself as the most important public event in the Orisha calendar.[24]

Orisha Family Day at Lopinot, 1998

The first Orisha Family Day took place in March 1998. Its main purpose was to introduce the elders of the faith to the community and especially to the youth. The day began at the Lopinot junction near Arouca where a group of about one hundred people, most in full African dress, gathered and, to the beating of the drums, marched and chipped (a Carnival dance step) their way to the meeting site. They sang Orisha songs as they marched and the procession moved fairly slowly, taking about a half-hour to cover the distance of about one mile. Orisha elders at its head included Iya Rodney and Baba Sam Phills. The site itself contains the remains of an old cemetery where the remains of some African slaves are interred. This sacred site was consecrated during the visit of the Ooni of Ife in 1989. As the procession entered the large open area, it made its way to a makeshift stage. The stage was decorated with three paintings donated by Leroy Clarke for this occasion.

A number of tents containing rows of chairs had been set up. Iya Rodney walked onto the stage and blessed its four corners with olive oil, water and burnt ashes. The group began to sing to Eshu, followed by songs to Ogun. In attendance at the first two Family Day celebrations was Chief Patricia Oluwole from Nigeria, who brought special greetings from the Ooni.[25]

The programme for that first day included greetings from other organizations, including one of the major trade unions in the country. Several members also made comments about this first auspicious occasion. Professor Rawle Gibbons, head of the Creative Arts Centre at the University of the West Indies and one of Orisha's main administrators, spoke at length about the development of the religion. He spoke about the Orisha conference that had been held in California in August 1997 and announced that the next conference would be held in Trinidad and Tobago in 1999. He also discussed the research being conducted by himself and a colleague. This included visits to all the current shrines, about seventy-five in number, in order to hear what most people want. Important themes were unity of all the groups, more education and more understanding of what the different groups do.

Professor Gibbons spoke passionately about the land at Lopinot, much of which had been overtaken by squatters. The many houses built on it were illegal. The Orisha movement was trying to maintain a sacred burial ground. He noted that, at this point, everything at the site was temporary – the stage, the chairs donated by a member, even the bakery products donated by a local bakery. He said, "There is now pride in what we are doing."

He further noted that Trinidad's hosting of the next Orisha conference was a step towards the building of the pride and profile of Orisha internationally as well in Trinidad. He asked the group to help in dismantling the myths and stereotypes about Orisha and to assert themselves in many ways through art, music and dance. He also discussed the disunity among the various groups and factions, and concluded by stressing that their main objective should be to bring about the unity of all groups.

During recess Eintou Springer, one of the administrators and main organizer of this and subsequent Family Day celebrations, called a press conference. Seated at a long table with her were Iyalorisha Rodney, chair of the Council of Elders; Babalorisha Sam Phills; and other elders. Springer spoke about the Orisha religion, its origins, its Africanness, its place in society today, and the plans for the future, including a building centre at the Lopinot site and the planned World Orisha Congress to be held in Trinidad in 1999.

A steady stream of people arrived at the site and, by early afternoon, approximately three to four hundred were in attendance. About two-thirds were women, and most were dressed in African garb. One Orisha elder was dressed in a Muslim-style tunic and pants. The audience greeted each speaker or event with enthusiasm and often with the traditional West African sound called "ululation", which sounds like a loud yodel. The remainder of the day was spent in workshops on music and drumming; African-style crafts and food were offered by private vendors in small booths.

Figure 10 President Robinson hosting a dinner for delegates to the Sixth World Orisha Congress, Port of Spain, 1999

The keynote address was delivered by a Nigerian lecturer at the University of the West Indies, Dr Fosi Mbantenku who, in his talk, reinforced the notion of pride in the African heritage of people in the New World. Entertainment was provided by a chorus of children singing Orisha songs, led by Ella Andall, the calypsonian and popular singer who is also a member of the Orisha faith.

Lopinot 1999

The following year the Family Day lasted for three days, including a market and food day. The ceremony began with a march, introduction of elders, prayers to all the gods and a welcome by Babalorisha Sam Phills as chair. The programme also included the distribution of achievement awards to persons who had made a valuable contribution to the Orisha religion. The awardees were Chief Patricia Oluwole from Nigeria, who also gave the feature address; Ras Tafari of Cheemok Bakery, who donates products to Orisha events; Isaac McCleod, a prominent businessman and supporter of the religion; and Eintou Pearl Springer, whose work in organizing events and administering the new infrastructure of the religion was recognized. Several government ministers, past and present, were there, as well as notable members of society.

The media presence was again extensive and the event and its participants were widely covered. That year's celebration was notable, however, for the official government legitimation it received. The prime minister, the Honourable Basdeo Panday, accepted an invitation to attend the event and, as Springer noted in her welcome, "It wasn't the first time he had come to be part of the Orisha people business", referring to his earlier support of their request for a holiday while in opposition.[26] The prime minister promised the deed to their lands at Maloney in the near future, and the revocation of laws and bylaws that discriminated against the faith. He also "publicly affirm[ed] [his] support for the National Council of Orishas in its continuing struggle to elevate Orisha to its righteous place in the republic of Trinidad and Tobago". He specifically added that his government "would guarantee to Orisha, and indeed all other religions, the right to observe every major life change – birth and marriage and death – in accordance with conventions of your religion".[27] Upon his arrival the prime minister, surrounded by elders and prominent members of the faith, ritually blessed a stone that marks a sacred spot at the Lopinot site, using the traditional method of pouring oil and water onto the stone. On the following day, under a huge red headline – "Shango Rising" – the *Trinidad Express* featured a photo of the prime minister, surrounded by elders and prominent members of the faith, holding a clay vessel of holy water in his left hand and touching his forehead with the other, stooping over the stone. The *Trinidad Guardian* published a similiar photo, but it shows the prime minister with both the oil and water vessels in his hands.

The 1999 Family Day celebration featured two of the major dynamics affecting this religion in the society today. The prime minister's presence and public affirmation of the religion demonstrated political legitimation, providing evidence of the importance of the external forces effecting changes in the status of the religion in society. At the same time, in another part of the programme, an important internal dynamic of change was also highlighted. The presence of the newly revived Egungun Society of Princes Town confirmed the importance of bringing genuine African Yoruba elements back into the faith.

The masked dancers representing the ancestors were led into the open space in front of the stage where they performed a ritualistic dance, accompanied by their drummers. One woman member became possessed by the spirit of an ancestor and blessed the people present. They performed for about a half-hour and were much appreciated by the crowd. They wore masks that are supposed to represent life and death and that delicate state between life and death that provides a link between the living and their dead ancestors.

The day also included a singing presentation by Ella Andall. She took the occasion of the prime minister's presence to make some comments about the state of the religion. She asked the government to "remove shackles to [their] identity as a religious group" by providing them with a marriage act and a deed to their lands. As noted earlier, the prime minister promised in his talk that both would be granted.

Lopinot 2000

The third annual Orisha Family Day took place on 19 March 2000 at the Lopinot site. The growing permanency of the site was evidenced by the building of a permanent concrete stage, as well as several benches that had been donated by a sponsor. Again, several hundred people attended and there was substantial media coverage. The programme was similar to that of earlier years: the procession from the junction to the site, opening prayers and welcome remarks and greetings. The moderator for 2000 was Khafra Kambon, who is the chair of the Emancipation Support Committee as well as the Orisha representative to the IRO. The afternoon's programme included entertainment by both Ella Andall and the country's leading soca calypsonian, David Rudder, who sang one of his Shango-inspired songs. Several members of government also spoke, including a representative of the Ministry of Education, and the minister of culture and gender affairs. Official representation centred on the president of Trinidad and Tobago, His Excellency A.N.R. Robinson or Chief Olokun Igbaro. The president was accompanied by his wife and members of his entourage. Ella Andall performed for the group and Eintou Springer and others made brief comments. The president delivered an impromptu speech, saying that he had not planned to speak at this occasion but that he was moved to do so because it was only when he arrived that he realized that the day marked his third year in office. He noted that it was indeed fortuitous that he was present at this important occasion on his "anniversary".

Figure 11 Babalorisha Sam Phills at the Orisha Family Day celebration, Lopinot, 2000

The Family Day featured two main addresses. One was by prominent Orisha member and sponsor, Isaac McCleod, who addressed the need for progress and unity in the Orisha movement. I had also been invited by the executive committee of the Council of Elders who planned this event to present a talk about Ebenezer Elliott, Pa Neezer, and I was happy to do so. Many of the younger generation of Orisha worshippers know very little about Ebenezer Elliot and, for many, he is merely a name from the past. One woman even said that she thought he was a character from a folk tale! In any case, the committee and especially Eintou Springer and Babalorisha Sam Phills, himself a spiritual child of Pa Neezer, thought it might be educational for the younger members to hear a talk about personal experiences with the great Pa Neezer. The paper (included in the appendix) discussed Pa Neezer's background, his grounding in the religion and his general view of the world. It also suggested that he be honoured by the nation for his contribution to spirituality and religion in Trinidad and Tobago.

These secular events received considerable media attention. The attendance of the prime minister or the president and his comments about the faith politically legitimated the group. The media continued to carry stories and photos of the Family Day celebrations for days after the event.

Reclaiming African Identity

One of the most interesting questions raised by the growing reassertion of Africanisms into the syncretized Orisha system is the motivation that drives the innovators of the movement. It must again be emphasized that the innovators consist of a relatively small group of people, themselves further divided into even smaller units. The first group of innovators are primarily motivated by political ideology, and their main interest appears to be getting the religion to a point where it is accepted by the mainstream and particularly by government. This small group of innovative activists were responsible for obtaining the lands at Maloney, the passage of the Orisha Marriage Act and, more recently, lobbying for the removal of old statutes. Their second objective is to develop a centralized administrative infrastructure. Members of this group include Eintou Springer, Professor Rawle Gibbons, Khafra Kambon and many others currently working in administrative positions with the Council of Elders. Although these innovators are also religious and believe fully in the spiritual values of the Orisha religion, their primary objectives can described as secular rather than sacred.

There is small sub-set of innovators also somewhat involved with administrative matters, but their primary objective in Africanizing the Orisha movement comes from a spiritual or sacred base rather than a secular one. The most important of these are probably Patricia McCleod (Iya Sangowummi), Valerie Stephenson Lee Chee and Brother Oludari. They are driven by the need to bring back what they construct as the true and authentic Yoruba source religion to the Orisha worship. For example, Valerie Stephenson Lee Chee has been working on the restoration of the Egungun ancestor festivals. Patricia McCleod has brought back the rain festival devoted to Shango. Brother Oludari is bringing back festivals and Orisha who had not been worshipped previously in the Trinidadian form of the religion. They are directly involved in Yorubanizing the practices in Trinidad. What is interesting about this group is that they are not satisfied with current Orisha practices although they revere the elders who managed to keep aspects of the religion alive during times of slavery and colonial oppression.

Another group, not quite identical to the secular or sacred innovators in either membership or ideology are some members who are currently or were associated with the Cyrus shrine in Enterprise. Although the practices of that shrine are still heavily syncretized with Christianity, Mother Joan Cyrus has many African implements in her *chapelle*, some of which date back to the founding of the shrine a century ago. Moreover, it is a very popular shrine and many visitors to the country are led there. A special section for visitors has been constructed on one side of the *palais*. Mother Joan is somewhat involved in the secularization movement, since she was a delegate at the World Congress in San Francisco and her brother was the main organizer of the 1999 World Orisha Congress.

Several members of the Council of Elders generally support both the secular and spiritually motivated changes to the religion. The present chairman, Babalorisha Sam Phills, in particular, is in favour of these changes that he calls "progressive". It is to Baba Sam's credit that he manages to negotiate and mediate between the various groupings in the faith today. Others such as Babalorisha Clarence Forde and Iyalorisha Rodney, older leaders, not only retain the syncretized beliefs and practices by which they were socialized, but also do not interfere with the new developments. Still others such as Olori Biddeau, Sister Gonzales and a few other leaders apparently do not take a position on the attempt to revive or re-Yorubanize the religion as practised in Trinidad today.

The innovating group as a whole share a common history of participation in the Black Power movement that swept through the Caribbean and created what has been termed a "revolution" in Trinidad.[28] The leading proponent of the Black Power ideology in the Caribbean was Walter Rodney, whose ideas influenced many young West Indian students and intellectuals. In Trinidad a political group called the National Joint Action Committee was formed and devoted itself to the dissemination of a Black Power ideology. While its appeal was primarily to young Afro-Trinidadians, it also attempted to mobilize support among the East Indian population, with some moderate success. Their ideology was described by the then prime minister, Dr Eric Williams, as "the insistence on Black Dignity, the manifestation of Black consciousness and the demand for Black economic power". He concluded, "If this is Black Power, then I am for Black Power."[29] The essence of this ideology revolved around the concept of race, since blackness and its place of origin in Africa was its mobilizing dynamic. This political ideology is still evident among the leaders of the Africanization movement in the Orisha religion but, as in other areas, Black Power as a radical or militant movement has gradually become identified with the more intellectual ideology of Afrocentricity.

In casting about for any institution or "survival" from the original homeland in Africa (and the Yoruba region of Nigeria in particular), these political ideologists or Afrocentrists found it in the practice of Orisha – a religion that could clearly be traced to African origins. In the intervening years, however, a strong element of syncretism with Christianity and especially Roman Catholicism (and later, Spiritual Baptism) became pronounced. Thus, their mission became not only the rediscovery of original Yoruba ritual but also the rejection and removal of Christian elements.

Underlying these objectives, however, is, I believe, the need to reassert African ethnic identity as an African-derived people, even while living in multi-ethnic Trinidad. At the heart of their dedication to Orisha is a political commitment to the philosophy of Afrocentricity and its valorization of African identity.

This doctrine takes many forms but, in the most basic sense, it evolves from a sense of place. Molefi Asante defines it as follows:[30]

> All knowledge results from an occasion of encounter in place. But the place remains a rightly shaped perspective that allows the Afrocentrist to put African ideas and values at the centre of inquiry . . . The Afrocentrist will not question the idea of the centrality of African ideals and values. The Afrocentrist seeks to uncover and use codes, paradigms, symbols, motifs, myths, and circles of discussion that reinforce the centrality of African ideals and values as a valid frame of reference for acquiring and examining data. Such a method appears to go beyond western history in order to re-valorise the African place in the interpretation of Africans, continental and diaspora.[31]

He further notes that studies of Africans in the diaspora must recognize that their history and culture stem from an African source. Afrocentricity or "Africalogy", in Asante's terminology, has been strongly criticized because it lays greater emphasis on the glories of the African past, thereby minimizing the slave experience in the New World. Paul Gilroy notes that

> there is a danger that, apart from the archaeology of traditional survivals, slavery becomes a cluster of negative associations that are best left behind. The history of

the plantations and sugar mills supposedly offers little that is valuable when compared to the ornate conceptions of African antiquity against which they are unfavourably compared. Blacks are urged, if not to forget the slave experience which appears as an aberration from the story of greatness told in African history, then to replace it at the centre of our thinking with a mystical and ruthlessly positive notion of Africa that is indifferent to interracial variation and is frozen at the point where blacks boarded the ships that would carry them into the woes and horrors of the middle passage.[32]

There is a danger, then, of centring one's African identity too closely on a mythic ancient model and ignoring the many multilayered components of modern ethnicities. As Kwame Anthony Appiah notes, "Identities are complex and multiple and grow out of a history of changing responses to economic, political, and cultural forces, almost always in opposition to other identities."[33]

Appiah thinks in terms of a "network of points of affinity" that create multiple identities that will be different, however slightly, for every person. Given the nature of the African diaspora to North and South America, the Caribbean, parts of Europe and elsewhere, it is highly unlikely that a single African identity can be shared across such vast historical and cultural differences.

In a similar vein, Gilroy suggests that African identities are composed of different strains and variants, depending on historical and local cultural influences.[34] He describes the cultures and ethnic identities of the many diasporic places as hybrids, since they are all the result of the historical discontinuities that occurred after the middle passage, or as he metaphorically terms it, "the Black Atlantic". For Gilroy, the Black Atlantic, culminating in the experience of slavery, becomes the locus of identity formation, but it is influenced and changed by local influences, producing a variant or hybrid.

One view of the people who conform to the philosophy of Afrocentrism in Trinidad today, and who are at the forefront of re-Africanizing the rituals of the Orisha religion, is that their understanding of the African world and their place in it would fit more closely with the thinking of Gilroy and Appiah rather than Asante's more rigorous version. Their ethnic identity seems clearly grounded as Afro-Trinidadians but their view of the world is informed, first and foremost, by their being the descendants of African slaves. African origins, in both cultural and individual identity terms, are highly regarded and, in fact, eagerly sought after, but there is also full acceptance of the hybridization brought by Trinidadian time and place. Thus, there is no apparent cognitive or emotional conflict or contradiction in wanting to replace syncretic Christianity with what are defined, and sometimes imagined, as traditional African rituals. As with the Ooni of Ife and his followers who are also Christians, some of the Trinidadian innovators worship in both Christian churches and Orisha *palais* and will probably continue both personal religious traditions. Khafra Kambon, a strong proponent of both Afrocentricity and the Orisha religion, summarizes the perspective of the newer innovating devotees:

> The Black Power movement of the 1960s and 70s . . . changed our psychological relationship to Africa, our heritage and its manifestations. In making the re-connection with our roots, which was a part of the revolutionary consciousness, in searching for an authentic identity, a number of Africans re-immersed themselves in the Orisha tradition. Orisha traditions and practices survived in Trinidad and Tobago and other parts of the West as an act of conscious and unconscious political rebellion. When the social and psychological forces opposed to its survival finally seemed to be on the verge of triumph, the Orishas were revived by political rebellion.[35]

The Orisha religion has provided these new leaders, and the many younger people who are beginning to develop an awareness of and interest in Orisha, with a cultural vehicle through which they can express that part of their identity which is African. Being able to worship traditional Yoruba deities, following ritual practices that originated in Nigeria and are centuries old, and defining aspects of their world through the prism of such "original" religious tradition are far stronger stimuli to African identity than are the wearing of a style of clothes or even the assumption of an African name.

> I really don't believe that the Orisha and the Catholic saints are one from what is my understanding of Orisha as primordial energies. The Catholic saints have a different kind of energy for me. Oshun could never be St Philomen, Oya could never be St Ann.
>
> – *Patricia McCleod (Iya Sangowummi)*

CHAPTER SIX

The Role of Syncretism in the Orisha Religion Today

Christian Syncretic Elements

In the earlier period, the main Christian syncretisms in Orisha worship were taken from Roman Catholicism.[1] Thus, Catholic prayers such as the Lord's Prayer, the Hail Mary and others were routinely chanted at the beginning of feasts. Sometimes the entire Litany of the Saints was recited. Hymns, more often than not, were derived from the Catholic mass. Most Orisha members then were also Roman Catholics, but there was considerable multiple religiosity and attendance at as many as three to four denominations and their events throughout the week was not unusual. Ebenezer Elliott chanted Catholic prayers at feasts but was himself a staunch member of the London Baptist Faith. He is buried in that church's cemetery near the Fifth Company Village on the Moruga Road, and Baptist prayers and hymns were sung at his funeral.

There was no particular distinction made between the Orisha and their Catholic-saint identities. It was commonly believed that they were two manifestations of the same spiritual force, "two heads of the same coin". The issue of the syncretic merger was not discussed often and rarely disputed amongst the people themselves. During the 1950s no particular Hindu syncretic elements were evident. The spirits of the Kabbalah were invoked by some Orisha worshippers, but not to any great extent. Leaders and spiritual children of Pa Neezer rejected the worship of Kabbalah and would have nothing to do with its practitioners.[2]

In more recent times the syncretism between Spiritual Baptism and Orisha has become more pronounced, while the Roman Catholic elements have been reduced. Christian syncretism, however, remains firmly entrenched in Orisha worship; it is just that one Christian denomination has been replaced by another. Research conducted in 1956 and 1958 shows that Spiritual Baptism was not very evident in Orisha ritual. It may have been established by the marriage between Tanti Silla, a prominent Orisha leader, and Shepherd Breton, a Spiritual Baptist practitioner, that took place in the late 1950s. Tanti Silla had a large compound on St François Valley Road, and she was one of the principal spiritual children of Pa Neezer. He officiated at her feast every year. Shepherd Breton came from the Fifth Company Village in southern Trinidad, where he was known as a Spiritual Baptist, and his name, "Shepherd", actually refers to his position in that church. He and Tanti met at a feast in the mid-1950s and began a relationship that culminated in a legal marriage. Shepherd was much younger than Tanti and seemed to have had a strong controlling influence on her.

When I arrived in Tanti's compound Shepherd was already well established there, but I do not think they were formally married at this time. Shepherd began having Baptist meetings in Tanti's large and well-equipped compound and he gradually introduced Baptist elements, such as the brass bell and Baptist hymns, into the Orisha ritual. Wednesday evenings would be devoted to the "Baptist Work". By 1958, when I returned for my second field trip to Trinidad, this amalgamation had more than taken root, and Tanti and some of her immediate followers began calling themselves "Shango Baptists". From then on, that term and the syncretism that it identified became quite popular. The syncretism then involved not only Baptist elements – implements, flags, designs, hymns and prayers – that were inserted into Orisha ritual but also mutual attendance at each other's ceremonies. Pa Neezer, by this time had stopped officiating at Tanti's feasts, explaining to me that "she doing the Baptist work now . . . I'm not able with that". He made a strong distinction between his formal English-derived London Baptism and the more fundamentalist Spiritual and Shouter Baptism.

Today, despite the assertion by some that "Shango Baptists"[3] do not exist and despite the strong attempts to Africanize the religion, the syncretism with Baptism is still very strong and much evident in Orisha ritual and ceremony. One senses, however, that it is still an area of contestation and some Orisha people admit, somewhat reluctantly, to also being Baptist. Even a well-known member of the religion who has written about Orisha does not accept the confluence of "Shango" and Baptist. Eastman, cited in the *Sunday Express* of 15 August 1999, states categorically "that animal does not exist. It exists only in the minds of the uninformed." He thinks that the Baptist practice in Trinidad is like the Aladura faith in Nigeria in terms "of the mixture of Christianity along with traditional religious practices". Other members of the faith use a theological argument, saying that Spiritual Baptism is Christian whereas Orisha is African in derivation.[4] Iyalorisha Rodney also distinguishes between the two, explaining that there are two spirits and that a Spiritual Baptist mother can be "attack[ed] and manage to get in . . . the power taken from them and they get involved. But the difference is between the bell and the drum"[5] where the bell and drum are used as symbolic manifestations of Christianity and Africanness.[6]

While it is normally assumed that Orisha people bring Baptism into their worship, today the process is also being reversed. There are a number of people well versed in the Yoruba tradition who are actually teaching Baptists some of the Orisha traditions. One such person claims to have knowledge of the Ifa in Nigeria as well as connections to Oyatunyi village in the United States. He helped one Baptist church perform a goat sacrifice to the Orisha.

A considerable amount of time at most feasts is still spent in Baptist prayer, chanting and singing. At Sister Gonzales's *Ebo*, for example, the congregation was kept on their knees chanting and singing primarily Baptist prayers for well over one hour before the drumming began. At the famous Cyrus shrine, one of the best known in the island, elements of Baptism are extremely pronounced. The compound itself is very large and contains two houses, a *palais*, a *chapelle*, a shrine dedicated to the Cyrus ancestors and many stools to the Orisha deities. It also has a mourning ground or house directly adjacent to the *palais*. This shrine meets regularly every Thursday evening, following instructions by the Orisha to Mother Joan Cyrus, its leader. At least half of the evening is spent in Baptist songs and prayers. Members of this shrine must go through a Baptist mourning period for three days before they become members in good standing. The well-decorated *palais* contains decorative satin banners in different colours suspended from its rafters. A Baptist symbol is embroidered on each banner. Even the title "mother", which identifies Joan Cyrus, is adapted from the Baptist religion. Its annual feast follows pretty well the same agenda as the Thursday meetings, opening with Baptist songs and prayers, followed by the Yoruba invocation to the Orisha and drumming and singing to the Orisha.

Of equal significance to Baptist elements at the Cyrus shrine are the African carved wooden statues of the various Orisha and their implements in the *chapelle*. Some of the statues are quite old, having been collected by the current leader's father and grandfather. In commenting on the Africanness of the *chapelle*, one of the leading members of the shrine said, "Oh, yes, we don't do those syncretisms here." At that very moment, her congregation was singing a Baptist hymn. What this suggests is that the Roman Catholic elements have been somewhat reduced in importance in the ritual but they have been replaced by Spiritual Baptist practices and accoutrements.

During the course of one visit, I observed an event that could very well be identified as a metaphor for this transitional stage in the syncretic process. Towards the end of the evening, which had been dedicated to Ogun, a circle of worshippers was formed, holding hands while they recited in unison an invocation in the English language to the Yoruba Orisha, calling each one by name. It is ironic that a hand-holding circle is Christian in origin, the language is that of the colonizer, but the deities are Yoruba.

On the several occasions this shrine was visited, only the mother manifested power and only for a brief period. At another feast no manifestations occurred. Several observers at *Ebos* or feasts have also noted that there are now fewer manifestations of the powers. Burton Sankeralli, a local journalist and long-time supporter of the Orisha, has also noted the relative absence of powers at many feasts held today. One can only speculate as to the reasons for their absence. One possible explanation is that as the movement becomes more middle class – and most of the leaders would qualify for that designation in terms of income, housing and other material possessions – perhaps they have lost the need to publicly display their power. Their status is assured merely by maintaining the elaborate compounds. As well, the dress worn to *Ebos* today is also elaborate and clearly expensive and not suitable for rolling around on the ground. What has also been noticed is that many of the strictures, prohibitions and commandments of the Orisha are delivered to the leader through dreams. Dreams and visions have always played a major role in determining the actions of Orisha worshippers, as has divination. Although there is no way of measuring whether the reliance on dreams has increased for today's participants, certainly most of the commandments from the Orisha are delivered by the leaders to their congregation as coming from a dream or vision in which the Orisha have appeared. Today, as in former times, divination by the casting of the *obi* seeds is also routinely done in order to determine most major decisions. Perhaps there is today a greater reliance on dreams and divination so that leaders can transmit their messages without the frequent mechanism of actual possession.

Iyalorisha Rodney's feast in September 2000 also provided evidence for the transitional nature of Orisha ceremonies. On the first evening, Monday, members sang a Yoruba song followed by the evocation in Yoruba, and translated into English, to each Orisha honoured at the feast. No Christian prayers were said at this time. On Tuesday evening, however, the small group spent most of their time sewing and then planting the flags of the Orisha at their stools and around the compound. At the end of the flag planting ceremony, Iyalorisha Rodney suggested that they say prayers and promptly launched into the Roman Catholic Our Father, followed by other Catholic prayers. It was probably not coincidental that the group of the innovators who do away with Christian prayers were not present during the flag ceremony, but they had led the Yoruba prayers on the first evening of the *Ebo*. On the Wednesday, a cattle feast was held in honour of *Elofon* – this ritual is only practised during leap years. The ritual at that event included both Yoruba ritual and Christian prayers and hymns.

Some Orisha shrines have abolished Christian elements entirely. One such is Brother Oludari's shrine, at which only African rituals are performed. Iyalorisha Rodney's *Ebo* has reduced the amount of time spent on Christian prayers. In commenting on this, one of her spiritual children says:

> In the *palais* of Iyalorisha Rodney on the opening night of her *Ebo* . . . Iya would give an hour or so to her Baptist colleagues as a mark of respect and spiritual bonding. Now, the movement for orthodoxy no longer makes that possible. In the shrine, any attempt at Christian prayers brings frowns and restlessness from many. Now the young people show off their skills, saying their prayers in Yoruba.[7]

However, it was observed that Christian prayers were said when innovator members were absent. These observations were also corroborated by some of the members who no longer attend Iyalorisha Rodney's *Ebo*, precisely because she does not carry on enough Christian prayers. A number of people said that they no longer attend her shrine, and one young man said that he continued to do so only to respect Iyalorisha but he feels that "the path she is on is wrong, nothing bad in praying"; his take on the lesser number of manifestations was "because the Christian groundwork has not been laid". In many of the other shrines throughout the country and especially those far removed from the capital, "innovators", who are primarily city based, are rarely present and the older Christian practices are still much in evidence.

Some prominent members of Orisha acknowledge the relationship between it and Spiritual Baptism, especially in terms of common African-derived elements. Valerie Stephenson Lee Chee is a good example of a well-versed Spiritual Baptist practitioner who was eventually directed towards the Orisha. She was and, to a certain extent, still is actively involved with the Spiritual Baptist faith, rising to the position of mother. She was born Anglican and practised that faith for some years before moving to Spiritual Baptism. She has not left that church but has, as she puts it, "graduated". Apparently her move to Orisha also reflects her need to progress and identify more closely with her African origin. She is also active in women's issues that have led her to criticize Spiritual Baptists because they do not accept women leaders. Even as a mother in the church she could not officiate at the altar, and only men are allowed to preach. Orisha, with its stronger role for women leaders, provides her with an opportunity to combine feminism with her intense religiosity.

Hindu Syncretisms

Hindu syncretism is also evident in some Orisha shrines. At least two were observed but there are likely more throughout the country where this is the case. The nature of the syncretism consists largely of Hindu pictures of deities, such as Ganesh, Saraswati, Vishnu, Hanuman, that were placed beside a chromolithograph of the Sacred Heart of Jesus. In one shrine there is even a stool for Lakshmi in the yard. There is also a triangle of flags or handis for the "Indian powers". The leader also said that sometimes he manifests Shiva, but in the form of St Francis. He also claims to work with "Chinese Powers". During the course of an evening in which several initiates were baptized, the Orisha Aba Koso manifested on the leader and the group sang to him. Shortly afterwards they reverted to Baptist hymns, chants and "doption". Several person "spoke in tongues" and, in general, the main proceedings were very Baptist oriented.

At another shrine Hindu pictures are also found in the *chapelle,* as well as a statue of Mother Kali. This particular leader does not appear to include elements of Hinduism in his practice, which he describes as "I do Catholic, then Anglican, then African", but he is married to an Indian woman and has many pictures of Hindu gods in his *chapelle.* Hindu elements are sometimes found in the ritual, as when a Hindu deity is identified as possessing an individual. Osain is said to be an "Indian" deity but he is also addressed as the Christian St Francis. Occasionally an Indian Osain manifests, and it is said that there are also Indian versions of Ogun.

Kabbalah

Several leaders, even well-respected ones, also practise Kabbalah. These include Baba Forde and Olori Jeffrey Biddeau. A well-respected deceased leader named Isaac Lindsay was also a Kabbalist. Kabbalah worship has been going on in Trinidad for some time, but respondents today do not know how or why it arrived in Trinidad. Even in my earlier ethnography, I was told of the "dark powers" and that some evil persons practised this form of supernaturalism.[8] Houk speculates that it was brought by Spanish colonists, whose African slaves might have observed the Kabbalah practices.[9] He also suggests that it was practised in secret and its banquets were generally not open to outsiders. Houk also notes that it reappeared in about 1970, at the same time as the Black Power revolution in Trinidad. Although not African in origin, Houk thinks that Kabbalah appealed to Africans who were already familiar with spirit possession through the Orisha. Kabbalah is still practised but, according to Houk, only within the Orisha network.

A major practitioner of Kabba, as it is known, is Baba Forde, today one of the leaders in the Council of Elders. He practises Kabbalah because it "educates". He described the activities at a Kabbalah banquet, saying that the singing invokes the spirits. There is also drumming, but it is merely to help along the music. The spirits are invoked and they are promised food and drink. Two kinds of spirits are invoked: Astral and Infernal. The former live anywhere in the universe and are benign spirits, but the latter dwell in the nether regions. People are afraid of Kabbalah because some of the infernals are rough and aggressive. "You need to control them . . . they can educate too but you must control them."

The way Baba Forde explains it, Kabbalah is close to the original Jewish mysticism. It involves another level of the supernatural, and the idea is to enter into a mystical world and reach the spirits who live there. The devotee does this to reach another realm and learn from these spirits, often called "entities".

Another perspective on Kabba as it is practised in Trinidad was provided by Brother Oludari, who is a former Kabbalist himself. He confirms that its practice brings one into another level of the supernatural, but the techniques used are largely drawn from the realm of magic. He thinks that the reason Kabba was practised was that it provided a means of reaching the dead. Since the Yoruba strongly believe in ancestor worship – during the Egungun festival the dead are re-enacted – earlier worshippers needed a way of maintaining contact with their ancestors and Kabbalah provided such a means. Many of the Kabba spirits are in fact the spirits of deceased human beings. With the resurgence of Orisha worship and with their emphasis on the veneration of ancestors, the mechanisms of the Kabba are no longer necessary. Oludari left the Kabba world when the Orisha began to be more meaningful to him. His Orisha mentor strongly disapproved of the Kabbalah and confirmed his wish to remove himself from their power. Baba Forde maintains that several Orisha practitioners who also practised Kabbalah were warned to stop.

The Role of Syncretism in the Orisha Religion Today

When they failed to do so, they experienced misfortune and/or early death. He cites the death of Isaac Lindsay as an example of one who was warned off the Kabbalah; he subsequently died at the early age of thirty-four when he failed to heed the warning.[10]

Respondents, in talking about the Kabbalah, are unanimous in their feeling that Kabbalah is separate from Orisha worship. Baba Forde was adamant that "Kabbalah is not Orisha" and that the two are not practised together, although the same persons might participate in both systems. Neither the spirits, songs and drumming nor the level of possession are the same as those in Orisha. If this is indeed the case, and respondents here feel that it is, then Kabbalah cannot and should not be considered a syncretic element of Orisha but a separate system of mystical belief and practice. Kabba spirits or entities do not normally manifest at Orisha feasts, nor do Orishas attend Kabbalah banquets, but Kabbalah practitioners do maintain altars, stools and flags to their entities in a different section of Orisha compounds. Houk maintains that it is only in the last twenty years or so that Kabbalah has been openly associated with the Orisha religion. In view of the strong views held by practitioners that the two are not the same, perhaps the ethnographer should take note and not claim that Kabba is a syncretic element in the Orisha religion.

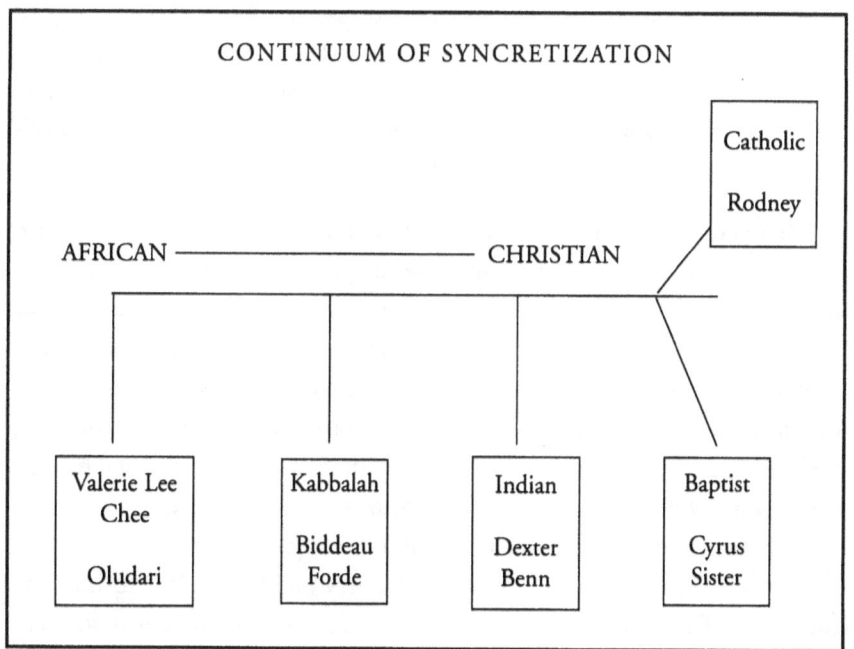

Case Study

The World Congress of Orisha: Contested Issues of Syncretism

During their attendance at the Fifth World Congress of Orisha in San Francisco in 1998, the Trinidadian delegation was invited to host the next congress, to be held in 1999. The idea for an international Orisha organization was apparently developed in New York City by the Caribbean Cultural Centre – a group dedicated to the study of African and African-derived traditions. The first conference took place in Ife, Nigeria, in 1981 and subsequent ones were held in Brazil and the United States. The conference brought together "traditional leaders and scholars, experts on the religions of Santería (Lucumi), Candomblé, Vodun, Shango and other belief systems that maintain the philosophy, traditions, and culture of Africa in the Americas".[11] An informal network of leaders and scholars involved in the study of Orisha religions was established. This network confirmed that the Yoruba-derived religion has been maintained in the diaspora. Moreover, these conferences also

> highlighted that the belief systems were the foundation of movements of cultural resistance and affirmation, which have shaped the lives and experiences of Africans on the continent and in the Americas. The conferences highlighted that followers of the African-based belief systems were at the vanguard of liberation struggles, the forging of independence movements, and the development of culturally grounded communities, societies, and institutions.[12]

What is of interest here is that the international network appears to have the objective of not only continuing the religious practices but also placing them historically within the context of resistance movements. As well, at least the American-based arm of this movement is concerned with how the religion can serve the greater needs of modern disadvantaged African Americans in education, community organization and economic viability. While earlier conferences may have dealt with these themes, the one held in Trinidad in 1999 did not deal with them in any extensive manner. Instead, this conference focused on ideological and theological issues.

This was the first time a Caribbean country had been asked to host the conference. Trinidad accepted the invitation and a committee was formed.

The Role of Syncretism in the Orisha Religion Today

The theme of the congress was "The Orisa, Ancestors, Community and the Family in the New Millennium, Strategies for Survival". The World Congress is an organization whose patron is the spiritual head of the Orisha religion, the Ooni of Ife. It has an international steering committee currently headed by a Nigerian professor, Dr Wande Abimbola. Constituent countries including Nigeria, Brazil, Cuba, the United States, and Trinidad and Tobago, and one or two others are represented on the steering committee. There are also regional sub-committees. One of the members of the National Council of Orisha Elders, Jeffrey Biddeau, is the Trinidad representative for the region.

The hosting of this conference itself became a contested issue, as differing versions of how this invitation came to be received have been told. According to some, it was a few politicized participants from Trinidad who secured the offer. To others, it was the purity and sincerity of their religious faith that convinced the international executive committee to select Trinidad. The dynamics surrounding the invitation lead to further contestation with respect to the "ownership" of the conference.

A secretariat was formed in the offices of I.T. McCleod, a businessman and surveyor who, along with members of his family, are Orisha worshippers who occasionally attend the Cyrus shrine located in Enterprise, a village near Chaguanas. McCleod's office is located on a street in St Clair, formerly the area in which expatriate English people lived. It contains large and luxurious homes, some of which have been bought by wealthy Trinidadians. A few have been converted to bed-and-breakfasts or business offices. The congress secretariat therefore, right from its beginning, was located in an area of the city long known as home to the elite, wealthy and privileged. The secretariat was largely staffed by volunteer members of the faith, especially those associated with the Cyrus shrine. Invitations were sent out to the member units of the international congress and a call for papers and presentations was also distributed. An information packet produced by the secretariat included information about accommodation, meals and tours of sites in Trinidad and Tobago. The papers were to be submitted in a word-processed format and complex instructions about typing, margins and the like were to be followed.[13] The congress was to be held in the downtown Holiday Inn. Registration fees for foreign guests was to be US$250, and TT$500 for locals. The Ministry of Culture and Gender Affairs provided two of its officers to help with organization, and some financial support was promised to defray accommodation and hospitality expenses of the Nigerian delegation, to be headed by the Ooni of Ife.

From the outset and looking only at this arrangement, it seemed clear that there would be very little local participation. Orisha practitioners and devotees are largely drawn from the working class and are not accustomed to attending events at one of the country's most prestigious hotels. Moreover, the TT$500 registration fee was felt to be excessive; most practitioners would find it a hardship to pay that fee. In addition, many of them live out of the city and would either have to find accommodation with friends and relatives or alternatively travel back and forth each day, incurring more expenses. Lunch was available at the hotel's high-priced restaurant but most participants ate at a local restaurant across the street from the hotel. Although its rates are moderate, having lunch there for a week also added to the cost of attending the event. The congress proceedings were also available for an additional TT$100, not included in the registration fees. As well as precluding local participation, the high cost of the congress also led to apprehension among some locals about how the money was being spent. A few people voiced concern that money might be mismanaged. Some of the volunteers who were supposed to contact shrines and provide information apparently failed to do so, which also contributed to the lack of local participation.

It should be noted at this point, however, that the rental of conference facilities at the hotel, the costs of printing the proceedings and other administrative costs incurred, even though much of the work was done on a voluntary basis, would be fairly high, necessitating a substantial registration fee. On the other hand, this was a catch-22 situation, in that the high fees discouraged attendance, which in turn reduced revenue. In the final analysis, about two hundred persons attended the congress, most of whom came from abroad. There was insufficient attendance to meet budgetary requirements and a debt was incurred.

The main highlight of this congress was to have been the attendance of the Ooni of Ife, Oba Okunade Sijuwake Olubuse II. Up until the first day of the congress, 15 August, his presence was expected. Formal arrangements to meet him at the airport, including representatives from government and other officials, were in place. By the next morning, however, word was received from London that pressures of state in his own country would keep him from attending the congress. While his absence generated concern on the part of the organizers, who felt that attendance and interest in the congress would diminish as a result, the majority of participants did not appear to be unduly affected by his cancellation. He was represented by Chief Omotoso Eluyemi, the Apena of Ife of Nigeria.

The congress programme was quite varied. Morning and afternoon sessions were on a wide range of topics, including Orisha practices in Nigeria, Brazil, Cuba, Haiti and the United States. A theatre arts professor from a Chicago university brought a production of a play about the Orisha performed in African-American dialect; drumming recitals and a few other cultural events were also part of the programme. The congress organizers had also arranged for a marketplace at the cruise complex, across the street from the hotel, where vendors sold a variety of products, clothes, jewelry, books and food from booths. Several government ministries provided help so that the cruise complex could be used for this purpose. In addition, a local art organization was contracted to put together an art exhibition featuring paintings and sculptures, especially those with African or Orisha themes. The exhibit was also in the cruise complex.

The congress received a considerable amount of publicity. Articles and photographs were in the newspapers, and local television featured some events. Both the media and the public focused on the opening ceremony that took place in the festival ballroom of the hotel during the first morning of the congress and was widely televised. It was very well attended, as the large ballroom was filled to capacity and people stood ten deep at the doors.

It began at about 9 a.m. with a group of Orisha drummers and singers chanting in the halls, slowly making their way into the ballroom and down the aisles, where they took their seats towards the front of the stage. The prime minister was "drummed" down the aisle to the side table where leading executives of the international steering committee were seated. Iyalorisha (mother) Joan Cyrus (Iyalorisha Ifakorode Oyayemi in full African dress), as the vice president of the Caribbean branch of the steering committee, was also seated there. Moments later the president and his wife were also welcomed to the accompaniment of the drums. The members of government were dressed in Western attire, but many Trinidadians in the audience – which included academics, artists, and many notable persons from the community – were dressed in African garb.

The national anthem was followed by a prayer and invocation delivered by Brother Oludari who, speaking primarily in Yoruba, called for the blessings of the ancestors and invoked Orisha leaders of the past (including Ebenezer Elliott). This was followed by a short speech given by Professor Abimbola, president of the steering committee: "Thanks to the government and people of this island . . . we couldn't have done it without the support of the government of this island." Iyalorisha Joan Cyrus then made a few comments of welcome, followed by a dance performance given by the L'Antoinette Stines Dance Company of Jamaica. Stines is an Orisha priestess in Jamaica, one of the very few in that country, as well as a professional dancer. Her company performed an Orisha-inspired dance that emphasized the strong torso and sharp rhythmic movements with which African dance is associated in the Caribbean. The performance was accompanied by drumming and Orisha chants and was very well received by the audience. The Apena of Ife welcomed the group in the name of the Ooni of Ife, and read greetings from him. The Ooni's message brought blessings to the assemblage and noted how Yoruba is spread throughout the diaspora, in the United States, Haiti, the Caribbean islands and elsewhere. He called it a "common culture in the New World" and noted that the first conference was held in Nigeria in 1981. The next congress would again be held in Ife, "Nigeria that is the source" and he noted that now, because of the extent of globalization, there is particular need to return to that source. An Orisha calypso was then performed by the young daughter of Iyalorisha Joan Cyrus, much to the amusement of the audience. This was followed by the featured event of the morning: an address given by the prime minister.

The prime minister's speech was in the same vein as those he had delivered at Orisha Family Day celebrations and at the various Spiritual Baptist celebrations that he had attended. At the centre of the speech, a promise to bring about some desired change or event is made to the group. The prime minister uses these occasions to announce benefits that his government can bring to an organization. He took the occurrence of the World Congress to reveal that the Orisha Marriage Act had been passed and would soon become law. In a dramatic gesture as he concluded his speech, the prime minister noted that he had been informed that President Robinson had just "this morning signed the bill into law". Thus, this opening ceremony was again

The Role of Syncretism in the Orisha Religion Today

taken as an opportunity to display this government's good will, and its legislative support of the African religion.[14]

The morning ended with a vote of thanks and some more drumming and singing provided by a group called "the culture shop". All told, it was a well-planned formal event, carefully time managed, that showed both the government and the country to excellent advantage. Although there was some local participation in the programme, the Nigerian office holders of the steering committee and other members of their delegation were particularly featured during the ceremony. The African focus of Orisha was strongly emphasized in this ceremony, and most of the audience were of African descent. But the speeches, particularly the one made by the "Indian prime minister", also placed a great deal of emphasis on the local context.

What was totally lacking in these ceremonies was any hint of syncretism. To all intents and purposes, the ceremony as presented was that of a celebration of an event honouring an African religion. Nowhere in the speeches nor in any part of the programme was there mention of Christianity or its influence on Orisha. This was most obviously evident in the invocation, that was largely delivered in Yoruba and contained no element or even suggestion of Christianity. The "African" focus was also emphasized in the Ooni's message, calling for a return to the "source" for the next congress. The opening ceremony set the stage for a series of conference deliberations and papers on an African religion as practised in Africa and in the diaspora. However, the discourse that gathered most attention, in papers and in the many informal discussions held in workshops and hallways among the participants, was that of syncretism and the Christian influence in Orisha.

Congress Discourse: Syncretism and Authenticity in the Orisha Religion

Throughout the first days of the conference the African delegates, wearing full Nigerian dress, dominated the conference. As they walked along the corridors and hallways of the hotel and gathered in front of meeting rooms for brief discussions, often just among themselves, they exuded confidence and pride of ownership. The implicit message communicated in their demeanour and body language was that this was a conference honouring an African tradition and that they were the sponsors and champions of that tradition.

The afternoon following the opening ceremonies was devoted to country-specific reports. The first presenter speaking from the host country was Patricia McCleod, who set the tone for this Afrocentric discourse. The central question posed in her paper challenged the traditional practices of Orisha in Trinidad: "Do we want a Yoruba tradition or a New World Order with African traditional inputs? Do we want to continue in a dual system of Orisha, influenced by everything else?" Her answer to the question posed by the congress theme of strategies for survival clearly reflects her Afrocentric ideology; she argued that Orisha must move back to its traditions and reject syncretic Christianity as well as other influences. The presentation was well received and inspired considerable audience participation.

For the remaining days of the congress, this theme was raised repeatedly. Occasionally it would be touched upon in formal presentations and then it would become the focus of the audience participation. In one session, for example, some of the confusion and contestation surrounding Orisha practices in different areas of the world was noted by the speaker. The first audience participant, in strong clear ringing tones, almost shouted out that "all of this happen because we lose the African practice, all we do is pray, pray, pray . . . is time to stop the prayer, let's do what our ancestors tell us". The theme was taken up by other members of the audience.

On many occasions the discourse surfaced during the many discussions and debates that took place among delegates in informal talk in the reception area and hallways of the hotel. For example, a heated debate took place between several priests from the American Yoruba village of Oyotunji, some African American delegates whose heritage is Haitian and who practise Vodou in the United States, and a few local delegates. It followed a paper presented by Gro Mambo, the leader of the Vodou-centred National African Religion Congress of Philadelphia, who described the disunity and factionalism among "houses" in the United States. She criticized the movement by noting that many priests and priestesses were involved for power, were not initiated properly, and were not sufficiently educated in the religion. She called for a return to African gods for guidance in restoring harmony and unity. Her view was contested by a priest from the American Yoruba village of Oyotunji, who argued that the real reason for the disunity was that too many "houses" followed Christianity instead of the "pure African, the Ife source". He said that it is only by going back to that source and being initiated there that the true practice of the religion could be maintained. The Haitian group, coming out of a syncretized Vodou background similar to the practices of Orisha elsewhere in the Caribbean and South America, maintained that what had developed over the years should not change. Local delegates took positions on either end of this continuum, depending upon their ideological commitment to Afrocentricity. The debate continued for more than an hour and, while the atmosphere remained amicable, it was clear that there were sharply differing views on the issue.

In another session, a Trinidadian delegate was reporting on the development of the Egungun ancestral cult in Trinidad. She showed a video and it was clear that some of the participants were women. Her presentation was challenged by one of the Oyotunji priests, who asked her during discussion if she was aware of the fact that Egungun, according to the Nigerian Ife usage, was celebrated only by men. He further said that her festival could not therefore have any religious significance since it was not done according to traditional Ife rules. Another African American entered the discussion, saying that using women in the Egungun festival serves to empower them and that it is a positive development for women members. He stated that when he and his followers started Egungun in the United States, they were not aware of a prohibition against women. Meanwhile, the original Trinidadian presenter made an attempt to answer the criticism by saying that divination had informed her that it was all right for women to be involved in the Egungun. She said that women started the festival, maintained it and are doing it in Trinidad and should therefore continue its development. While she defended her position, her voice and quiet demeanor communicated the respect that devotees express towards elders and especially priests. Using strong and forceful language, the Oyotunji priest told her that they should meet afterwards so that he could educate her in the traditional practices, and she softly agreed to do so. In this encounter, the Afro-American priest was asserting not only the authenticity of the true African practices as compared to the rather, in their view, makeshift practices taking place elsewhere, but also bringing in a gender issue. It was quite clear from his behaviour that the original Yoruba Orisha religion, at least as he understood it, prohibited the participation of women in secret societies and that they should therefore not be allowed to play such roles.

In another session the theme of purging Christianity from Orisha practice was again raised, and when the formal session ended a vigorous, no-holds-barred debate took place among participants in the hallway. The session had been dominated by African Americans who held to the position that their form of Orisha practice, as learned both at Oyotunji and through their pilgrimages to Nigeria – and one or two had been initiated at Ife – was superior to that of the Caribbean countries where the syncretized form was still practised. Maintaining the Christian elements as was the practice here was just another way of not dealing with slavery and colonialism that had forced Christianity into Orisha worship. By continuing this slave tradition, the religion had become impure, inauthentic and "tainted with oppression", according to a priest from Oyotunji, one of the dominant speakers. Addressing some local devotees, he proclaimed, "You folks just ain't doing it right." He maintained that Orisha as practised in the United States was the only true and authentic form of the worship because Americans had learned it directly from the ancestral source in Ife without the unfortunate, but forced, intervention of Christianity. One of his followers took up the discourse, telling the group that "now is the time to get rid of the oppressor [meaning Christianity], we will help you". The offer of help was repeated several times in this discussion, and it was clear that the Americans thought that they had found the only true expression of the Orisha worship. The same somewhat patronizing offer of help was made in the example described earlier with respect to women in Egungun. The local participants in these discussions, lacking the African experience claimed by the Americans, were usually forced into the role of questioner or listener. When one asked how Christian elements could be removed in shrines that had been accustomed to these rituals for generations, a rather flip "you just do it, man" was the reply. Later that point was developed further, and the Americans admitted that more traditional African teaching would be required before devotees could be enjoined to give up the Christian practices.

The same point emerged again in informal discussion that took place at a reception given by the president of Trinidad and Tobago in honour of the congress delegates. In a small group of four local participants, one very sophisticated Orisha member began the discussion by laughing at those "arrogant Americans". He said, "They come down here and are trying to tell us what to do – just like Americans!" The counter-argument developed here was that the Americans easily sidestep the syncretic Christian influence because they "have no Orisha tradition". They are only modern adherents of the religion that "they picked up recently in trying to empower themselves as Africans in America". Countries such as Trinidad and Tobago and others in the Caribbean and South America have five hundred years of tradition in the Orisha religion that includes Christianity, he said, "You can't just change, get rid of something like Christianity, it's our tradition." Laughing, he continued: "All of those African guys are Christians too, so what's it all about?"

The effect of the American theological dominance in many of these arenas essentially led to two responses. On the one hand, some local practitioners listened carefully and were willing to learn from the Americans because they respected their closer links to the African source. More sophisticated and knowledgeable devotees, however, generally dismissed the American position because it did not reflect the local, historical reality of countries like Trinidad and Tobago, Brazil, Cuba, and others. There is, however, a third group within the Orisha movement whom I have termed the "innovators", who are thoroughly Afrocentric in ideology in that they fully support the Africanization of the religion and would like to eliminate Christian elements but know that this would require considerable time and patience. Some people in this category are going about Africanizing themselves and their immediate followers by slowly introducing more and more African rituals and festivals into their religious practice. Brother Oludari fits into this category as does Patricia McCleod, who has taken the initiative in introducing a rain harvest festival derived from African sources and who herself is a practising Afrocentric Orisha worshipper. Similarly, Valerie Stephenson Lee Chee, who created the Egungun society in Trinidad, which currently has a few practising members, falls into this group. Despite their agreement with the African-American Orisha position on this issue, they felt that the Americans were, as one put it, "out of place . . . they treat us like children".

Conclusion

There actually appears to be an increase in the crossovers between Orisha and Spiritual Baptism. The old term, "Shango Baptist", although decried by some, appears to still have salience.[15] If the process of syncretism is understood as coming about as a result of developmental evolution rather than as a mask designed to hide the Orisha religion during the period of colonization when it was outlawed, then it is not necessarily a pejorative term but merely describes the flexible nature of the religion. It also relates to the intense religiosity of Trinidadians. The viability of the syncretisms is evident in that they have gained strength over the years, with more and more crossovers between Orisha and Baptists appearing at many more shrines. There are also some interesting parallels between the two religions. For example, both use colours to signify deities and spirits. Astral "travelling" is common to both and some Orisha also "put people on the ground". This ritual, known as "mournin", is designed to bring an initiate closer to the spiritual world. Certain vessels, the use of the Shepherd's Rod and other symbols are sometimes shared. Many of these parallels can be traced back to original African sources.

Now I know Shango is mi culture,
Yoruba is mi tongue
Mi gods, mi Orisha, Ogun and Osain
Mi calabash, mi obi, mi candle
and mi oil
That is what they give me and say:
Son, go back and toil
— *Lord Nelson, "Alado Yeh"*

CHAPTER SEVEN

African Religions and Popular Culture
Calypsos, Steelband and Carnival

THE INFLUENCE OF AFRICAN religions on the popular culture of Trinidad and Tobago has been poorly researched. It is only in relatively recent times that some attention has been paid to this intriguing subject. In light of this paucity, this chapter will attempt to demonstrate that the African religions have always been represented, even if negatively, in the popular culture of this society. The term "popular culture", as used here, refers to the world of music, especially calypso and the steelband, and to the various arts that are reflected in the annual Carnival celebrations.

The Influence of African Religion on Calypso

Calypsos in Trinidad and Tobago have traditionally commented, negatively or positively, on all aspects of life.[1] Originally, calypsonians were restricted to live performances that allowed them to enhance their lyrics with dramatic devices such as costumes, facial expressions and actions. While recordings have permitted them to reach wider audiences, the dramatic tradition continues and facilitates the use of symbols in live performances.

The African tradition of rhythmic percussive music centred on the skin drum, call-and-response singing, and the use of the voice as an instrument (*doption*) are features common to the worship and rituals of both Orisha and Spiritual Baptist faiths. Likewise, movement and dancing (jumping and shaking, for example) is part of worship in the Orisha and Spiritual Baptist religions. The significance of music, in particular the drum, and of movement cannot be overstated in the practice of the African religions.

This aspect of Orisha worship was highlighted in the Senate debate on the Joint Select Committee Report on Public Holidays by temporary senator Edmund Mejias, who noted:

> The worship of Orisha consist [*sic*] of prayers, it consists of invocations. One thing that is important is the principal feature of our worship; that our prayers and invocations are mainly sung rather than spoken. No preaching is involved in our temples and our shrines because dance is our major expression of the will and the soul of all the worship. The musical accompaniment is not incidental; it is not taken as pleasure. It is integral to the act of worship because the worship of the Orishas largely depends on drums.[2]

Music and dance link the Orisha and Baptist faiths to the calypso and the Carnival in which it evolved. The origins of the calypso have been traced back to the folk songs of enslaved Africans, whose secular music was similar to their religious music except in its lyrical content. Often these songs, sung in the call-and-response pattern to the accompaniment of drums and other percussive instruments, provided the background for the performance of particular dances such as the *jhouba* and the *kalinda*. The connection between the calypso and the religions of the slaves and their descendants is, therefore, as old as the art form itself. Raymond Quevedo points out that some *kalinda* songs that were incorporated without modification into early calypsos shared the same tempo and rhythm as Orisha religious chants. He cites the following chant that was partially incorporated into a calypso in the 1960s:

> Ja Ja Romey Eh
> Ja Ja Romey Shango

Ja Ja Romey Eh Mete Beni
Ja Ja Romey Shango[3]

The common root in African traditional music constitutes an integral part of the creolized African heritage of Trinidad and Tobago. The appeal of this music was never lost to the Creole sensibility. However, colonial policy and practice resulted in ambivalence and contradictory postures towards things African. This was evident among all sections of the Creole population, including the predominantly African-descended calypsonians.

The Early Period: 1930–1940

In his seminal work on calypso, Gordon Rohlehr says that both religions provided useful themes for entertainment. He notes that several well-known calypsos with an Orisha theme were made in the 1930s[4] and the images presented by these calypsos were generally not favourable. They tended to treat Orisha activities as spectacles, and were usually graphically descriptive. Orisha was presented as a fearful, powerful activity as in, for example, Cobra's "Shango Song" (1937), where the venue is Laventille. The narrator claims to be an Orisha devotee and he recounts his possession experience:

> Now am going to tell you just what I see
> The night I had the Shango jumbie
> I saw a man sitting on a bed
> With lighted candles upon his head
> The man was like a grizzly bear
> And Jack Spaniels [wasps] all in his hair
> And the Oken [Ogun] kneeling down at his feet
> Drinking the goat blood and eating the meat
> Oh that night was a terrible sight
> The spectators was in a fright
> When I catch the thing I was in the ring
> To get me out was an awful thing
> When I look around upon the ground
> I thought a pig had ploughed up the ground
> I got a cut, I lose my shirt

> I even tear down a young lady's skirt
> Oh, but the child sympathise with me
> I promise to pay her and she agree
> So never again will I hang around
> When the Shango and the Oken [sic] beating they drum.

The calypsonian is not openly negative, but his portrayal is simplistic and evokes erroneous images of uncontrollable behaviours. Images such as Jack Spaniels in the hair and the drinking of blood communicate a negative image to the audience. The notion that this religion is frighteningly powerful is strongly communicated.

Lord Beginner's "I didn't know she was dancing Shango" (1937) also focuses on the ritual and describes the materials used in the ritual:

> A girl with an old broom who made a dash
> and hit Madam Debay with the calabash
> Then the fowl and Coo Coo pass with song
> The rum and the mauby that was so strong
> Agre, Agre, Agra, Agra, was the cry
> Ogre, Ogre, Agra was the reply
> Is then I came to know
> You were the Queen of the Shango
> Gal it gave me a blow.

Later in the song, the calypsonian describes a man coming out of the kitchen with a twisted mouth and pulling his hair out and "taking his head and digging the ground". The song mocks the rhythmic movements made by devotees in possession and even their facial features. The singer is shocked to find out that his girlfriend is a member of the religion that he mocks with his lyrics.

In 1938 Caresser sang about the usual ritual features of the ceremony but his opening words contain a negative tone, especially towards his own black people, whom he castigates:

> I don't know why some black people so
> Indulge in nothing but evil
> Plunging themselves below the level
> Boasting they could invoke the devil.

Thus, black people who are Orisha devotees are evil and their faith is really about calling the devil. Nothing about the true nature of the religion or its resistance during the periods of slavery and colonialism is discussed. Even the facts about the worship, like the others already cited, are wrong, demonstrating how ignorant the singers and the general population were about these religions. Not only does Caresser show ignorance but the song also portrays ridicule and even contempt:

> When the spirits started to manifest
> I laugh til I felt a lump in my chest
> I never saw a greedy woman like that
> She eat over ten pounds of flour flat.

Gordon Rohlehr notes that of all the calypsonians in this period, only The Growling Tiger, in a song called "What is the Shouter and Shango", has something positive to say about Orisha because he accurately and fairly sensitively describes the power of the drums:

> Anywhere you breathe in the atmosphere
> You bound to hear a Shango drum beating far and near
> A body of voices singing so loud
> As though they want to pierce a hole in the cloud.

Despite such a strong image of the music, the song goes on to describe the behaviour of people under possession, as doing ludicrous things that are hardly likely.

Activities, such as worship and the actual ceremonies, were often located far away and the narrators distanced themselves from the events they were describing, demonstrating their unfamiliarity with responses ranging from terror and panic to contempt. Invidious comparisons between the Orisha and the established religions of the colonial masters pervaded the calypsos, and open support for repression and police brutality was expressed. Rohlehr's assessment of the calypsonians' position with respect to Orisha and other African-derived religions is that

> if these practices constituted any deeply felt aspect of their lived reality, they generally endeavoured to conceal this fact under a cloak of nervous laughter or even open ridicule. The long process of cultural erosion had taken its toll, breeding ignorance and its twin brother, superficiality.[5]

Of Baptists, Rohlehr observes that in some instances their image was even more negative than that of Orisha worshippers. He points out that generally Shouters were not feared while the Orisha and their powers were, so that ceremonies of the former were presented as comic spectacles and those of the latter were attended by countervailing dread.

The Growling Tiger's "What is Shouter and Shango" begins:

> The Shango, of course, is quite disagreeable
> For the drum is miserable
> But the KooKoo and goat and the nice white rice
> I man the rum and coffee is nice
> But the Shouters is a husband children and wife
> And they living miserable a corrupted life
> If this that they call civilization
> It's a disgrace to my native land.

It continues by noting that there is "Roman Catholic, Anglican and Salvation but what is the Shouter band? If it is a religion, do tell me please I am tired with the nonsense: give me an ease."

Tiger compares standard religions with Shouter Baptism and suggests that the latter is not a religion. He also lauds the police, who rout the Baptists dressed in "some long night gown" and even "burst his head with the police butoo". In fact, he has nothing good to say about either religion.

Shouters tended to be treated by the police more as nuisances than as security threats.[6] These perceptions and attitudes inform the calypsos on Shouters in the early years. Shouter ceremonies were presented as strange, incomprehensible "pappy-shows", barely distinguishable from fetes and sprees. Themes such as mercenary leaders, scheming and sexual immorality among members, and very prolonged rituals, all attempts to ridicule the faith, were among those treated in calypsos of the 1930s.

Images of the Orisha and Spiritual Baptist Faiths: 1940–1970

The presentation of the Orisha and Spiritual Baptist faiths in calypsos between 1940 and 1970 indicates that neither calypsonian nor audience was entirely comfortable with these religions as legitimate and acceptable phenomena in the cosmopolitan, multi-religious reality of Trinidad and Tobago. Where these themes were treated, narrators did not represent themselves as devotees to the faiths. Ceremonies and rites were presented as strange, incomprehensible rituals. The tendency was still to treat them as spectacle and to ridicule them.

Some of the typical attitudes of the earlier period are expressed in Young Killer's "Baptist Funeral", written in the 1950s. The setting of the calypso is in the back of Sangre Grande, behind the backs of the authorities. The aura of secrecy that surrounds the rite suggests that it is prohibited. Some fun is poked at its top-heavy hierarchy: "So many leaders and teachers. It even had some brothers and sisters?" The narrator's imagery suggests confusion and disorientation. He is dazed by colours. It is a colourful Carnival masquerade that is somewhat "bazoodee", meaning extremely confused, because of the lighting and movements of the ritual.

His assessment of the faith is that one should be wary. He claims that he was happy to be joining a family but, ironically, is rejected by people who themselves cannot be trusted:

> They still bawlin?: Move! Move! Move! Killer Move!
> Well we have some provers here to prove.
> Imagine I feeling shame, the way they watchin' me.
> They have a sick woman in they back,
> You know they plannin' to bury she.

In this stanza the narrator appears to have deliberately misrepresented the Baptist rite of mourning. Having conveyed the impression that the rite is suspect, his subsequent jumping when the leader begins to ring the bell may be interpreted as an involuntary action. This suggests an unnatural (possibly occult) power in the rite that the narrator does not appear to take seriously. Rather, he uses it to highlight the ridiculous nature of the entire event. What is significant, however, is that, although his actions parallel their own, this does not serve to bridge the gap between himself and the rest of the congregation for he continues to be repulsed by the refrain: "Move! Move! Move! Killer move!"

Even as late as the end of the 1960s the Orisha religion was also given the same frivolous treatment in calypso. In Duke's 1969 calypso, "Shango", a female devotee invites the narrator to a ceremony. The ritual is referred to as "a Shango dance" and he is invited because she knows him to be "a Shango fan". Both devotee and narrator thus perceive the ceremony strictly as entertainment. The lyrics focus on the unusual events that take place at the ceremony:

> At twelve o'clock, they bathe a goat
> With two white cock, then they cut the throat.
> Brother Flood was the ringleader.
> The man drinking blood just like a vampire.

Duke also treats the Orisha faith as obeah. In his calypso, "Shango Jumbie", a woman faced with an errant husband seeks the assistance of an obeah man, who assists her in keeping the husband home against his will. The very casual identification of the obeah man with the Orisha worshipper is made in the second stanza:

> A neighbour say that she tie him
> With a Shango spirit name
> For every time he try to move and the spirit disapprove
> He does drop a whip on he back.

Here the Orisha is malevolent and an accessory to a woman's selfish cause. This is similar to Melda in Sparrow's "Obeah Wedding" of the same period. In this calypso Melda attempts to effect a marriage between herself and the narrator through the mediation of an obeah man. He is confident, however, that she will not succeed because "Papa Neeza is mi grandfather", a reference to the highly reputed Orisha leader Ebenezer Elliott. Sparrow's boast might be interpreted as another example of the identification of the Orisha with obeah. Read from another perspective, it asserts the power of the Orisha against witchcraft. The greyness of ambivalence, however, had not been dispelled in this period.

The Orisha faith as a source of supernatural power, whether good or evil, had been recognized in the earliest calypso recordings. Whether these powers were deserving of public reverence and respect by the calypsonians and the rest of the society, including devotees, was an entirely different matter. Sparrow's 1967 "Shango Man" provides an example of this duality. This calypso is narrated in the first person by a man who goes to an Orisha ceremony as a scoffer and is overcome by the power and begins to dance. The power is acknowledged but there is no pretence at reverence. In fact, the calypso continues the tradition of treating Orisha ceremonies as spectacle, and the narrator cleverly uses the amazing events of the occasion as a background for his own spectacular behaviour:

> Rolling on the ground, people dancing round.
> Then they lift me up, spin me like a top.
> Well they cut off the goat head in the mud.
> Lord! Mi belly boil!
> Then they make me drink up the goat blood,
> Mix with olive oil, singing:
> Ojo Romey O! If you see me dance the Shango!
> I want to hear the rhythm roll deep down in mi soul.

Apparently, the devotees are not offended that the narrator has emerged as the star of the show, which is what, in this calypso, the ceremony has certainly been reduced to – free-for-all entertainment, emptied of all sacredness: "Well everybody tell me I was great / They say I am a boss," he boasts.

Notwithstanding their irreverence, even mockery, some musical aspects of the calypsos of this era indicate that their composers had recognized the music of the Orisha and Baptists as a source of creative inspiration. Both of Duke's calypsos referred to above are introduced with drumming. Sparrow's is also introduced by drumming and goes further, with the partial use of an old Orisha chant in his chorus. There is little doubt as to the commercial viability of this recognition, in the light of the appeal of traditional African music to the Creole population. In fact, Rohlehr has pointed out that in the 1930s, Shouter hymns and chants rivalled calypsos commercially and that there appeared to be an unconscious merging of the two forms.

This process had been underway since that time and had achieved almost full expression in Small Island Pride's "Goin' Down Jordan" in the 1950s. Here a full range of musical devices – rhythm, doption, chanting and choruses – drawn from the Shouter tradition are used to great effect. This calypso also represents a significant departure in the attitude of the calypsonian vis-à-vis the Shouter faith. In this regard, it is one of the earliest expressions of positive identification with the faith. The calypso is the simple narration of an Anglican's conversion to the Baptist religion. The setting for the calypso is a meeting on upper Frederick Street. There is no vivid imagery or graphic description of possession or other aspects of the meeting; no attempt to present the faith as ridiculous spectacle. Unlike the protagonist in Young Killer's calypso referred to earlier, the narrator is converted and receives immediate acceptance from members of the religion. He elaborates on the spiritual and material benefits of conversion:

> Well before I baptize I had plenty pain.
> Now I catch myself, a fresh man again.
> Don't talk about the leaders, they treat me good:
> Plenty sweet oil and plenty food.

Apart from the single stereotypical reference to Baptist membership as a source of food, this calypso presents a complete reversal of the image of the Baptists. The street meeting takes place on the main street of the capital of Trinidad and Tobago, not in a remote retreat. The narrator begins almost apologetically: "Well, I were livin' very nice as an Anglican / Now ah tun tail to the Baptist religion." However, by the end of the calypso he completely rejects the established, respectable religion in favour of the despised, derided faith and recommends that "every man on this earth should be baptize". It is also especially noteworthy that the catalyst for his conversion is not the preaching but the music.

This calypso stands apart in the period before 1970. Its open embrace of an aspect of African culture that had long been spurned, legally and socially, quite possibly reflected the confidence and personal belief of the individual calypsonian far more than any significant change in the social status of the religion. The Shouter Prohibition Ordinance was repealed on 30 March 1951, thus liberating the religion from legal proscriptions. However, up to the 1960s, parents were still allowing their children to adopt the established Christian religions as a prerequisite for attendance at denominational schools.

Post-1970 Images of the Orisha and Spiritual Baptists in Calypso

Since 1970 more positive images of the Orisha and Baptist faiths have been presented in calypsos. This was marked by open identification of calypsonians with these religions, the increasing use of musical techniques and symbols (in particular, costumes) associated with them, and a corresponding decrease in the graphically descriptive calypsos that ridiculed and denigrated the Orisha and Baptist faiths.

The overt proclamation of religious identification came mainly from calypsonians who were themselves devotees or had been initiated into the faiths. The use of symbols and musical techniques by others was both the product of musicians' creative experiments and the recognition of the commercial value of indigenous musical forms. It is worth noting, in this regard, that this recognition was not confined to African traditional music but also included musical traditions drawn from the Indian community in Trinidad and Tobago and other traditions of the New World. Both trends were, however, part of a wider movement that involved the exploration of ancestral and national identities.

The nationalist contest for political power in Trinidad and Tobago had been won by the PNM, which formed the first government of the independent state from 1962. The backbone of the PNM was the urban-based Creole population, composed of large numbers of Africans who were the culture-bearers of the creolized African traditions, the main component forms of which were the calypso, the steelband and the Carnival. The rural-based and Hindu-dominated Democratic Labour Party was arrayed against the PNM. From 1956, when the PNM assumed political office, it sought to legitimize the popular culture of the Creole masses as national culture. Essentially, this project consisted of promoting Creole cultural forms at the expense of the state, while virtually ignoring those associated with the Hindu population.

The year 1970 was characterized by political unrest in Trinidad and Tobago. Disaffection was manifested within a number of sectors, including the army, the labour movement, the University of the West Indies and, significantly, the urban, predominantly African, dispossessed masses. Often referred to as the Black Power movement, it clearly articulated the failure of the new national government to meet the expectations of the African masses, and emphasized that continued social and economic hardships had historically coincided with race. The assertion of African identity was the natural cultural counterpart of the political struggle.

The cultural protest of 1970 underscored the historical reality that, since emancipation, Creole cultural forms had been subjected to a series of purges to eliminate the more obvious and offensive African elements. The national adoption of the African-derived cultural practices of the working classes was thus made possible through their cleansing by the respectable Creole classes.

The Orisha and Shouter Baptist faiths were not accorded the same status as the secular culture of which they were an integral part, perhaps because they could not be subjected to purging of their African essence.

However, one of the effects of the 1970 discourse was a new, or more confident, identification with the African self, that became increasingly evident in the more positive explorations of the Orisha and Baptist faiths, spiritually and musically, in calypsos. Individual calypsonians began to make their presence felt through personal testimonies and, in so doing, they combined the two major trends – musical and spiritual proclamation – that would establish the presence of the Orisha and Spiritual Baptist in the heart of Creole culture.

The two trends merged in the recordings of Calypso Rose in the 1970s. Rose, in fact, might be regarded as the standard bearer of the Baptist faith in this period. Prior to 1977 Rose's image as a calypsonian suggested that she was a member of the Baptist faith. This, however, might have been simply a matter of unconscious personal style. After Rose won the Road March title in that year she recorded "I Thank Thee", and there was very little question subsequently about the religious ground on which she stood. The calypso is a personalized outpouring of gratitude to all who had contributed to her success, among them: "The Baptist religion that gave me so much wisdom / Glory be! I thank thee!"

The expression of personal sentiments and her own spiritual convictions pervades Rose's calypsos in this era. On the same album, she records "Warrior". Here there is no explicit reference to the Shouter faith, but certain imagery and metaphors clearly point in that direction. The theme of the song is the victory of a much harassed and maligned woman. She refers to those who want to kill her because they envy her talent, others who want her to retire, and yet others who accuse her of being "dread" and "weird". Her response to all is a defiant boast:

> I am on the battlefield and I have me shield.
> Me soul they want to devour!
> But tell them me name Warrior! Warrior!

The real-life conflict is given a spiritual dimension. She is waging spiritual warfare with the shield of faith and the special Shouter's spiritual gifts of "travelling" – "I am a traveller. I could see every corner" – and "seeing" –

"Po' thing, they don't know that I could see them before they see me." Then Rose establishes the connection between the Shouter faith and Africa, between the spiritual and the natural:

> Some say I'm weird. They callin' me dread.
> But I think they goin' out they head.
> Because they don't know I come from the Congo.
> I'm a warrior from me head to me toe.

This calypso moves beyond referring to the Shouters as other. The pre-existing gulf between the calypsonian and the Shouter has been bridged, and there is complete reconciliation of the two personas. This serves to increase the credibility of the faith as a valid spiritual force, because the testimony is coming from a calypsonian who has been tried and proven in the world of calypso. Rose, a Tobagonian in a Trinidad-based art form and a woman in a male-dominated arena, has reached the pinnacle of success. In 1978 Rose again won the Road March title and became the first and only female, to date, to win the Calypso Monarch crown.

The old Shouter themes became issues of the past. Shouter beliefs and experiences were presented with reverence and a sense of awe, as the religion was openly proclaimed. In Rose's 1982 "Lyvere Oshun Tabukoo", she describes the mystical Shouter experience of "travelling". The narrator is disturbed by odd physical sensations, and finds herself transported to a strange land where she is made to wait "patiently as a lamb" beside a river. These references – "the lamb, the river [possibly Jordan]", and "the new born king" and the "new land" in the next stanza – are biblical images and symbols. The journey continues until revelation occurs:

> I started travelling further.
> I really thought it was a dream.
> I saw past, present and future.
> So much mysteries I have seen.
> As I look across the ocean, I saw the great I AM.

An identical trend was being established among calypsonians who were dealing with the Orisha faith. Nelson's "Alado Yeh" is very similar to Rose's "Lyvere Oshun Tabukoo". It is a spiritual journey narrated by someone who is professing the faith. Here, too, the narrator is transported to a new and strange land and experiences some alienation and confusion. These emotions are not the same as those conveyed in earlier calypsos. There is no scepticism; rather there is a sense of awe: "Watching what they doing, trying to understand / It was so amazing since I came from another land." By the third stanza the confusion is dispelled and the narrator comes away with new knowledge:

> Now I know Shango is mi culture, Yoruba is mi tongue,
> Mi gods, mi Orisha, Ogun and Osain.
> Mi calabash, mi obi, mi candle and mi oil.
> That is what they give me and say: Son go back and toil.

Again, there is the link between the spiritual and the natural, between Africa represented in the Yoruba tongue and Shango. In this regard, the calypso speaks of wholeness. It affirms the African spiritual tradition as a regenerative force for the lost child of Africa. The narrator is now possessed of confidence and strength. He is aware that he must continue to live among scoffers, but he is also fully persuaded of his ability to overcome:

> You may laugh and shun me and treat me with scorn.
> I know who go help me since I was reborn.
> So when you hear me chanting and knocking mi drum,
> All who stand there mocking, wait till mi power come.

One wonders whether it is simply the demands of rhyme in the last verse that prevent the full manifestation of the narrator's power.

Today the influence of the religions, when it is commented upon, is generally favourable and positive. The religious groups themselves are quick to protest any lyrics that they consider offensive to them. The unwillingness of the Spiritual Baptists to tolerate any further mockery of their faith was demonstrated by their response to a calypso sung in 1984. Blue Boy's "Soca Baptist" was met with well-publicized protests by religious leaders. The calypsonian makes reference to the music at a Baptist meeting that, to his ears, sounded like soca music. Baptists claimed that he was desecrating their religion. Even the then prime minister, Dr Eric Williams, entered the foray, saying, "Let good sense prevail", when asked by Baptists to ban the calypso from the airwaves.[7]

But Blue Boy was, in fact, at the forefront of a trend that was to become well established by the end of the decade, and the influence of Baptist music on soca is still evident today. Super Blue gained the Road March in 1991 with a song called "Get Something and Wave", in which he consults with a bell-ringing Spiritual Baptist mother about the status of the nation. Gordon Rohlehr notes that some singers today have internalized the "Shango/Baptist" beats, chants and structures: "The way Super Blue uses his voice, the chants, his overall style are a very genuine manifestation of Baptist music . . . and it always permeates Rudder's music." Andre Tanker's music, including the popular "Sayamanda" and "River Come Down", also shows the influence of Baptist rhythms.

References to both religions can be found, but it is perhaps in the music even more than in the occasional lyric that the spirit of the African religions is lauded. As David Rudder sang in 1987, in a song called "Engine Room":

> So I want a hard rhythm section
> So I could groove up this nation.
> We gonna let them know
> They couda never stop the drum
> When people fellin' the doption
> And they show their reaction
> Something in the rhythm
> Does tell them whey they comin from.

And as journalist Debbie Jacob concludes:

> Today, the Orisha/Baptist connection to music is seen as a powerful force. Neither the religions nor the music which emanates from them, are something to be shunned or mocked. Instead, they're viewed as noble faiths and powerful songs, arising from the soul. A struggling nation, in search of its lost soul, welcomes and respects both.[8]

Today both the Orisha and Spiritual Baptist religions have gained social legitimacy, and negative or pejorative commentaries in calypsos are not tolerated. Negative constructions are hardly found in contemporary songs. Moreover, many popular calypsonians today are Orisha devotees or supporters, and their lyrics show praise rather than scorn for African religions. The following case studies provide some examples.

Case Studies

Ella Andall

Ella Andall is a popular singer.[9] She performs annually at the calypso tents and at major musical functions throughout the year. She also performs abroad, and will soon go to England to perform in a Trinidad-based musical. She is a woman in her early fifties with a striking face set off by deep-set, large black eyes. In appearance Ms Andall looks African, and she enhances that effect by wearing African-designed clothes topped off by her trademark – a tall, multi-draped head tie – usually in a fabric that matches her dress. She appears to earn enough to live fairly comfortably.

She maintains that she has had a difficult time breaking into the calypso season because many calypsonians do not think she sings true calypsos. In the interview quoted below she challenges that view, maintaining that Orisha songs and rhythms form the basis of the "kaiso" or calypso song. Ms Andall performs Orisha songs even in the calypso tent. Her performance is always African-based. In addition to the ways in which she uses her identity and ideology in performance, Ms Andall has a remarkably beautiful, full-bodied mezzo-soprano voice. Her voice is untrained, but the listener would not know that because of her splendid delivery and stage persona. She does not read music although she composes it by playing on the drum and singing into a tape recorder. Ms Andall is a striking example of a popular artist whose life, creativity and work all derive from her faith and belief in the Orisha religion.

Interview with Ella Andall

EA: I was born in it, in Orisha. I never saw it as where I begin, it was always there, it was always around, the drums, the songs, the ceremonies. I was born in a small village in Grenada, so my aunt and my family we were all of it in that.

I know of it as a child. I knew, you see it wasn't something that I think that I learnt, it was the way, it was how it is, that we cleared spot, that we sweep and we prepare the ground and I see my aunt and they do that and to me that's normal.

Then I came to Trinidad I found that you know that you had to hide. In Grenada I didn't see it as hide, I was very young at that time so I was like a great feast happening, a wonderful time in my life with these things happening, we go by the sea, with all the drumming and the dancing and it was all excitement and all of that, we prayed the same way, you know we go to prayers and things like that.

When I came to Trinidad . . . well it's not like picking it up. It's still there even if there wasn't the shrine, I would get up in the morning and [points to a little shrine in bedroom] that's my little shrine right there, and there's Eshu and Ogun and Osain and Shango inside, so I pray that way so this is me, so it's not like picking it up, it never left me . . . the Christianity came in and the people tried to show me they way it supposed to be and what was heathen and what is all that, but I know where I draw my strength, when I finish pray in the morning and I sing my prayers I am good for the whole day, that's what I know, so I always hold steadfast to that.

Orisha is a philosophy of life, to me it's how one lives, you see I would always go for a day in a sense of the Orisha, like clear up the path way, so I know being a child of Ogun that I am never afraid to cross whichever paths because that is the energy that I would pull up and that Shango is there and Shango is a strategy for justice, and the iron and steel a symbol of never-ending justice. That's how I look at it . . . so is what I live by . . . this is the Orisha, and I go deeper than that to what that Orisha stands for, the energy that the Orisha is.

So for a lot of people that I have talked to, particularly younger people, they say they are in it because it's African and it gives them an identity, a sense . . . .

Of course that's a given. But it's deeper than that for me. You know, deeper than that.

[On songs]

I knew the melody from . . . from a child so I would be able to go a sister and say listen to this melody that I'm hearing, and she would say this is a old one, look I can't even remember all the words and then some of the words broke in, some of the words . . . because we have been really lucky to have so many different parts of Africa in this Trinidad, so you will get people mixed with those from Nairobi and from Nigeria. The medium I used to reach people is my voice so I learn the song fast and I sing the songs and then I would pull up some old melodies and then she will tell me well the words for that melody is that and that and that . . . but I sing it in my . . . I make it my music because it is my music and I love it, I love the melodies, I like the energy in which . . . and I like the language, I like the language and I did the *Ebo* . . . to give thanks for all the things . . . for the energy that manifest in me, I want to do Shango and I want to do all of it, I want to bring it where people in Trinidad are not afraid of it because there is still a lot of people that they are afraid of it, and it gives me a particular kind of spiritual strength, but you know . . . so I want to give it to other people and I think I have done it . . . . Even not in the big way that I would like to have done it but I've done it. Because children and people call up and I get some response and reaction from people in a very positive way, so I want to take away the fear of the Shango that people in Trinidad still have. They call it obeah and you know the terrible things that everyone talks, you know, and because of the voice people accept it, so I am going to work a little, to help them do the work a little better to get the language to the people.

Because people call me and ask me what it means and I will tell them what it mean, so that I did not have my brother who . . . from the University to translate all of it and I run out of funds because I did this project [referring to a CD of Ogun songs] on my own with the help of a friend and all the young people from Creative Arts Centre and then you use people who want it done. Yea, so people call me to ask me what does this one mean, and I said that the meaning is that is a song of praise or is a vocation song or is a song of entertainment and they understand and I tell them what it means.

FH: Do you consider yourself a calypsonian? I mean you perform in calypso tents, but from what I heard you sing Orisha songs.

EA: Watch nah, Orisha songs is the base of . . . is calypso, calypsonians who said about me that I am not a calypsonian, no problem, they could say whatever they want to say, but I am coming from inside of the belly of calypso, so I am that, but they don't call me that, a calypsonian will never tell you that, they will tell you that I sing African songs, because Africa is hard for people to identify with, to a great degree in Trinidad still you would not say Africa you prefer to say black, because Africa represent I believe pain to some people, when the whole term with the black and the ugly and the drum not good and everything that was black was not good, so then why do you want to identify with this Africanness that I am bring in their face, but the children love it, children love it, so I'm confident with it, and those who don't know where calypso come from I kind of feel kind of sad because when you know your root there is nothing that you cannot do. And I know that, and I know it too because I would talk to some, some of them who know it the Orisha timing with the three drums you get all the different instrumentations from those three drums and if I telling them to come to their face to this earth . . . but what I'm doing is opening new doors that was locked that has been established . . . if I'm making any sense with this theory. So that I'm doing like say let's trace, let's retrace our footsteps to the thing and through the years, this year, last year they had about five, this year we have a little bit more, where people talking about their roots, talking about the Orishas and carrying it into calypso, so I have done my work. So it has taken root, so now people say a song, a guy called Johnny King, John King he sang a calypso and he talking about the pan in relation to the drum from the Orisha yard. Yea, so it is taking root, and I happy I really happy about that.

Well I got a lot of flack when I started, I got a lot of flack . . . I got a lot of flack from some of the elders as well, and say but they still afraid and still feel after they pass the law that they still have to hide it, you know.

It has been accepted and blessed by them . . . And people doing it now and doing it with respect, you know, not just to become popular, they would call me and I would call Sister [her spiritual mother] and ask if it okay for it to be done in that way and she would give her advice on it and so we have now, I hope one day we would see like we have the Chutney festival [an Indian song festival] in Trinidad that we would have an African song festival, you know and people not be so afraid that you is a Shango and I am a Christian and we see ourselves as people of the world and expressing our beliefs. That would be a splendid idea. We believe in God in different ways.

FH: Your musical energy, your source of inspiration comes from the Orisha.

EA: Yes, yes, sort of unconsciously almost. And let me tell you what happen to me a lot of times, well I would get a song, I would do a song and I would get the chant and when I call Funso [a Yoruba-speaking professor at the university] to translate the song it would fit exactly, I would not have to change. I don't like to look for a chant, the chant would come and I would try sometime to remove it and say well I don't know what this one means, and then when I call Sister, and I speak to the elders and I call Funso, it is exactly fitting, exactly.

FH: How do you explain that?

EA: I don't. Orishas I think, I think ancestors I think I'm naturally a throw back from the ancestors, believe me. If you ask me to pray I would pray Ay, Wawry [she chants in Yoruba] . . . in Yoruba, that is what I know and I would say that things I want to say to the Almighty, to the Universe, to the biggest source there is in English if I can, but the prayers I was taught is where I would meet God. So if you say De Wra . . . and I saying Ay Wrawra, you should not be offended by that, because you should be thankful that through the years the ancestors kept it still, that's the important thing. Like through all that brutality, that somehow they managed to keep it for us and I give thanks to them all the time.

David Rudder

David Rudder, called "King David" by his many admirers, is a three-time Calypso Monarch, and one of the most popular soca calypsonians of modern times.[10] His popularity today might only have been equalled by the Mighty Sparrow in earlier times, but some would argue that Rudder is the greater performer. His songs often carry important social, political and economic messages. Globalization and transnationalism are among his favourite themes. He is not a devotee of Orisha, but is a very firm supporter of this religion and attended the Lopinot Family Day celebration in March 2000, where he entertained the group. There are many elements of Orisha in his songs: sometimes the use of African chants, references to the religion in favourable terms and complete songs in which Orisha provides the framework. One such is "Shango Electric", in which he sings:

> Elegba, ocumba, bay way, ashe ashe, eh baba ashe baba . . .
> Shango said to Legba, I am sad. What people do, they make me mad.
> They break the face of Africa . . . Legba, come send me through their cable . . .
> to their AM and FM bands Legba say look I've cleared a way for you, to touch them . . . Oh yeh, Shango, oh yeh, oh it's Shango electric baby Elegba to open up the door
> Shango, it's Shango electric baby who tell Legba to open up the door.
> Shango say bring the children, bring your offerings, make the revellers shake and shimmy, woman falling down . . . girls with their sexy figure . . .
> whose the jumbie who that pulled the trigger, lord the vibrations getting bigger . . .
> preacher tumble down . . .

who is the bad john, is he . . . is he is he who he who.
Shango electric baby who tell Legba to open up the door . . . everybody,
Shango said oh why do my children swear they don't even look to their elders today . . . like headless chickens running around . . . they don't even know where they're coming from . . . send me through their cables, through their AM And FM band Legba said look I've made a passage . . . go make them jump up and raise their hand . . .
Eh lebfa ah gunga, Oya, Oya, ow wah a wah.
Send me through their cables, I'll be coming in flaming red but to find a way to wake the children to make them stand tall and make them raise their head . . .[11]

David Rudder says about himself:

Basically all the things you hear in my music right now are the things I experienced as a child. These things manifest themselves now. In Belmont where I grew up I was surrounded by so many different influences, we had steelband yards, two of them, right on the road was a Catholic church and an Anglican church. On the hill just above where I lived, there was a Shango yard, and up the Valley Road, a couple of blocks from me was the Arada yard which was actually the first settlement in Belmont Valley Road, with Papa Nani, so that is how I got locked into these influences, really. When I create, they just tend to manifest, because I go back into where I came from and these things reveal themselves.

FH: In what way?

DR: In ways when sometimes I might mention a name, I might recall Papa Nani, or I might recall a chant that I heard growing up. I might recall a rhythm and sometimes all three of them come together. Sometime, I'm not even aware, till people come and say to me – something happened there when you were performing . . . something happened to me, I don't understand it – while you were singing so and so. So a lot of it is, I wouldn't even say subconscious, I think it's more, it just reveals itself.

FH: Are you a practising Orisha?

DR: No. I do go to festivals whenever I can, but to say that I am practising, no. I live on an aeroplane so it's only when I come into Trinidad and sometimes I go down to Iya Rodney's in Marabella. We are very close. She considers me one of her sons. I go down there sometimes.

FH: Are you initiated?

DR: No, I won't say I'm a hard-core devotee, I would say that I understand its significance in my life. The things I do and I pay respect to that.

FH: What is happening in Orisha today?

DR: It's something that should have been a given. Because of the whole things there is a sort of complex in the society. African people . . . maybe it's because of the history and the slave trade – everything in our culture is a "pappyshow".

In a society where there is a sort of feeling of a second, everyone feels second class. Things which to me are natural are seen as great achievements. And while I'm glad to see these things happening, none should have been passing laws or making it happen in a political way. It should have been natural. Should never have been oppressed.

FH: Is Orisha a way of identifying with the African past?

DR: Yes, it does. There is a strong sense with a link with the past. For example, when I go to Iya Rodney's, somebody will show me a shrine in a corner that was put there by Papa Neezer and it might be a hundred years old. So, seeing something that's so old and is still there. Same feeling I get when I used to go up to the Arada yard with Papa Nani, this is a man who came straight from Africa, and founded this colony so there's . . . even though it's shut down now, you go into Antoine Lane and you get a strong sense of something that is really beyond comprehension.[12]

FH: But it doesn't bring you back to Africa?

DR: My vibrations start from right here and it just helps me to create some sort of a linkage, a key to how it might have been but that is as far as I go.

FH: What is the future of Orisha?

DR: The last time I was at Iya Rodney's I saw about thirty or forty teenagers with Nikes and Reeboks in the yard, and they are just fashion statements of North America but they are in the yard! So I just smiled. There are so many youths searching for something and some are going back to seek that aspect of their lives. I think it's growing and what is interesting also is that I heard Barbadian accents, and most of all, I heard Jamaican accents and Jamaica has

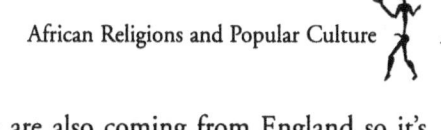

no history of Orisha. Some of them are also coming from England so it's interesting to see that development also. These are people who didn't have that sort of history – like, Cuba, Haiti, Trinidad, Brazil, but I'm seeing people coming from places who know nothing about Orisha and being there is most interesting.

FH: Do you know all the songs, chants?

DR: No, the things I do I just remember from childhood. I don't know, there are a lot of them I don't know. Sometimes I pick up something here and there. There was a programme on "faila ransom" life and the programme opened with a series of chants I never heard before so I incorporated some of that in my music also. There are many things I haven't picked up on yet. So much to learn but I never worry about these things because I feel all in good time.

FH: Is Orisha an inspiration to people?

DR: Oh yes, yes, whenever I perform I see things happening with people, I know that something more than just music is happening here.

FH: Does it reach them through ecstasy, trance?

DR: Yeh, more than music is happening here, something way beyond me. A concert is a strange thing. It can be very sterile, depending if it's a laid-back audience like sitting in a kaiso [calypso] tent. If you have one of those audiences where you have closeness, where it's a community and there is energy, it happens.

Interview with Composer (a Calypsonian)

Composer is a calypsonian who has been singing professionally for a number of years. He is in his fifties and appears to have made a modest living from his entertainment. He does not appear in the major calypso tents anymore, but in 2000 performed in a club that featured old-time calypsonians and their songs.

Composer: Involved in Orisha for a long time. When I was ten, eleven, twelve, playing around there was an Orisha priest who carried on feast, he chose me out of all the little boys romping around and he confided in me.

My father was a wild Indian king, played it in Carnival . . . if you play a character for Carnival you automatically become that character for life.

The customs are similar, songs, to the Orisha. So when I was adopted by this priest, I could relate to him. Eventually I became interested and started following it, but very quietly. I grew up understanding wild Indian culture and the Orisha culture. My mother came from Iacocos, Catholic area but Orisha was around. I began studying the songs, learned them as a little boy, stuck in my head. Melodies, haunting melodies. These are the oldest songs that we have heard . . . they came with slaves and who knows how long these songs were around before then. And the nice thing about those songs is they never get stale, never get tired of singing or hearing them . . . that tells you about the spirituality in those songs. The songs that hail out to the deities, the tone, melodies, structure, you get the feeling that they are calling out, calling (yah weh, yah, weh). I live by the spirit . . . I allow things to shape.

FH: How has Orisha influenced your career?

Composer: The Orisha has a very profound effect on calypso and steelband. Many people do not see the connection but there is a very strong one. If you saw the older bards, the older calypsonians performing, Roaring Lion, Growling Tiger, Dictator, Attila the Hun – the steps that they made on the stage were basic Yoruba Orisha steps. Later, Bomber, Pretender, others, had the same steps on stage . . . [chips and steps]. Sparrow changed the movement to pelvis. Even today, older bards use the same steps as Orisha feasts on stage. The call and response that permeates calypso was taken from the African pattern of singing. The appeal, the melodies, that seem to reach out to the astral, into the stratosphere – these are some of the basic things which drew me and kept me glued to Orisha influence and it influenced my calypsos.

FH: In what ways were you influenced?

Composer: It was in me, I felt and need to express myself as I had belonged to it. I had formed a family singing group that used to go round singing ballads and in our repertoire were one or two chants from the "chantwells" that preceded the calypso. I felt I needed to express myself. I felt I needed to address the imbalance that had gone on between the colonial masters and the slaves and that sort of thing.

FH: Do you compose Orisha lyrics?

Composer: Yes, I stayed away from the exact melodies and the essence of the songs in the Orisha tents . . . I believe that they are sacred items. I am still grappling with the thought of whether it is right to pull them into a commercial setting. I don't know. Maybe the Orishas have designed it that way but I am not qualified to say. There are those of late who have begun to sing the Orisha songs on stage. I don't know if that's right or wrong. I did not tamper with the songs.

But I have used the language with a view of having the language accepted as a form of communication by the sons and daughters of Africa. That was my reason for using some of the words in the following song:

> When anything gets out of control, its best to call the gods of the world.
> The major races in this island are the Africans and the East Indians but them politicians have a plan . . . they say they only want *douglarization* [literally "bastard" in Hindi – the term is applied to a child of mixed African and Indian heritage].
> Our ancestor, Babawao, your children in danger, the gods of our forefathers, eh wah la, the gods of Orisha. Now they gone so far, they want to change the looks of your children from Africa . . . let me explain, there is a purpose for every man, whether evolution or creation, our presence on earth is by god's command. Each one according to distinction and for identification, man cannot unite with man, they want to mix up with douglarization. Baba Orisha. Our ancestor, Eshu, babala, your children in danger, gods of our forefathers, eh wah, eh wah. Now they gone so far, Yemanja, they want to change the looks of your pickninnies from Africa. Assimilation, douglarization, this mixing of race was never god's plan. He put different fish in the ocean, birds in the air, man on land . . . is only mankind mix up in confusion.
> Mama lata, peaceful coexistence is the solution for Indians and Africans, mutual respect and to hell with them politician . . .
> Shango, ba ba wa; iya Orisha, iya Oya.

Composer is a very serious Orisha worshipper who has injected some Orisha lyrics and meanings into his songs. The most obvious is the one quoted above, in which he declares himself against racial mixing and calls on the Orisha to help keep races apart. Aside from the strong socio-political message in that song, the appeal to the Orisha is obvious.

Another notable calypsonian, Sugar Aloes, is also a serious Orisha worshipper and has been seen in Orisha manifestation at several feasts. Unlike Composer, however, he does not inject any element of Orisha into his calypsos, which are mainly biting, satiric political songs.

The Influence of Orisha on Steelband

The relationship between the development of the steelband and the Orisha religion has been part of public understanding for some time. But only recently has this relationship been documented. Stephen Stuempfle in his major work, *The Steelband Movement in Trinidad and Tobago*,[13] notes that there were many "Shango" *palais* as well as Shouter churches in the East Dry River area of Port of Spain, the so-called behind-the-bridge section of the city whose residents were, and still are, poor, working-class people. It is in this area of the city that the steelband is said to have developed. In another book, local scholar Kenrick Thomas traces the development of the steelband in Tacarigua.[14] One of his seminal contributions is to show how the steelband was influenced by the Orisha religion.

The use of drums, especially at night, was banned in the ordinance of the 1950s. This played a role in the search for a new method of percussive expression. It led to the development first of the "bamboo tamboo", or the beating of sticks of bamboo together, that gradually evolved into the steelband. The latter was also, of course, facilitated by the abundance of the steel drums left by the Americans during their presence in Trinidad during World War II. Thomas notes that many of these early drummers were members of the Orisha faith. Thus, many of the early participants in steelbands during and after the war were devotees, who brought the skills and rhythms learned on the Orisha drums to the steelband. One striking experience is recounted by Thomas.

In 1945, a Shango feast was being held at Mother Gerald's palais in Tacarigua and it was attended by Andrew "Run-in" Beddoe, who was already a member of the Destination Tokyo steelband of John-John (in Laventille, a poor, working-class area located on one of the hills surrounding Port of Spain). That band is today known as Carib Tokyo. Beddoe was also a well-known Orisha devotee and famous for his drumming of the African rhythms. His brother, Jeffrey, who was also a member of the religion, accompanied him. Andrew Beddoe died some years ago but Jeffrey (who spells his name "Biddeau") is still an active Orisha priest whose shrine is located in Matura. Another devotee who is described as "a scary looking character known as 'Brassy'" and others attended. "They were all top leaders in the Orisha religion and carried with them an eerie aura." A pan yard featuring the Dead End Kids was next door to Mother Gerald's shrine and "most of those visiting steelbandsmen who were devotees of the Shango religion found themselves at the pan yard during the day time. Andrew Beddoe took one of the rudimentary steelpans and made some convex indentations and began playing Orisha tunes". Thomas notes that this was the first time some of these steelbandsmen had ever heard a melody, and they were Orisha "tunes". Beddoe and other Orisha devotees became regular visitors, injecting a considerable amount of Orisha content into the playing. He also organized the metal or iron section of the band that provided the main source of the rhythm.

Even today, the part of the steelband called "the engine room" provides the rhythmic drive to the music. Using metal percussive instruments in the engine rooms confirms the Orisha god Ogun, who is the god of iron. The relationship, therefore, between metal and Ogun, although largely symbolic, provides another Orisha influence.

In fact, that relationship has been systematically studied by Candace Goucher in a paper called "The Performance of Iron: Stoking the Furnace, Sailing the Seas".[15] She maintains that during the slave period, "the spirit of Ogun was onboard Atlantic voyages" because every ship had to carry a blacksmith who had to maintain the ironwork aboard ship. She notes that the "performative aspects of iron technology and its historical memory on land and on sea" probably combined technological production with human performance of ritual and practice. In a direct linkage to the evolving Carnival in Trinidad, Goucher speculates that there was a close relationship between the steelband with their Orisha drummers and the development of the Fancy Sailor mas.[16] The early sailor bands were known to include bad behaviour and violence, but they also produced some distinctive Yoruba dance movements, performed to drumming, that recall the presence of Ogun. They not only performed the movements of Ogun but also carried iron implements, suggesting his spiritual presence with them. Even after World War II sailor bands "were known for their distinctive dance, which contains elements of the dance steps familiar to local manifestations of Ogun in Orisha rituals".[17] Thus, in developing this theory based on the memory of ritual performance transformed through time to the production of Carnival in the New World, a link with the old African past and into modern performance is created.

The Influence of Orisha on Carnival

Although there is a significant literature, both popular and scholarly on the Trinidad Carnival, the influence of African religions has not been treated in serious research.[18] What follows therefore is largely speculative or, as Springer notes, the influence must be examined at the "philosophical and metaphysical" as well as the literal level. In fact, Springer's paper delivered at the Third World Carnival Congress held in Port of Spain in October 1999 is the only one to deal explicitly with this subject. This is a summation of her paper entitled "The Role of Orisha in Carnival".[19]

Many West African peoples had masking traditions, including important ones such as Egungun in which masked people played the role of the ancestors. It is quite likely that many of the slaves and their immediate descendants brought to the Caribbean remembered masked festivals. At the same time, the French in Trinidad brought their own versions of masks to hide the identity of players during their pre-Lenten Carnival celebrations. Both origins of Carnival in Trinidad therefore brought the idea of masks to the New World, and it is no wonder then that the masquerade, or mas, as it came to be known in Trinidad, provided the main format for Carnival celebrations. Rawle Gibbons and Aiyejina note that the passion with which Africans accepted Carnival demonstrates that they saw it as a legitimate way of expressing their earlier Yoruba traditions of masking. Springer, however, goes one step further and suggests that Egungun, or the Yoruba festival of the dead, was practised in her childhood and that it is this ancestor tradition, so vital to Yoruba religion, that survived in the memories of Orisha worshippers. She sees a clear connection, therefore, with the masked tradition coming out of Egungun, surviving through the Orisha religion and moving into Carnival practices. A famous Carnival character, the Moko Jumbie, or stilted walker, is also a revered ancestral spirit, as is the Pierrot whose face is also covered. The Pierrot is also directly linked to the *commedia del arte* style of theatre in eighteenth century Italy and France.[20] Springer sees Oshun and

Shango in the Carnival characters of Tan Tan and Saga Boy in the eternal dance of courtship. The hat of the Midnight Robber comes from the Orisha Oshun. She even sees significance in the colours of the national flag of Trinidad and Tobago, designed by two mas men and bearing the colours of Eshu and Shango.[21]

Springer sees further relationships between African religion and Carnival in the "qualities of spirituality" in the use of natural features such as rivers, sun, sea, sky, wind – Oshun, Yemanja, Olokun and Oya – in the Carnival bands. She notes that Shango, the god of thunder and lightning, appears on many Carnival banners in the form of his double-headed axe. Mas bands have actually played elements of nature such as Rain Forest, Cosmic Aura, Jungle Fever, Carnival of the Sea and others. There have also been individual portrayals of Papa Bois, sun kings and queens and others. Papa Bois, the keeper of the forest in Trinidadian folklore, is a primordial element of nature and is thus, Springer believes, closely tied to Orisha deities of nature. She also sees ritualistic significance in another Carnival character, the Dragon, who crosses through fire and water – dangerous elements that must be propitiated by ritual.

Another aspect of relationship deals with the regenerative powers that fuel Carnival celebrations. Springer notes that some Africans such as the Bakongo believe that masked processions carry spiritual rebirth and good fortune to the entire village; their songs bringing their inner messages of what life and death are all about. Carnival as practised in the early days in Trinidad also brought about a regeneration to its players, and even today revellers say that Carnival recharges their energy. Springer concludes her paper by saying, "My obeah, my Orisha survived, masked, in the masque; masked in syncretic formulations."[22]

Orisha "Mas" in Carnival: "401 meets 2001"

The Background

Shrine leader, Brother Oludari Massetungi, whose African-oriented philosophy was described at length in chapter 5, became the centre of a new controversy that pitted his organization, the Egbe Onisin Eledumare, against that of the National Council of Orisha Elders. Oludari has, for a number of years, thought about bringing out a mas band for Carnival, but his efforts only came to fruition in 2001. Beginning the planning as late as December 2000, the shrine and its active members nevertheless managed to design, develop and organize a Carnival presentation in time for 26–27 February 2001. It was entitled "401 meets 2001"; 401 signifies the number of Orisha deities in the traditional Yoruba pantheon.

Oludari and his shrine are on the margins of the more traditional Orisha mainstream, largely because he subscribes to a fully Yoruba-oriented worship devoid of any vestiges of Christianity.[23] His shrine and its members, many of whom are young people, participate in council activities to some extent but the group basically runs to its own agenda. While this is in keeping with the atomized and individual nature of Orisha shrines and their leaders, his is particularly distinguished by their total dedication to the "African sacred sciences". In this regard, his shrine is similar to that of Patricia McCleod – both of whom were earlier identified as Afrocentricists who are motivated primarily by spiritual and doctrinal commitments to the Yoruba Orisha, as compared to other African-oriented innovators inspired primarily by political and ideological dynamics. Oludari and McCleod do share, however, the need to identify with their African origins and cultural heritage, for which the Yoruba-derived Orisha religion provides the ideal forum.

The decision to mount a Carnival mas met with criticism, especially from the National Council of Orisha Elders. Their opprobrium is contained in the following letter sent to shrine leader Oludari and to the *Express* newspaper:[24]

> The Council of Orisa Elders wishes to advise it is viewing with grave concern the developing trend of disrespect for the religion in the Carnival arena. The council is mindful of the strong links between the religion and the evolution of the mas. This was at a time when the Carnival was the sole means of public expression for an otherwise persecuted belief system . . . the Council of Orisa Elders now invokes the wrath of all the Orisa on all who dare feature any Carnival characters named after the Orisa. It views any incorporation of the Orisa into Carnival as an attack on the sacredness of the religion . . . The present Carnival no longer includes the elements of African spirituality, with which it was imbued in its earlier years. We respect and give recognition to all those elders of the mas and the pan, who bravely expressed their religion in the Carnival, at a time when it was illegal to do so at any other time. It is the view of the council though, that such a forum is now no longer suitable or necessary . . .

(signed: Babalorisha Sam Phills, Chairman, for and on behalf the two chief shrine leaders, Iyalorisha Rodney and Babalorisha Forde and three other members of the council)

The media has, thus far, not taken a stand on the issue. However, a long article by Leroy Clarke was published in the *Trinidad Guardian*.[25] In it, Clarke takes a generally positive position, saying, "The advent of this performance can be viewed objectively as a ritual of utterance meant to revisit and re-evaluate our social practices, in this case, mask or mas playing."

Oludari himself believes that it is important to bring the cosmic and spiritual energy of the Orisha into a Carnival that has become too secularized. It is an attempt, in his view, to regenerate Carnival and bring it back to what it was in earlier times. He believes that the distinction between the sacred and secular is too rigid and that the Orisha and their energy are part of nature and permeate all of social life. Carnival, as part of the social life of the country, is therefore an appropriate arena for the display of Orisha powers. Gordon Rohlehr makes much the same point when he notes that "the unity of secular and sacred existed in many traditional African societies and was part of what was lost or obscured in the New World encounter between African systems of thought, belief and performance and Manichean Christian, particularly Calvinist Protestant modes of perception".[26]

Another member of the Egbe group supports the mas because "within us all the Orisa are present . . . and the portrayal of nine Orisa deities will liberate the awesome power of the cosmos to help reestablish the equilibrium and balance in our nation as we resanctify Carnival".[27] Oludari and his members emphasize that their decision was sanctioned through the divination processes of Ifa. As one of its members stated, "Nothing is done without the blessing of Ifa. When [we are] in doubt about what to do [we] do divination. This was authorised by higher forces than ourselves."

The decision to play an Orisha mas in Carnival is not really new. Orisha, or Shango bands as they were once known, paraded through the streets of southeast Port of Spain in earlier times. Older Trinidadians, now in their seventies and eighties and raised in this area of the city during the 1930s, clearly remember that they were sometimes accompanied by steelbands "when they came down from the hills". They also recalled that mothers would take their children inside and close their windows when these bands passed because they were afraid of the obeah that Shango people were believed to practise.

Despite the earlier tradition, the decision to mount a Carnival band in 2001 brought out some of the ideological and doctrinal differences, further illustrating the conflict between authenticity and syncretism already discussed. This controversy provides more evidence that such doctrinal divisions are evident in the practice of the Orisha religion today.

The Mas

The band consisted of about forty members, most of them younger supporters of the shrine. It was registered in all of the events of Carnival, including Jouvert, Monday night mas and the Parade of Bands on Tuesday. Its Jouvert portrayal was called "A Tribute to Piparo" and featured a number of members wearing mud-stained pareos and head ties and mud decorations on their faces. Oludari was with the band, carrying two African sacred staffs in his hands. Painting the body in mud is a traditional feature of Jouvert Carnival bands and is called "mud mas". Piparo is the name of a village in southern Trinidad where small, but occasionally active, mud volcanoes are located. What distinguished this group from ordinary "mud mas", however, was the way in which it was made to relate to the Orisha religion. Brother Oludari stated that "this is a tribute to Aganyu, the primeval Orisha god of volcanoes and a fitting way to begin the Carnival".[28]

A ritual initiated each event; prayers, offerings and thanks were made to the Orisha. Chanting and songs were also part of the ritual. On Monday evening, for example, the band played a Monday night mas. A small group of twelve members assembled in a park in Woodbrook, Port of Spain, the centre of many Carnival activities. Some were in their complete Orisha costumes, others in partial costume. The women portrayed Oya, Oshun and Yemanja; the men Eshu, Shango, Ogun and Orunmila. The band also included the "unformed", played by young children. The costumes used the colours of the deities as researched by Oludari and therefore differed somewhat from their portrayal in the more conventional Orisha *Ebos* or feasts. At about 9 p.m. the group formed a circle, holding hands, around a flagpole. Oludari placed a small calabash of water, one of seeds and a bottle of sweet oil on the floor. He was holding an African sculpture staff, possibly an Eshu dance staff from Nigeria, that he used throughout the ritual. Libations were made, followed by the ritual blessing of people past and present. Aiding in the ritual was another Orisha elder, Esmond King, who has an extensive background and knowledge of the early steelband movement and Carnival mas, who specifically called the names of many individuals who played significant roles in the popular culture of an earlier era. People living and dead, all African people, elders and the nation as a whole were included in the blessings, each of which was accompanied by a few drops of water sprinkled from the calabash onto the ground. Singing and drumming followed. The band was awaiting the arrival of their steelband accompaniment that failed to arrive in time, so the evening ended at this point. The mixture of the sacred and secular – ritualistic celebration versus the worldly and profane Carnival rites – was especially obvious, albeit in a small way, during this event.

As the religious ritual was being celebrated around the flagpole, a steelband of about twenty players atop a flat-bedded truck, surrounded by about one hundred Carnival revellers, several of them white tourists, slowly made their way on the street facing the park. The band was playing an old-fashioned ballad and the people were singing along, many of them holding on to the truck's sides with one hand and managing beer bottles with the other. At one point the two music sounds merged together and created an almost surrealistic, other worldly ambiance. In addition to this particular event, the night sounds were punctuated by the calypsos of the season, particularly those of calypsonian Shadow.

On Carnival Tuesday, the band came out with about forty players. Unlike other Carnival bands, however, they were accompanied by traditional Orisha drummers as well as by the steelband, comprised of younger musicians who had agreed to play despite the controversy created by this event. They did not play the calypsos of the season but concentrated on those composed by the late and great calypsonian, Lord Kitchener. They also played ballad music. The participants danced with the traditional movements of the Orisha deities, resting now and then with the small "chip" movement moving to the music. They did not "wine" – the sensual and erotic hip and pelvic gyrations that are the conventional movement of Carnival merrymaking. Even at competition points, they played their own music interspersed once or twice with the Yoruba Orisha singing of Ella Andall.

Most Carnival bands create a King and Queen of the band, whose costumes are the most elaborate and costly. The Orisha band did not portray a

King but they did create a special costume for their Queen. The Queen portrayed Oyeki Meji, one of the sacred scriptures or *Odus* associated with the Ifa system of divination. The band's press release describes this mas thus: "The invocation of this first *Odu* is the primary first stage of all initiation ceremonies. It is the portal through which the ancestors may return to share their wisdom with the living." This *Odu* symbolizes the female principle, the costume depicted a woman wearing a head tie flowing with straw-like locks, a full skirt in blue and white and a stylized torso displaying large bare breasts. Yellow-white streamers, symbolizing milk, flowed from her breasts. She was entered in the Queen of the Bands competition but did not progress beyond the preliminary stage. In fact, the *Trinidad Guardian*,[29] reporting on the competition, headlined its article "Orisa Queen fails to impress". In noting that a calypso singer played the mas, the article reports that the "costume did not resemble any of the other huge, iridescent queens, her blackened, droopy 'Odo-Oyeku Meji', who lost a few stringy hair strands, resembling ole mas". (This refers to the Jouvert mas where ugly, dingy and often-ridiculous costumes are worn.) Its religious significance was clearly not understood by this reporter. The band was not able to cross the grandstand stage at the Savannah, as is customary for all Carnival bands, because the Queen costume was damaged during the course of the day. However, they paraded all day and joined in the other competition venues. Oludari and his shrine members were pleased with their first entry into Carnival mas and they hoped to bring out a more elaborate and larger band the following year.

In 2001 Patricia McCleod (Iya Shangowummi) and her shrine had also planned to bring out a Carnival mas band because they too had the permission of Ifa, obtained through divination, to do so. It was to have been entitled "Yoruba Cosmology – Faces of Oshun" in honour of the Orisha Oshun but they decided to delay their presentation. Although McCleod too received the same condemning letter as Oludari, she feels that both groups are doing nothing disrespectful to the Orisha religion and, in fact, "the two Iles getting the vision around the same time shows the Orisha was sending a message".

In 2002 Patricia McCleod did, in fact, mount the "Faces of Oshun". The band consisted of her shrine members, many of them also young people. The mas camp – a small shop – was located on one of the streets leading off the Savannah. On Carnival Tuesday morning the band of about sixty persons, accompanied by a rhythm band, played their mas. About six pan players (steelband) and their instruments travelled on a small truck, while a bamboo tamboo rhythm section on a wheeled platform was attached to the truck by stout ropes. Bamboo tamboo instruments are hollowed out rods of bamboo, pitched to different levels, that preceded the development of steeldrum or "pan". The players were dressed in the different faces of the Orisha Oshun, celebrating her femininity as well as different aspects of her power. One very elaborate gold and sequined section called "bangles, beads and combs" portrayed the feminine and beautiful side of Oshun, while green-costumed players demonstrated her earthy qualities. The Orisha Shango also had a prominent role in the band, being shown in several of his manifestations including the "King" of the band, who portrayed Shango as the lord of the skies in the form of giant white eagle.

Mrs McCleod, all of whose decisions were guided by divination, did not take the band through the main competition point, the grandstand at the Savannah, but they did pass the smaller downtown competition points. As well, they traced a route through some of the older areas of the city associated with the historical African slave presence. Throughout the day they were treated respectfully and with interest. Their costumes, which markedly differed from the more commonplace bikini-type costumes of most of the larger Carnival bands today, attracted considerable interest. A few spectators mistook them for "the Minshall band", referring to mas band leader Peter Minshall, who has for some years developed the most innovative, artistic and creative presentations.

Oludari's Orisha shrine and their participation in the Carnival of 2001 created a controversy between themselves and the National Council of Orisha Elders. (By contrast, the Oshun mas the following year, although also criticized by the council, did not attract as much attention.) The event was played out in the newspapers, thus adding more friction to the situation. In addition to furthering the distance between Oludari's and McCleod's shrines and the shrines represented by the council, however, the event lends support to the ideological and doctrinal differences within the Orisha religion today. It also provides some provocative insights into the nature of public and private ritual, the roles of performance and spectacle in Trinidadian popular culture, and as the growing trend towards minimizing the difference between the sacred and secular.

Orisha in Performance: The Musical Play
Tales of the Orisha

This overview of the influence of African religions on popular culture would not be complete without mention of a highly innovative and entertaining musical, written by Professor Rawle Gibbons. Based on a Cuban play that features Santeria, Gibbons developed a Trinidadian version that relates the story of the origin of the Orishas and provides incidents and highlights of their lives as deities. The play is a mythical piece accompanied by Orisha drumming, music and spectacular songs performed by Ella Andall. Several Orisha elders are known to have said they thoroughly enjoyed the play and felt that it provided an entertaining and educational vehicle for the audience. The very idea of performing such a piece invites acceptance of the Orisha faith today. One of the play's objectives is to inform the audience of the distinguished and noble history of the Orisha, and that it is a proper religion with its own origin myth about the creation of the earth. The fact of the play also confirms an earlier point, that the Orisha religion has a wide following in the artistic world. The playwright, director and several of the performers are, in fact, Orisha devotees.

> It's not Shango, it's the
> African Work
> – *Ebenezer "Pa Neezer" Elliott*

CHAPTER EIGHT

Conclusion

THERE ARE SEVERAL ISSUES or questions that I want to discuss in this concluding chapter. One of the most important relates to the status of Orisha as a religion or as a cult. The early literature identified it as a cult and I too, in my ignorance, called it such.

It is instructive to go back to one of the earliest and still most influential theorists in this area, Emile Durkheim,[1] who identified religion as a powerful institution whose main function is social control of the population and the need to provide society with values of cohesiveness. Another eminent anthropologist, Peter Worsley,[2] defines religion as a set of beliefs that, in some way, refer to and look for validation in a dimension beyond the empirical-technical realm. Wallace describes the universal formal properties of religion as: (a) the supernatural premise, (b) elements of ritual and (c) beliefs all held together in a pantheon that includes myth and values.[3]

Emile Durkheim identified seven characteristics of religion:

- a recognition of a belief, or power, or force
- a belief in the ambiguity of power – sacred things are both physical and moral, positive and negative, helpful and dangerous
- "non-utilitarian" – work is utility and everyday but the sacred is beyond the everyday
- non-empirical – the sacred is beyond empirical nature
- it does not involve knowledge – it is not based on knowledge from the five senses
- it is supportive and strength giving; it raises the individual above him- or herself
- it impinges on human consciousness with moral obligation and an ethical imperative, and elicits intense respect

According to an anthropological perspective, religion can be defined as a system of beliefs and practices through which people struggle with the ultimate problems of human life. The main function of religion is to provide a link between the natural world of lived experience and the supernatural world of gods, deities and spirits. The institution of religion includes three major components:

- beliefs about the supernatural
- myths
- rites and rituals

The belief system can include the relationship between the natural and the supernatural, while myths provide answers to questions about human origins and the mysteries of life and death. Some religions include a belief in the afterlife. Rites and rituals include prayer and many other forms of religious behaviour. Other components found in some, but not all, religions include an organized structure, a place of worship, formal practitioners and other elements.

By all accounts, the Orisha faith contains all the elements normally associated with a religion. It has even acquired an organized structure and is formalizing its practices. Why, then, was it designated as a cult in earlier times? Even today there are people who tend dismissively to relegate it to cult status. While there is nothing inherently wrong with the designation "cult", it has taken on pejorative and mostly negative meanings. A cult in the common discourse is something less than a religion. The term is usually applied by "Christian apologists as a cudgel to attack small religious groups, or, even worse, minority Christian faiths which do not adhere to all the traditional Christian doctrines".[4] For many a cult is a false faith, yet some of the very elements of cult behaviour are also applicable to mainstream Christianity. But the last word on cults may be that of writer Tom Wolfe, who noted that "a cult is a religion with no political power".[5]

Beyond the actions of the state is the important dynamic of public consciousness. In former times African religions were despised, feared and rejected. Today they have become part of the public consciousness in positive and energetic ways. Their social acceptance is a sign of the maturity of Trinidadian society, that can now not only accept that half of its population has African origins but also assert this identity with pride. The transformation of the Orisha religion is spearheaded by Afrocentric innovators who, as part of their ideology, believe in the power and supremacy of their African heritage. While this new-found African supremacy may be related to the ever-present ethnic competition in this plural society, it is also apparent that segments of the Indian communities share in, and support, the need to create equal opportunity for all religions practised in the country. The benefits to the society as a whole of recognizing and supporting old, African, virtually indigenous religions can only be regarded as a positive measure of the maturity and growth of the country.

The African religions and specifically Orisha have become multi-levelled institutions in this society. They serve not only the obvious religious needs but also as a source of inspiration for personal identity somewhat similar to the case of secular Jews who nevertheless identify, themselves as Jews. Many people, motivated by the need to reclaim their African heritage, can now openly support the religions because they see in them a source of understanding and a coming to terms with their slave and colonial past. It is a source of amazement for Orisha believers and supporters that this religion could have been maintained undercover for so many years, thus allowing it to survive under the most brutally oppressive conditions. The strength of belief in the traditional African gods was therefore extremely prevalent among the early slaves who brought it with them. This strength allowed the religion to survive. It is a mark of respect for these elders that the religion is today being brought back to the African traditions that the elders knew and respected before enforced Christianity changed Orisha's beliefs and rituals.

For many of the artistic supporters of the religion, Orisha is far more than a set of rituals. It is a source of creative inspiration that transforms their consciousness and brings them closer to their African origins. It brings them in touch with a historical reality that for many years was rejected. One need only look at the lyrics of some modern calypsos or study the rhythmic percussive sounds of soca music to hear the African influences. The subtle nuances that speak to African forms and designs are clearly evident in the works of visual artists such as Leroy Clarke and Makuma Kenle. The Orisha gods and goddesses themselves are portrayed in some of these pictures.

On a more mundane and secular level, both religions have served and continue to serve the needs of the state as a vehicle through which electoral support can be garnered. Finding such vehicles is a particular requirement of the state at this time, when the Indian-led government is attempting to influence a crossover vote of Afro-Trinidadians to their cause. The last election in 1996 necessitated a coalition between the National Alliance for Reconstruction and UNC parties in order for Basdeo Panday to form a government. Another election was held in December 2000, and the government did win a slim majority. An election was also held in 2001, resulting in an 18–18 tie between the two parties. While there was crossover voting in both recent elections, it has not been demonstrated that members of the African religions voted for the so-called Indian government. Providing a new national holiday, legislating Orisha marriage rites, donating land and promising to remove old oppressive legislation have given the present government a considerable amount of mileage. All of these events are covered in depth by the media, and the prime minister takes every public occasion to remind the public of some of the perks given to these religions – all in the name of providing an equal place to every race. While these changes clearly benefit the members of the religion, their very need has provided this government with a chance to confer benefits on a predominantly Afro-Trinidadian population. Who can fault a government that is attempting to help African religions find their rightful place in society after years of marginalization and rejection? This is especially so in a multi-ethnic society such as Trinidad that places a very high value on religion and whose members are, generally, deeply religious. Providing benefits to these religions demonstrates that the government is willing to ensure the equality of all its citizens without recourse to ethnicity.

Another function served by the African religions is that they have become a source of synergy between the Indo- and Afro-Trinidadian segments of the society, providing a means of coming together symbolically to achieve their ends. One example of this synergy deals with the controversy surrounding Orisha's membership in the IRO. It took the combined efforts of the Maha Saba and the Orisha's Council of Elders to highlight the discrimination that had been faced by the Orisha religions in their attempt to gain membership. The media made much of the meetings between Eintou Springer and Babalorisha Sam Phills's public attendance at a Maha Saba–led Hindu festival and their subsequent appearance on television a few days later. The Indian community in Trinidad also contains some marginalized religions, and thus their coming together to champion the equality of all religions crosses over the ethnic boundaries in this society. Clearly, any mechanism that encourages ethnic solidarity in an often competitive and sometimes hostile environment can only lead to greater accommodation between these two, often antagonistic groups.

Trinidad is an extraordinarily complex society despite its small size. It is also one rent with paradoxes. Therefore, it is no surprise that the growing strength of the African religions, focusing on the Afrocentricity of their innovating members, also serves to provide a buffer against the growing Indo-Trinidadian hegemony in this society. Indo-Trinidadians not only run the present government but also appear to be increasing their participation and power in all areas of the public and private sectors. Research also provides evidence that more Indian children are succeeding in schools and postsecondary institutions, so that even greater participation in decision making capacities are predicted for them.[6] In the face of such growing hegemony, Afro-Trinidadians fear for their place in society. The African religions, especially Orisha with its growing Afrocentrism, provide a mechanism for Afro-Trinidadians to refocus and reclaim their identities.

There have been significant changes within the Orisha religion. The trend towards secularization and centralization has not detracted from the spirituality of the religion. In fact, there are now more rituals and festivals being introduced into the religion in order to bring it back to its African roots. Attempting to remove its syncretic Christian rituals will not undermine the richness of its ritual expression; it will in fact enhance the rites and ceremonies that are becoming more varied. As far as its ceremonial life is concerned, the increased Africanization will only make this religion more interesting and more available as a vehicle for finding and enhancing personal identity.

At another level, both religions are growing in the diaspora. Both are experiencing transnationalistic expressions. In the United States the Orisha movement is rapidly growing among African Americans, and while they dispute the authenticity of its expression in the Caribbean, they nevertheless recognize its viability and at least part of its African derivation. In the United Kingdom both religions have active followings, and in Canada the Spiritual Baptist religion is well represented. Even the Orisha movement is beginning to be practised there. Both religions are being transported abroad as Caribbean people migrate, bringing their religious expression with them. Thus, from small beginnings in the tiny countries of the Caribbean, African-derived religions are making their presence felt in the large metropolises of the world.

Finally, I want to come back to the criticism increasingly directed at these religions in Trinidad: disunity. It has indeed become fashionable for politicians to harangue these groups in their public meetings on the issue of disunity and factionalism. It is probably safe to assume that government finds the competing factions within one community difficult to deal with. The present government included, until recently, a senator from one of the Spiritual Baptist communities who does not represent the other Spiritual Baptist groups and is perceived by them to be overly political. Criticizing the African religions for disunity indicates ignorance of how religious institutions develop in society. One has only to read any history of religion to realize that disunity and factionalism have always been endemic in practically all societies. Most religions experience break-away factions – probably because of differences in the understanding of cosmology and ritual. The ideological nature of religion readily lends itself to difference and dissension. Consider, for example, that early Christians were a breakaway sect of Judaism; that there are a number of groups within Islam; that modern Christianity itself is split between Roman Catholicism and Protestantism, that is itself divided into innumerable groups. The list of religious factions and sects, some of which have formed new religions themselves, is endless. In postmodern societies there is an increase in what are called "new religious movements", attracting the young and disillusioned members of society. New religious movements are born when a new leader emerges and seeks a following, adding yet again to the number of religious groups in human societies. One need not belabour the point. Yet, the African religions in Trinidad are accused of factionalism to denigrate the validity of their religions. Recently, a letter published in one of the newspapers expressed this commonly held point of view. The writer notes that "there are so many leader who believe they are the ones who should be boss . . . [they appeared on television] and made a mockery of themselves, they almost fought on the TV".[7]

Finally, one of the most powerful arguments with respect to the discourse of "unity" and "disunity" relates to the origins of these religions. It should be remembered that Orisha in Nigeria, as well as its manifestations in the diaspora, is based on oral tradition. The sacred texts or *Odus* in the Yoruba religion are constantly in dispute because priests differ among themselves with regard to their interpretation. There are also regional variations in the practice of the religion. Thus, an orally based religion gives rise to differences and disputes. "Disunity" is almost built into such a structure. Difference and contestation is also part of African-based performance culture,[8] and its most obvious manifestation takes the form of social and political "speechifying" such as occurs at the University of Woodford Square and in other public places throughout the Caribbean.

Scholars of religion have noted that religions are neither mirrors of reality nor static models of it, but ideological fields composed of multiple models and mirrors in constant competition.[9] This means that as change and transformation take place in society so too are they reflected in its religious organizations. Dissension between and within religious organizations reflects the wider societal arena of which they are part. From this perspective, disunity merely reflects the segmentation of race, class and gender that is already endemic in this society and the individual religions should not be criticized for it. They and their members are as much influenced by the wider dynamics taking place in Trinidadian society today as are all its institutions.

Moreover, the popular discourse of disunity should not be used to influence the individual expression of religions that have always been atomistic and individualistic. When a religion has traditionally been organized along lines of individual leadership, the presence of many groups is the obvious consequence. Furthermore, the unity discourse also fails to understand the generation gap between the modern innovators who are attempting to restructure both the organization and its rituals and the older, traditional members. Segmentation by ideological traditions and age are therefore part of the very structure of this organization.

Over-riding the challenges brought by ideological and personal factions, so characteristic of all religions, however, are the common elements shared by all devotees of these African religions. There is a common ground of understanding that brings all members of these faiths together and it is their deep-seated faith in the spiritual and supernatural forces of their religions. Devotees of Spiritual Baptistism and most members of Orisha have a profound faith in Christianity and the divinity of Jesus Christ. As well, they believe in the presence and powers of the Orisha to guide their lives and footsteps. Their overwhelming faith and spirituality, their deep-seated religiosity is what brings them and keeps them together. Differences created by personality conflicts or even by some ideological conventions are superficial in comparison to the spirituality expressed by believers in the African religions, with or without the Christian syncretism. All devotes of Orisha and all worshippers of Spiritual Baptism share far more in common than the petty differences that attempt to divide them. Among Orisha believers, the faith in *ase* or an inanimate power that resides throughout the world and that resides in some people, defines a view of the relationship between the natural experienced world and that of the supernatural. In a similar manner, the belief in the Holy Spirit is pervasive among Spiritual Baptists and helps define their existence.

The words of Pa Neezer introduce this chapter. He identified Orisha as "the African work". His own ritual was, however, strongly influenced by Christianity and his own identity was influenced by his deep-seated Christian faith. On the other hand, Pa Neezer was an extraordinarily complex thinker despite his humble farm origins. He went to great lengths to be taught the Orisha faith and its rituals from his grandmother, herself a child of slaves. He believed in the all-encompassing power of the Yoruba Orisha. He gave pride of place to these Orisha and performed in their service for many years. For his time, he can be considered a forerunner of the Black Power movement, not in any political sense, but certainly in terms of his pride in learning and doing the "African work". Being an African was as important to Pa Neezer as any other aspect of his identity, and this in a time when all things African were marginalized and rejected. One can only wonder and speculate on how Pa Neezer would receive the theological changes being introduced into his religion today.

I began this book by explaining something about the personal journey that led to my interest in the Orisha religion. Perhaps it should also end on this note. Re-exploring the nature of African religions and particularly their newly found place within Trinidadian society has given me a deeper respect for the vitality and validity of this religious form. The miracle of its survival, as well as its current revitalization as it attempts to find its place in a postmodern society itself undergoing massive socio-political change, suggests that its supernatural foundations as well as the personal faith and conviction of its adherents are indeed strong. Re-studying the religion after so many years has completed the circle for me and perhaps led to a more profound understanding of my own connection to spirituality.

APPENDIX

My Life with Ebenezer Elliott (Pa Neezer)

A Talk Given to the Orisha Family Day Celebration,
19 March 2000, at Lopinot

Dr Frances Henry, Professor (Emerita) of Anthropology
York University, Toronto, Canada

Honoured elders, guests:
Conrad Mauge in his book *The Lost Orisha* says a few words about Ebenezer Elliott: "He was a man of the people and for the people. It is unfortunate that devotees whom I spoke to under the age of thirty-five did not know of Papa Neza."

Well you may be wondering why someone like me is here to address the Orisha Family Day – and one of the reasons is that I knew Pa Neezer very well and I am here to share with you, the younger generation of Orisha devotees, something about his life and work. But let me tell you a little about myself first.

I came here in 1956 as a graduate student doing a PhD in anthropology and my interest was to study the Orisha religion, then known as the "Shango cult". I became interested in this topic because even back then I wanted to know what African culture traits and elements had survived into the New World. I had heard that Trinidad had this African religion but little was written about it. So, I came here.

My first introduction to the religion came from people who I met here who told me that it was African, barbaric – that they engage in terrible practices like blood sacrifice and that Shango is obeah and the people who do it are obeah people. I was warned time and time again not to have anything to do with "Shango" people.

Naturally I didn't listen because even then I felt that people who talked that way did so out of ignorance. Not a one of them had ever seen a feast or talked to an elder.

Eventually I came to Tanti Silla's *palais* on St Francois Valley Road. Tanti and her congregation welcomed me and my research made a lot of progress. I had already heard a lot of talk about Pa Neezer – people today refer to him as *Papa* Neezer but he was really known as *Pa* – people told me that only Pa could give me real answers because he knew more about Orisha than anyone else in the country. But they also warned me: "Pa will talk to you but only if he had a mind to – he don't talk to just anybody, you know." Some of the Orisha people painted a picture of Pa Neezer as a somewhat frightening man, somewhat stand-offish but certainly someone to be respected.

I must admit to feeling a little apprehensive as the first evening of Tanti Silla's feast arrived and Pa was to come up from Lengua to conduct it. Nothing I had heard about the great Pa Neezer prepared me for the man I met on that late Tuesday afternoon. A somewhat bulky man, about 5 ft. 10 in height, slouching at the shoulders, shuffled into the compound. He was wearing an old pair of brown pants and a white shirt rolled up to his elbows and on his head, his trademark, an old wide brimmed hat pulled low over his forehead. In his shirt pocket was the ever-present pipe. He was in his mid-fifties when I first met him. He shuffled in, very slowly. He looked harmless enough and not especially authoritative.

It took me a while before I summoned up the nerve to go and talk to him. As the feast was under way, he got up and went into the kitchen for some coffee, which he loved. One of the ladies asked if I wanted some and when I said yes, she brought it to the table where Pa was sitting. I introduced myself and stated my purpose. He was polite but distant. I talked some more. He said very little. The only thing he asked me was why I wanted to know about Orisha. I explained about sharing the religion with students abroad and then he said, "Me don't know nothing, ask others." He finished his coffee and walked out. He stayed at Tanti's for the days of her feast as it was too much to travel up and down to Moruga and back to Port of Spain. The next afternoon, I returned and saw him having a meal. I went up to him again and said that people had told me that if I wanted to know anything about Shango, I would have to speak to him. I said I know your knowledge about Shango is extensive and what other people tell me would not be accurate. His eyes, large and deep set, sparkled and he began to laugh, a slow rumble coming from his chest. "It's not Shango, it's the African work, the Orisha work," he said. I knew then he was beginning to accept me. We spoke some more during the week and as he left for home, he told me to come down to see him in Lengua and, "We go talk some more."

I could not believe my luck and rapidly made plans to go down to Lengua which I did the following week. Pa Neezer talked to me about the African work and a little about himself and why he did it. As I was leaving to go back to Port of Spain, he came with me in the taxi and stopped at the main Moruga Road near the Fifth Company junction in front of a house. We stepped out and he said this was his other house and if I wanted to come down to spend some more time, I could use his house. I gladly accepted, returned to Port of Spain, packed a bag and the following week journeyed down to Fifth Company again. He met me at the house later that day, bringing with him his sister-in-law, Miss Eva, who he said would cook my meals. The house was old but there were two bedrooms, one of which I used, and a sitting room, a coalpot and a "safe" in the kitchen. The outhouse was in the back, as was a hand-made shower dispensing rain water. The house also had about a hundred bats that lived in its rafters. I got used to them. A lodger, Mr Peters, lived in the cookhouse in the back of the property. As it turned out, Pa would come up to the main road house every Friday afternoon and spend the weekend at this house. On Sunday morning he would attend the London Baptist Church up the road. For that purpose, he kept his gray suit, a clean white shirt and tie in the house to change into when he attended church. Of course, he would wear a gray hat on his head to complete the church outfit.

Thus began one of the most exciting and rewarding periods of my life. I spent many months living with Pa Neezer. I watched him do his bush doctoring because he allowed me to sit in with him as sometimes a hundred people or more would come on the weekend to seek his counsel. Pa Neezer was a renowned bush doctor and his knowledge of herbs and natural medicines was unbelievable. I attended all of his feasts and many more in various parts of the country. He would take me with him – he never owned a car but the taxi containing one or two drummers, himself and me would arrive at a house. Eyebrows would be raised as I got out but since I was with Pa, I would be welcomed too. Remember, back in those days, Orisha was still practised in secret and underground – strangers were not exactly invited. As time went on, Pa Neezer trusted me and he would answer my questions. I even did little errands for him, sometimes going to the bank for him or buying him something he wanted. We became friends.

Samuel Ebenezer Elliott was born in 1901 in the Third Company Village. His family originally came from the United States and were part of the "Merikans" who were settled in the villages in southern Trinidad in the early part of the nineteenth century. They are still known as the "company" villages. These were slaves who had fought on the side of the British during the American war of independence. They were given sixteen acres of land to work as farmers. Pa Neezer's maternal grandmother was a famed Orisha woman named "Ma Diamond", from whom he learned his African work. Ma Diamond's mother came from Africa as a slave and taught her daughter the Yoruba religion. Pa Neezer therefore learned the religion and its practices from an African source. Ma Diamond also passed on her vast storehouse of knowledge of bush medicines to the young lad. He attended school in Moruga up to the seventh standard. Pa worked for a while in the oil fields of Point-a-Pierre. Sometime during the early 1930s, Pa won a lottery of $1,200 – then a very substantial sum. He purchased additional land with his winnings and settled in Lengua Road. He made a good living farming about fifty acres of productive land, raising mainly bananas and cocoa. He was married to Miss Ada and had four children and several adopted children.

During his early thirties, two things happened in his life. He was able to settle down and farm his land and he was able to hire workers to help him. During this time, he began receiving dreams and sometimes visions from the Orisha. He was told that he had remarkable healing powers and that he should begin to help people by healing them of sickness. The Orisha, he thinks it was Ogun, also told him that he should hold feasts. The deities told him that he had special powers and that it would be selfish of him to deny his power to other people. He would hold at least four feasts a year and a special one around Christmas time for the children. There, St Nick would arrive and give gifts and sweets to the assembled children. Pa Neezer devoted the next thirty-five years of his life to the service of the Orisha and to the people.

Pa's spiritual powers were awesome. He did nothing without divination, usually with the obi seeds. He never made a move without this consultation, and in his work with people, he divined their problems using his special powers.

Pa would not attend just any Orisha feast – only those of his spiritual children. Among his favourites was Mother B, an already elderly woman who lived at Bastor Hall in Couva with her family. She, like Pa, was considered a respected "old head". And here with us are two of his children, Iya Melvina Rodney who I knew when she was a young woman working with Pa Neezer, and Baba Sam Phills. (There may be others present as well.) He dismissed many as practising "fakes" who were not true to the African religion. He imposed very strict rules at his feasts. There was no drinking or bad language allowed. People had to remain silent except when singing or praying. Only real manifestations were allowed. Others whom he did not know or their followers were led out of the *palais* – he feared that they were not genuine manifestations. He also was a devout Christian and paid a great deal of time and attention to the Catholic and other prayers at his feasts. Sometimes, when he was annoyed with his flock who were not living right or flaunting his rules, he would keep them at prayers for hours at a time. He fully believed in the dualism between Christianity and the Orisha. For him there was very little difference, as they were one and the same.

Pa Neezer was most impressive when the power was in his head. He had three main Orisha: Ogun, Ajaja and Aba Lofa. On the first evening of his own feast, Ogun would always manifest on him. When in manifestation, Pa Neezer was truly awesome and not a little bit terrifying. He would appear to grow to seven feet tall, his body was straight – he did not walk, he stomped, his bare feet hitting the earth hard with every step. There was no sign of the rheumatism that plagued him in everyday life. The power took all of that away. The powers worked Pa Neezer hard: he would talk, give orders and actually deliver a sermon. I once heard Ajaja talk for forty-five minutes exhorting the crowd to behave, to live cleanly and to obey the words of God. People listened in absolute silence and if any other powers were there, they departed when the power hit Pa Neezer. There were several hammocks strung under his house during feast time for people to rest in during the days. One night, however, Ogun noticed that a few people were sleeping in the hammocks. Angrily, he stomped over and dumped out each sleeper onto the floor.

On the second night of his own feast, Aba Lofa would manifest on Pa Neezer. At that point in time, Pa was the only "horse" who received this ultimate deity. He had to prepare himself to receive that power. He was not in the *palais* but sat on the gallery of his house in total silence and completely still. It was as if he was clearing his mind of everything in it, preparing to receive that power. Finally, his eyes closed, his head shook and his body quivered. Slowly, he got up, eyes closed and hands clasped in prayer as he walked into his bedroom. When he emerged, he wore white trousers, shirt and white headband. A long white cloak hung from his shoulders. He walked into his *chapelle* and when he emerged at the door of the *palais*, a freshly killed cattle head rested on his own head. With blood splattering down over his face, and the white garments and the long cloak billowing out behind him, Aba Lofa walked, marched, displayed himself with hands on his hips and finally danced. He danced a vigorous African rhythmic dance – moving and gyrating his entire body. He never said a word. The crowd was electrified, although most of them had seen this manifestation before – but no one moved or said a word. I stood there watching in total admiration – I had never seen such a display of power and magnetism in my life. No one doubted that a god was in their midst.

When the power left Pa Neezer, he would revert to the slow, shuffling middle-aged man suffering from rheumatism.

His other important role in life was to heal people. Every weekend he came up to the Moruga Road house where dozens of people would be lined up waiting to see him.

He would sit in the gallery, a Bible next to him – the obi seeds with which he divined were in his hand. A patient would come up, sit in the chair facing him and he would look into his or her eyes as they told him of their complaint. He would then diagnose the problem – too much hot blood, wind in the belly – and tell them what to take for their ailment. But he would also tell them why they were suffering and here was his opportunity to try to convince people to "live right" – not to be envious of their neighbours, to live like a Christian – he would recite the Ten Commandments to some of them and then pick out the commandment that they had disobeyed. People were often astounded that he knew of their transgressions. Often, he threw the obi seeds and by reading their patterns would not only know the illness but more importantly what caused it. He also told people that they must pray and keep their faith in God. He rarely mentioned the Orisha, because many of his clients were not devotees.

Pa had an extensive knowledge of bush medicines and he dispensed these or told people how to make them. The therapy he gave consisted of both psychological counselling and physical healing. He was especially good with people who had psychological problems because he would give them a reason for their distress that they could understand and relate to.

Pa Neezer had a very good knowledge of illness and disease. He knew instinctively what he could treat and what required medical attention. Many is the time I have seen him shake his head and tell a person, "Is not me to help you, go to the hospital." These were people suffering from cancer and other diseases he could not cure. Once I saw him look at a young child a woman was holding and, just by looking at the crying child, he told its mother that he had "appendix" and take him to the hospital right away. Another time, he turned away a woman, telling me afterwards, "Not that one, she have cancer, I can't do anything for she."

Pa Neezer did not take money for his consultations. If pressed, he would say, "You could leave a little something", usually less than $1. Oftentimes he would take money out of his own pocket and give to somebody to take a taxi to the San Fernando hospital. He would take the gifts people brought him, some candles, animals for the sacrifice, some ground provisions. Most of the time these payments would be used at his next feast. Along with his gifts, Pa read books and especially the *Home Physician*, from which he learned a great deal. He sometimes mixed regular medicines along with his own herbal mix. One time, when I was suffering from sand fly fever, Pa gave me a lotion that was made of calamine lotion, herbs he had put into it and a dead scorpion. He said the scorpion released some fluid into the lotion, which was good against itching. He also gave me a drink to combat the fever – the very next morning I was hale and hearty again.

Pa's patients were ordinary kind of people but that is not to say there weren't many middle-class and even well-known people who would consult him. Some of them were Indians. These people came at night, often late, since they did not want to be seen consulting the "obeah" man.

This brings me to a very significant point about Pa Neezer – one that I don't need to tell this audience about – but one that is important for the rest of this society to know. Ebenezer Elliott was not an obeah man. The perception of him in Trinidad society was that he was a famous and skilled obeah man. Many people, including the calypsonian Sparrow, believe this – remember a calypso called "Obeah Wedding" in which a woman uses obeah to catch Sparrow in marriage and the refrain is, "Melda, Melda, you don't seem to understand / Obeah can't upset my plan because Papa Neezer is my grandfather."

Whenever I told Trinidadian friends that I was working with Pa, they would jokingly say, "You learning obeah too?" Obeah is black magic designed to cause harm and evil. Pa Neezer stood for exactly the opposite – for good and well being. He worked for the good of the spirit or soul and of the body. He never did harm to anyone nor did he cause harm to happen. What he could do, however, was to undo the harm that an obeah spell had created. So, if someone was suffering as a result of obeah having been worked against them, Pa Neezer, by using the right incantations, prayers and divining tools, could remove that spell. I personally saw him remove such a spell from a man who had to be carried into the gallery – he appeared to be paralysed and couldn't even talk. Pa cast the seeds, read them and then said the person was suffering from "mal jeux". In less than an hour, after his ministrations, the young man walked out of the yard, beaming and giving thanks. Later we learned that a neighbour of his had cast the spell because he wanted the man's wife.

In his last years Pa Neezer suffered from onset diabetes – "sugar". He tried to control his diet to some extent but he took only bush medicine. As his sugar levels rose, the medicines no longer worked. He was taken to hospital where a leg was amputated. A short time later he passed away. Pa was unable to cure himself and apparently he had a great fear of hospitals. So he did not go for medical treatment for himself. What irony for a man who helped so many people go to hospital.

Knowing the man as I did, I believe that he had a deep belief in fate and that there comes a time when the human life is over. I believe that he knew his time had come and that he would soon join his beloved Orisha. I don't think he had any regrets about leaving this earth. He died in 1969 and had one of the largest funerals southern Trinidad had ever experienced. He is buried in the London Baptist Church cemetery in Fifth Company Village and his body was interred in a double coffin, the inner one made of lead, so that people would not try to steal his skull in order to use it for evil purposes.

Conclusion

Let me tell you that Samuel Ebenezer Elliott, the bush doctor and the highest Orisha priest in Trinidad and Tobago, was one of the greatest men I have ever met. This simple farmer living in a small village in southern Trinidad, without electricity or running water, was a kind, caring and very spiritual man. He had a relationship to the spiritual world, the world of the supernatural, unmatched by any man or woman. He was a man truly in touch with the world of nature and with the universe. He was part of the Orishas and also part of the gods of Christianity. I have travelled a great deal in my life and have met many people, but I have never met his like again – he was a rare creature among men. I am fond of telling people that there were four men in my life – my father, I have been married twice so my two husbands, and Pa Neezer. I feel honoured and privileged to have known this great man.

And, friends, in conclusion, let me leave you with this thought. Trinidad and Tobago is still a young country in need of historical icons and role models. There are political leaders and historical figures, community workers and leaders in all walks of life who are or should be honoured for their contributions to the building of this society. Samuel Ebenezer Elliott is such a man. It was his work that kept the African Orisha religion alive in this country at a time when it was threatened from external oppression and internal carelessness. He led a life of goodness, charity and inspired thousands of devotees. His life and work should be honoured both within the religion as well as in the whole society. A monument to his memory should be erected and his life and good works should be taught in every school in this country.

Notes

Preface

1. George Simpson, *Religious Cults of the Caribbean: Trinidad, Jamaica, Haiti* (Rio Piedras, Puerto Rico: Institute of Caribbean Studies, University of Puerto Rico, 1980); James Houk, *Spirits, Blood and Drums: The Orisha Religion in Trinidad* (Philadelphia: Temple University Press, 1995); Kenneth Lum, *Praising His Name in the Dance: Spirit Possession in the Spiritual Baptist Faith and Orisha Work in Trinidad, West Indies* (Amsterdam: Abingdon, 1999).

Introduction

1. Since 1996 I have lived part-time in Trinidad, spending about five months per year there. My fieldwork took place during these periods of residence.
2. The population of Trinidad and Tobago includes two main ethnic groups: people of African heritage and those brought by the British from India in the nineteenth century as indentured labourers. There are also significant numbers of English- and French-derived "creoles" who are white or near white; Chinese, Portuguese, Syrians, Lebanese and others. Its system of social stratification is based largely on ethnicity and social class and its recent political history is dominated by these two elements. Trinidad's political history, like that of Guyana, is structured in terms of ethnic politics. During the 1930s an anticolonial strategy involving labour unrest in the black-dominated oil-field sector and among the agriculturally based Indian sugar workers culminated in the development of a trade union movement. Following universal suffrage in 1946, candidates for political office began to appeal to their ethnic constituencies and political partisanship based on ethnicity became institutionalized. In 1956 the People's National Movement (PNM), led by Dr Eric Williams and largely backed by the people of Afro-Trinidadian or black heritage, swept to power. Its chief opposition was the Indian-dominated and -led party, the Democratic Labour Party. Despite attempts by the PNM in subsequent years and the renamed Indian Party, now the United National Congress (UNC), to create inclusive parties, voting along ethnic lines has been maintained. See Selwyn Ryan, *Race and Nationalism in Trinidad and Tobago* (Toronto: University of Toronto Press, 1972) and Selwyn Ryan, *The Jhandi and the Cross* (St Augustine, Trinidad: Sir Arthur Lewis Institute of Social and Economic Studies, 1999).

3. Morton Klass, *Ordered Universes: Approaches to the Anthropology of Religion* (Boulder: Westview Press, 1995).
4. Aisha Khan, "On the 'Right Path': Interpolating Religion in Trinidad", in *Religion, Diaspora and Cultural Identity: A Reader in the Anglophone Caribbean*, ed. J. Pulis (Amsterdam: Gordon and Breach, 1999), 248.
5. John K. Nelson, "The Anthropology of Religion: A Field Statement" (Department of Anthropology, University of California, Berkeley, 1990).
6. Mary Douglas, cited ibid.
7. Nelson, "The Anthropology of Religion".
8. This and other quotes in this section are from Lorne Dawson, "The Cultural Significance of New Religious Movements and Globalization: A Theoretical Prolegomenon", *Journal for the Scientific Study of Religion* (December 1998).
9. Susanna Rostas and Andre Droogers, *The Popular Use of Popular Religion in Latin America* (Amsterdam: CEDLA, 1993).
10. Stuart Hall, "Cultural Identity and Diaspora", in *Identity: Community, Culture, Difference*, ed. J. Rutherford (London: Lawrence and Wishart, 1990), 222–37.
11. Jean Muteba Rahier, introduction, *Representations of Blackness and the Performance of Identities*, ed. J.M. Rahier (Westport, Conn.: Bergin and Garvey, 1999), xiv.
12. Kenneth Liberman, "Truth and Authority in Tibetan Religious Practice", in *Religion and the Social Order*, 6, ed. L. Carter (New York: JAI Press, 1996); B.R. Hertel and M. Mehrota, "Authenticity in Hinduism: Who, What, How?", in *Religion and the Social Order*, 6, ed. L. Carter (New York: JAI Press, 1996).
13. L. Carter, introduction, *Religion and the Social Order*, 6, ed. L. Carter (New York: JAI Press, 1996), ix.
14. Ibid., x.
15. Stephen Glazier, " 'Authenticity' in Afro-Caribbean Religions: Contested Constructs, Contested Rites", in *Religion and the Social Order*, 6, ed. L. Carter (New York: JAI Press, 1996), 207–25.
16. Peter Sutherland, "In Memory of Slaves: An African View of the Diaspora in the Americas", in *Representations of Blackness and the Performance of Identities*, ed. J.M. Rahier (Westport, Conn.: Bergin and Garvey, 1999).

Chapter 1

1. The traditional Yoruba religious system is complex and multilayered. Their cosmos consists of a supreme deity, Olodumare or Olorun, many hundreds of lesser divinities called "Orisa", spirits of deceased ancestors and other spiritual beings. Some Orisa control the forces of nature while others are heroes who have become divine. The Orisa have cults devoted to their worship that are sometimes based on kinship-related descent groups, or a particular divinity may have their centre of worship in a region, town or village. The main Orisa are associated with distinctive dress, colours, foods and rituals. Some are derived from elemental forces of nature that they are believed to control, while others are folkloric heroes who have become divine. Rituals include those that are practised on an individual basis,

those associated with the shrines of the Orisa and, finally, large-scale annual festivals. Divination is a central feature of Yoruba religion as in ancestor worship. See W. Bascom, *Ifa Divination: Communication between Gods and Men in West Africa* (Bloomington: Indiana University Press, 1980); also many Internet sites devoted to Yoruba culture and religion.

2. James Houk, *Spirits, Blood and Drums: The Orisha Religion in Trinidad* (Philadelphia: Temple University Press, 1995).

3. This is not to suggest that African-derived religions are not found in the Protestant Caribbean. In Jamaica, for example, several African-derived groups flourish – among them the Convince Cult and Pocomania. See D. Hogg, *The Convince Cult in Jamaica*, Yale Publications in Anthropology, 58 (New Haven: Yale University Press, 1960); Kenneth Bilbey, "Neither Here nor There: The Place of Community in the Jamaican Religious Imagination", in *Religion, Diaspora and Cultural Identity: A Reader in the Anglophone Caribbean*, ed. J. Pulis (Amsterdam: Gordon and Breach, 1999).

4. Older ethnographic sources include: M.J. Herskovits, *Life in a Haitian Valley* (New York: Knopf, 1937); M.J. Herskovits, "African Gods and Catholic Saints in New World Negro Beliefs", *American Anthropologist*, no. 39 (1937): 635–43; George Simpson, "The Vodun Service in Northern Haiti", *American Anthropologist*, no. 42 (1940): 236–54; George Simpson, "The Belief System of Haitian Vodun", *American Anthropologist*, no. 47 (1945): 35–56. More recent works include: George Brandon, *Santeria from Africa to the New World* (Bloomington: Indiana University Press, 1993); Maureen Warner-Lewis, *Guinea's Other Suns: The African Dynamic in Trinidad Culture* (Dover: Majority Press, 1991).

5. Donald Pierson, *Negroes in Brazil: A Study of Race Contact in Bahia* (Carbondale, Ill.: Southern Illinois University Press, 1942); M.J. Herskovits, "The Southernmost Outposts of New World Africanisms", *American Anthropologist*, no. 45 (1943): 495–510. More recent works include: Robert Voeks, *Sacred Leaves of Candomble: Magic, Medicine and Religion in Brazil* (Austin: University of Texas Press, 1997).

6. John Mason, *Four New World Yoruba Rituals* (Brooklyn: Yoruba Theological Archministry, 1993).

7. David Trotman, "The Yoruba and Orisha Worship in Trinidad and British Guinea", *African Studies Review* 19, no. 2 (1976): 1–17. See also Philip Sher, "Unveiling the Orisha: African Religions and Public Relations in Trinidad", in *Africa's Ogun: Old World and New*, ed. Sandra Barnes (Bloomington: Indiana University Press, 1997).

8. In *The Lost Orisha*, Conrad Mauge claims that an ancestor of his, Ifayomi, a slave, was transported from Guinea to Martinique and thence to Trinidad in 1808 where he and his master settled in what is today Princes Town in southern Trinidad. He credits him with re-establishing the Orisha religion there a few years later. It then spread during the nineteenth century throughout the country, as more Yoruba

were brought to Trinidad. Unfortunately, Mauge does not provide any historical sources for this story, so its authenticity is open to question.
9. See George Brandon, *Santeria from Africa to the New World* (Bloomington: Indiana University Press, 1993); Kamari Clarke, "Genealogies of Reclaimed Nobility: The Geotemporality of Yoruba Belonging" (PhD diss., Temple University, 1995); and Marta Vega, "Yoruba Philosophy: Multiple Levels of Transformation and Understanding" (PhD diss., Temple University, 1995).
10. Supposedly the order in singing is from Ogun, Omela, Omira, Gabriel, Shakpana, Osain, Shango, Aireelay. In actual fact, the singing order is quite flexible and almost any power can be sung to at any time, with the exception of the singing to Eshu and Ogun at the beginning of the ritual.
11. Possessions, or manifestations as they are now called, ranged from two to twenty-four in one evening during my earlier fieldwork. During the present fieldwork period, far fewer manifestations were observed.
12. See chapter 6 for more detail on the Africanization of the religion.
13. For more on Yoruba songs in Orisha ritual and elsewhere in Trinidad, see Maureen Warner-Lewis, *Yoruba Songs from Trinidad* (London: Karnak House, 1994).
14. Frances Henry, "Social Stratification in an Afro-American Cult", *Anthropological Quarterly* (April 1965). There is now a new class of membership composed of high-profile, notable people from the artistic and professional communities who have recently and publicly affirmed support for the religion.
15. N. Mahabir and A. Majaraj, "Hindu Elements in the Shango/Orisha Cult of Trinidad", in *Indenture and Exile: The Indo-Caribbean Experience*, ed. Frank Birbalsingh (Toronto: TSAR, 1989).

Chapter 2

1. References on this religion include: P. Stephens, *The Spiritual Baptist Faith* (London: Karnak House, 1999); C. Jacobs, *Joy Comes in the Mourning* (Trinidad: Caribbean Historical Society, 1996); H.A. Gibbs-De Peza, *Call Him by His Name Jesus* (Trinidad: Fishnet Publications, 1996); Stephen Glazier, *Marchin' the Pilgrims Home* (Westport, Conn.: Greenwood Press, 1983). Excellent research is being conducted by a doctoral student from the Department of Anthropology, University of Helsinki, Finland, on the cosmology of Spiritual Baptists in Tobago. See Maarit Laitenen, "Seeking Wisdom, Knowledge and Understanding: Mythology on Trial" and "The Global Mythology of a Local Religion: A Tobagonian Twist to Discourses of the Diaspora", unpublished papers.
2. The first truly indigenous people in this region were the Carib and Arawak, who had their own religious systems.
3. Earl Lovelace, *The Wine of Astonishment* (London: Heinemann, 1983), 32.
4. Some of the following material on the history of the faith, including citations, comes from Jacobs, *Joy Comes in the Mourning*.

5. Because of its earlier history as a Spanish and later a French possession, the main religion in the island was Roman Catholicism.
6. S.D. Glazier, "Mourning in the Afro-Baptist Traditions: A Comparative Study of Religion in the American South and in Trinidad", *Southern Quarterly* 23, no. 3 (Spring 1985): 141–56.
7. Cited ibid.
8. Many of the smaller islands in the Windwards, such as Grenada, St Vincent and others, also practised Spiritual Baptism. Many people from these islands migrated to Trinidad, where they were denigrated as "small-island people". Some of the negative perceptions of the faith in Trinidad may be influenced by the origins of many of its adherents.
9. These stories are related in the video *Spirit Water Deep* shown on Trinidad and Tobago Television in March 1998.
10. Cited in Gordon Rohlehr, *Calypso and Society in Pre-Independence Trinidad* (Tunapuna, Trinidad: Gordon Rohlehr, 1990), 157.
11. By the then acting governor, John Higgins. Cited in Roy Thomas, ed., *The Trinidad Labour Riots of 1937: Perspectives Fifty Years Later* (St Augustine, Trinidad: Department of Extra-Mural Studies, University of the West Indies, 1987).
12. Martin Daly, Senate debate, cited *Sunday Express*, 29 March 1998.
13. These descriptions are largely drawn from James Houk, *Spirits, Blood and Drums: The Orisha Religion in Trinidad* (Philadelphia: Temple University Press, 1995); Stephen Glazier, "New World African Ritual: Genuine and Spurious", *Journal for the Scientific Study of Religion* 35, no. 4 (1996): 421–32.
14. This group is the one originally led by Bishop Elton Griffith, whose fight against the Shouter Prohibition Act led to its repeal in 1951.
15. The difficulty with the numbers is that the census uses the aggregated category of "Baptist" but there are many versions of Baptism practised in the country including, for example, the London Baptist Church and the Independent Baptist Church, as well as those of the Spiritual/Shouter Baptist faith.
16. *Newsday*, 31 August 2000.
17. Dated 21 October 1993.
18. *Trinidad Express*, 30 March 2000.
19. Ibid.
20. Interview, 14 April 2000.
21. Section 63 states: "Any owner or occupier of a house, building, yard, or other place who:
    a) without license . . . permits any persons to assemble and play or dance therein to any drum, gong, tambour, bangee, chac chac, or any other similar instrument of music, at any time between the hour of ten o'clock in the evening of one day, and the hour of six o'clock in the morning of the next day or
    b) Permits any person to assemble and dance therein the dance known as 'bungo' or any similar dance, is liable to a fine of four hundred dollars; and any constable may, with such assistants as he may take to his aid, enter any house, building, yard or place where any persons may be so assembled, and stop such dance or seize and carry away all such drums, gongs, tambours . . . and forfeit them."
22. *Trinidad Guardian*, 30 March 2000.

Chapter 3

1. *Trinidad Guardian*, 31 March 1996. I have personally attended all the national holiday celebrations of the Spiritual/Shouter Baptists from 1997. I did not, however, witness the celebration in 1996 and this account therefore is from the newspaper.
2. Ibid.
3. President Robinson is from Tobago.
4. The Savannah is a very large grassy plain in the middle of Port of Spain, willed in perpetuity to the people of the country.
5. The reference is to Brian Lara, a major cricketer who comes from Trinidad.
6. The term "spirit lash", which means being hit by a spirit for some transgression, is associated with the Spiritual Baptist faith.
7. *Trinidad Express*, 8 April 2000.
8. This is a square located in the heart of downtown Port of Spain in which Dr Eric Williams held many political speeches in his attempt to educate the masses politically, hence its "University" title.
9. Cited in "Commentary, Licks over Spirit Lash!" in the University of Woodford Square column, *Trinidad Guardian*, 17 April 2000.
10. These allegations were also made in interviews conducted with other Spiritual Baptists. Archbishop Burke's appointment as a senator was not renewed after the elections of December 2000.
11. *Independent*, 21 April 2000.
12. A general election was held on 11 December 2000. It is, however, difficult to disaggregate the returns by religion and only a rough approximation based on riding demographics might be possible. However, in a column dated 7 April 2000 and written by Sean Douglas for the *Trinidad Express*, it is noted that "ethnic voting and the 17–17 tie in the last general election, now means that any political party that can grab a small but key group of its opponent's seats in the East–West Corridor, can tilt the 2000 general election its way. *One such group is the Spiritual Baptist Shouter faith, a traditional bulwark of the PNM but now wooed by the UNC granting them a public holiday plus land for a 'Spiritual Park'*" (italics mine).
13. George Chambers led the PNM government after Dr Williams died. The National Alliance for Reconstruction was led by A.N.R. Robinson. In 1996 the two Tobago representatives of the National Alliance for Reconstruction supported the UNC, thereby insuring them as the government of the day and their leader, Basdeo Panday, as prime minister. Mr Robinson was later made president of the Republic of Trinidad and Tobago.
14. It should also be mentioned that this highly politicized reporting comes from the *Trinidad Express*, a newspaper that the prime minister has often castigated as being one of his "enemies". However, my main point here is that both political leaders are doing their utmost to gather support from this potential constituency, which in itself is a strong indicator of their legitimation and acceptance by the society and its state.
15. This debate also aroused the ire of segments of this divided society. At a meeting of Baptists held in Woodford Square on 17 May 1995, and reported in the *Trinidad Express* the following day, Archbishop

Randoo said, "Instead of a National holiday, government granted us a festival day. What does government mean by a festival day?" Over two dozen members of the faith attended the House sitting to hear the debate. University of the West Indies professor Merle Hodge wrote an impassioned letter to the newspapers (29 May 1995) in which she asked, "Why should African religion in Trinidad and Tobago, triumphing at last in its long heroic struggle against repression and scorn settle for a 'festival day'? Why should other religions have 'holy days' but we a 'festival day'?" She maintained that "the real problem is Afrophobia. It is the fear of the African element in our heritage . . . . There must be nothing that might lead African people to think that they are somebody." She also criticized the numerous Christian holidays, asking why "are Catholic holidays taboo? Why must one group hog four out of a total of six religious days . . . ?"

16. "Loud Shout for African Spirituality", *Trinidad Express*, 29 May 1995.
17. Interview with Senator Burke, 3 February 2000.
18. Ibid.
19. Cited in *Hansard*, ct 95.07.04.
20. Interview, 20 May 1998.
21. *Hansard*, ct 95.07.04.
22. Ibid.
23. Statement by the Hon. C. Imbert, *Hansard*, 1 May 1995.
24. *Hansard*, 1 May 1995.
25. *Trinidad Guardian*, 30 May 1995.
26. Some members of the Christian communities were unhappy with the removal of one of their holidays.
27. *Trinidad Express*, 2 August 2000.
28. The term "high priestess" is not even used by devotees themselves.

Chapter 4

1. The structure and organization of the Spiritual Baptist religion has not changed much in recent times. Its organization is described in chapter 2.
2. Interview, February 1999.
3. At least one member, Rudolf Eastman, has challenged the leadership of Iyalorisha Rodney. Eastman, a very knowledgeable Orisha practitioner, claims that he helped Iya organize and register her shrine and that he should now be leader. Iya and her followers were extremely distressed by his action and brought the matter to a lawyer. After receiving a "cease and desist" type letter from the lawyer, Eastman has apparently withdrawn his claim. Many people, however, think that he will become the next head of the religion after Iyalorisha Rodney.
4. *Trinidad Express*, 7 August 1988.
5. Interview, 1998.
6. Reported in *Hansard*, ct 95.07.04.
7. This quote comes from discussion held at the council's convention in 1999. Arrival refers to a holiday similar to that of Indian Arrival Day. Quoted in the *Trinidad Guardian*, 5 September 2000.
8. *Trinidad Guardian*, 5 September 2000.
9. A breakaway group from Islam, the Amadiya do not accept the divinity of Jesus Christ as does traditional Islam, and they also revere other prophets in addition to Mohammed. In Trinidad, many traditional Muslims believe them to be blasphemous.

10. *Trinidad Guardian*, 5 September 2000.
11. Ibid.
12. This point will again be addressed in more detail in the concluding chapter.
13. E.P. Springer, "Orisa and the Spiritual Baptist Religion in Trinidad and Tobago", in *At the Crossroads: African Caribbean Religion and Christianity*, ed. B. Sankeralli (St James, Trinidad: Caribbean Council of Churches, 1995), 89.
14. Ibid.

Chapter 5

1. David Trotman, "The Yoruba and Orisha Worship in Trinidad and British Guinea", *African Studies Review* 19, no. 2 (1976): 1–17. See also Philip Sher, "Unveiling the Orisha: African Religions and Public Relations in Trinidad", in *Africa's Ogun: Old World and New*, ed. Sandra Barnes (Bloomington: Indiana University Press. 1997).
2. John Comaroff and Jean Comaroff, *Revelation and Revolution* (Chicago: University of Chicago Press, 1991).
3. Homi Bhabha, *The Location of Culture* (London: Routledge, 1994).
4. C. Stewart and R. Shaw, eds., *Syncretism/Anti-Syncretism: The Politics of Religious Synthesis* (London: Routledge, 1994).
5. Ibid., 7.
6. W. Abimbola, *Ifa Divination Poetry* (New York: NOK Publishers, 1977).
7. Glen Jacobs, "On Observations and Queries on Santeria: A Report from the Field" (Department of Sociology, University of Massachusetts, n.d.).
8. See the case study of the World Orisha Congress.
9. Cited in Jacobs, *Joy Comes in the Mourning*.
10. V.Y. Mudimbe, *The Invention of Africa* (Bloomington: Indiana University Press, 1988), 185.
11. "Belief Systems and Religious Organization of the Yoruba" (http://lucy.ukc.ac.uk/yorubaT/yt6/html).
12. Peter Sutherland, "In Memory of Slaves: African View of the Diaspora in the Americas", in *Representations of Blackness and the Performance of Identities*, ed. J.M. Rahier (Westport, Conn.: Bergin and Garvey, 1999). The name of this religion is variously spelled "Vodou" or "Vodun" or, popularly, "Voodoo".
13. Anthony Appiah, *In My Father's House* (New York: Oxford University Press, 1992).
14. Proceedings of the Sixth World Congress of Orisa Tradition and Culture (Trinidad, August 1999).
15. Ibid., 29.
16. What is still contested, however, is the spelling of the name. Some local worshippers use the Yoruba spelling of *Orisa* in an attempt to be more authentic, but the *h* is still included in many written texts, including this one. The words are pronounced the same.
17. *Ashe* or *ase* represents the commonly held belief in a supernatural, animatistic and impersonal energy, force or power that is found everywhere and anywhere in the universe.
18. Maureen Warner-Lewis, *Trinidad Yoruba: From Mother Tongue to Memory* (Tuscaloosa: University of Alabama Press, 1996), 87.
19. Kamari Clarke, "Genealogies of Reclaimed Nobility: The Geotemporality of Yoruba

Belonging" (PhD diss., Temple University, 1995).
20. Ancestor worship or veneration is found in other parts of the New World including Brazil and the Caribbean. For example, M.G. Smith has noted the presence of the saraka (ancestor dance) in Carriacou and Grenada in *Dark Puritan*, Department of Extra Mural Studies (Kingston, Jamaica: University of the West Indies, 1963). It has also been noted in Jamaica; see Maureen Warner-Lewis, "The Ancestral Factor in Jamaica's African Religions", in *African Creative Expressions of the Divine*, ed. K. Davis and E. Farajaje-Jones (Washington, D.C.: Howard University School of Divinity, 1991), 63–80.
21. V. Stephenson-Lee Chee, "Our Ancestral Heritage" (proceedings Sixth World Congress of Orisa Tradition and Culture, Port of Spain, Trinidad, August 1999).
22. Conrad E. Mauge, *The Lost Orisha* (Mount Vernon, NY: House of Providence, 1996).
23. Ibid., 11.
24. I have been fortunate to attend all three of them and, in fact, participate in two.
25. In private conversation, Chief Pat told me that the Ooni was very impressed with the practice of Orisha in Trinidad.
26. *Trinidad Express*, 22 March 1999.
27. The deed to the Maloney land was given in July 2000. The official Marriage Act was granted in 1999 but the regulations implementing it were not finished until 2001.
28. Conference on the Black Power Movement, University of the West Indies, February 2000.
29. *Trinidad Guardian*, 23 March 1970.
30. Molefi Kete Asante, *Kemet, Afrocentricity and Knowledge* (Trenton, N.J.: Africa World Press, 1990), 6.
31. Asante's doctrine also states that its inquiries should begin with the ancient civilizations of Africa, mainly "Kemet" or Egypt and others, rather than European civilizations such as Greece.
32. Paul Gilroy, *The Black Atlantic: Modernity and Double Consciousness* (Cambridge: Harvard University Press, 1993).
33. Appiah, *In My Father's House*.
34. Gilroy, *The Black Atlantic*.
35. Personal communication.

Chapter 6

1. For a historical analysis of the development of Christian syncretism in African worship, see Rawle Gibbons, "Syncretism and Secretism in the Manifestation of African Spirituality", in *African Caribbean Religion and Christianity*, ed. B. Sankeralli (St James, Trinidad: Caribbean Council of Churches, 1995), 67–85.
2. Houk provides a description of Kabbalah today (James Houk, *Spirits, Blood and Drums: The Orisha Religion in Trinidad* [Philadelphia: Temple University Press, 1995], 169–80). He also notes that of fifty-one shrines surveyed, Kabba flags were found in sixteen, and over half of forty-two worshippers surveyed said they had attended a Kabbalah banquet within the last year.
3. "No Such Thing as a Shango Baptist", *Trinidad Express*. In an interview, a Spiritual Baptist archbishop claimed that "the name came

about through the fact that some of the Spiritual Baptists left their churches to join the Orisha movement and vice versa. There is nothing like a Shango Baptist. You are either Baptist or Orisha."

4. E.P. Springer, "Orisa and the Spiritual Baptist Religion in Trinidad and Tobago", in *At the Crossroads: African Caribbean Religion and Christianity*, ed. B. Sankeralli (St James, Trinidad: Caribbean Council of Churches, 1995).

5. Ibid.

6. Houk distinguishes "orthodox" and "non-orthodox" Spiritual Baptists (*Spirits, Blood and Drums*, 85) but this demarcation appears to be too simplistic. For a detailed discussion of the way in which differences between Spiritual Baptists and Orisha are constructed by Togabonian Baptists, see Maarit Laitenen, "Seeking Wisdom, Knowledge and Understanding: How Tobagonian Spiritual Baptists Demarcate their Religion" (typescript, Department of Anthropology, University of Helsinki, Finland, 2000). Given the substantial number of Spiritual and Shouter Baptist groups in Trinidad and Tobago, however, there are many versions of difference between the two religions. Among Shouter Baptists there is considerable recognition of the African traits in their ritual.

7. Springer, "Orisa and the Spiritual Baptist Religion in Trinidad and Tobago.

8. I did not personally attend any Kabbalah banquets during my earlier fieldwork. The mainstream network of Orisha elders, including Pa Neezer, strongly disapproved of its practices. In a small country such as Trinidad, my attendance at such an event would have quickly spread throughout the network. I did not want to jeopardize the excellent and close rapport I had with my respondents and therefore chose not to attend any Kabbalah ceremonies.

9. Kabbalah is a system of Jewish religious and mystical knowledge that is thought to have been communicated to Moses. Most of its knowledge was passed on through oral traditions, but during the Middle Ages its teachings were recorded. It became popular in Spain and France during the early medieval period. Houk speculates that some of the early Spanish and French settlers might have brought the Kabbalistic philosophy to Trinidad.

10. When I mentioned that I had heard that Lindsay was extremely overweight and that he had died from a heart attack brought about by the stress on his heart due to his weight, Oludari said that there are many people in the world who are overweight and who do not die at the age of thirty-four.

11. Franklin H. Williams Caribbean Cultural Center. Web site, 21 May 1999.

12. Ibid.

13. The instructions were so complex that only a person skilled in word processing could have followed them. The proceedings published by the congress reproduced the papers exactly as they were submitted, and it is evident that only a few presenters were able to follow the formatting instructions.

14. There were other significant political references in this speech, discussed in chapter 4.

15. The term is not favoured by participants in the faith. There is a strong tendency to identify each religion as individual and, although Baptist elements may be practised in an Orisha ritual, the ritual itself is identified as Orisha.

Chapter 7

1. This chapter deals only with popular culture. It does not explore the frequent use of African religious practices and symbolism in the literature and poetry of the region. Writers have always understood and accepted the importance of these traditions in their work, even in times when Afro-Trinidadians rejected their African roots. See, for example, the treatment of Spiritual Baptism in the work of Earl Lovelace in *The Wine of Astonishment*.

    I am deeply indebted to Dr Ann Lee who did much of the research on calypsos in the early part of this chapter. Dr Lee also wrote a draft of the section on calypso that I have used here almost in its entirety.
2. *Hansard*, 11 July 1995.
3. Raymond Quevedo, *Attila's Kaiso: A Short History of Trinidad Calypso* (Trinidad: University of the West Indies Extra Mural Department, 1983). See also Maureen Warner-Lewis, *Yoruba Songs from Trinidad* (London: Karnak House, 1994).
4. *Calypso and Society in Pre-Independence Trinidad* (Port of Spain: 1990), 152.
5. Ibid., 153.
6. Ibid., 152–59.
7. Cited in *Sunday Express*, 28 March 1999.
8. Ibid.
9. Interview, 18 February 2000.
10. Interview, 21 February 2000.
11. These lyrics were taken from a performance.
12. See Andrew Carr, "The Rada Community in Belmont", *Caribbean Quarterly* 3, no. 1 (1953).
13. Stephen Stuempfle, *The Steelband Movement: The Forging of a National Art in Trinidad and Tobago* (Kingston, Jamaica: The Press, University of the West Indies, 1995).
14. Kenrick Thomas, *Panriga: Tacarigua's Contribution to the Evolution of the Steelband Phenomenon in Trinidad and Tobago* (Washington, D.C.: Original World Press, 1999).
15. Candace Goucher, "The Performance of Iron: Stoking the Furnace, Sailing the Seas" (paper presented at the Third World Carnival Conference, sponsored by Trinidad Industrial Development Company, Port of Spain, Trinidad, October 1999).
16. This term is a contracted form of "masquerade", the bands of Carnival.
17. Goucher, "The Performance of Iron", 24
18. There is, however, a literature on the role of Candomblé and other forms of Orisha in Brazil and its relationship to the Carnival celebrations. Boyce Davies, for example, has written about the performance of the "filhas d'Oxum" (the daughters of Osun), who perform regularly in the Brazilian Carnival. What is particularly interesting about their participation is that unlike the stereotyped portrayal of the scantily clad, sexy Afro-Brazilian women who are members of Samba schools, the filhas d'Oxum present a different portrayal of the Afro-Brazilian woman. They emphasize "a carnival of beauty and

joy in femininity that emanates from the Orisha Oxum (Oshun) as she is interpreted in Afro-Brazilian (Yoruba) Orisha tradition" (Carol Boyce Davies, "Filhas d'Oxum in Bahia Carnival", in *Representations of Blackness and the Performance of Identities*, ed. J. M. Rahier [Westport, Conn.: Bergin and Garvey, 1999]).

19. Eintou Pearl Springer, "The Role of Orisha in Carnival" (paper presented at the Third World Carnival Conference, sponsored by Trinidad Industrial Development Company, Port of Spain, Trinidad, October 1999).

20. The Pierrot is a traditional Carnival character whose roots go back to the European origins of Carnival but whose behaviour also includes elements of African-derived stick fighting. The Midnight Robber and the Dragon are also traditional Carnival characters. The former appears to derive from American cowboy influences in the early twentieth century, while the latter is part of the traditional devil bands of the Trinidad Carnival. See Errol Hill, *The Trinidad Carnival* (Austin: University of Texas Press, 1999); *Trinidad Carnival*, a republication of *Caribbean Quarterly* 4, nos. 3–4 (1956).

21. Tan Tan and Saga Boy refer to two Carnival characters created by mas designer Peter Minshall. They are very large puppets.

22. E.P. Springer, "Orisa (Orisha) Tradition in Trinidad" (paper presented at the Sixth World Congress of Orisa Tradition and Culture, Port of Spain, Trinidad, August 1999).

23. This incident became public in early February 2001 and, at the time of this writing, not all the "facts" are in. I have been able to follow it as events unfolded and have been able to interview some of the key participants to the controversy, but time and publication pressure have not allowed for more extensive examination of this interesting and timely issue beyond this brief summary. I plan to write a more extensive paper on the subject in the near future.

24. This is not the first controversy that involved the use of religious symbols or practices and Carnival. In 1998 soca singer David Rudder was strongly criticized for a calypso called "High Mas" that invoked the Catholic "Our Father" and repeatedly used the word "amen" in its chorus. Although Rudder and his song were enthusiastically received by many, some religious leaders were outraged and expressed their criticism in public discourse prior to and even after Carnival. Similarly, mas creator Peter Minshall's "Hallelujah" band in 1995 created an uproar amongst those who felt that he had transgressed into sacred areas that should not be expressed during Carnival. Nevertheless, as Rohlehr notes, there has been a steady "transgression from the ranks of the holy into the realms of the secular". Citing the growth of the Gospelypso, which uses the rhythms, melodies and power of Calypso, "its aim . . . is that of penetrating the secular ethos of Calypso and Carnival towards a goal of social transformation through the winning of more souls for Christ" (Gordon Rohlehr, "Change and Prophecy in Calypso", part 2, *Trinidad and Tobago Review*, March 2001).

25. *Trinidad Guardian,* 18 February 2001.
26. Rohlehr, "Change and Prophecy in Calypso".
27. *Trinidad Guardian,* 23 February 2001.
28. *Trinidad Express,* 14 February 2001.
29. *Trinidad Guardian,* 25 February 2001.

Chapter 8

1. E. Durkheim, *The Elementary Forms of Religious Life* (New York: Collier, 1961).
2. Peter Worsley, *The Trumpet Shall Sound* (New York: Schocken, 1968).
3. A. Wallace, *Religion: An Anthropological View* (New York: Random House, 1966).
4. G. Simmons, "Cults and Psychology", 19 May 1999 (http://atheism.about.com/library/weekly/aa051999.htm)
5. Cited ibid.
6. Selwyn Ryan, *Indo-Trinidadians and the Labour Market in Trinidad and Tobago* (St Augustine, Trinidad: Institute of Social and Economic Research, 1993).
7. *Newsday,* 31 August 2000.
8. I am indebted to John Stewart for drawing my attention to this point.
9. Gustavo Benavides, *Religion and Politics* (Albany: State University of New York Press, 1989).

Glossary

Baba	Term of respect used to designate a knowledgeable and often elder male of the religion.
Babalorisha	The senior male leader of the religion.
Buttoo	A protective wooden stick used by the police in earlier times.
Carrat	Dry palm fronds used to thatch roofs.
Cattle feast	A ritual that occurs every four years or during a leap year and is dedicated to the Orisha Obatala (or Elofa).
Chapelle	A small chapel containing the ritual accoutrements of the Orisha.
Horse	Refers to a person who serves as a medium for a spirit possession or manifestation.
Hummingbird Medal	The Hummingbird Award, a medal, is bestowed on meritorious persons by the government of Trinidad and Tobago.
Iya	A term of respect to designate a knowledgeable and usually elder female in the religion.
Iyalorisha	The senior female leader of the religion.
Mongba	Originally a Yoruba priest, but now used mainly to mean the man who leads the ritual in singing and drumming.
Obi	A multi-sided seed.
Palais	The ceremonial area in a leader's compound where the ritual is held.
Santeria	The name (literally, saints) applied to the African-derived syncretic religion in Cuba and in the Cuban communities in the United States.
Shango Jumbie	A Shango or Orisha spirit.
Shrine	Now used to designate an Orisha compound.
Tamboo bamboo	A music band of primarily percussive instruments made of bamboo – precursor to the steelband.
University of Woodford Square	A large grassy square in downtown Port of Spain in which Trinidad's first prime minister, Dr Eric Williams, delivered long political speeches in order to educate and politicize the public, hence its nickname of "University".

www.ingramcontent.com/pod-product-compliance
Lightning Source LLC
Chambersburg PA
CBHW021823300426
44114CB00009BA/305